THE OXFORD

Essential Writer's
Reference

THE OXFORD

Essential Writer's Reference

BERKLEY BOOKS, NEW YORK

THE BERKLEY PUBLISHING GROUP
Published by the Penguin Group
Penguin Group (USA) Inc.
375 Hudson Street, New York, New York 10014, USA
Penguin Group (Canada), 10 Alcorn Avenue, Toronto, Ontario M4V 3B2, Canada
(a division of Pearson Penguin Canada Inc.)
Penguin Books Ltd., 80 Strand, London WC2R 0RL, England
Penguin Group Ireland, 25 St. Stephen's Green, Dublin 2, Ireland (a division of Penguin Books Ltd.)
Penguin Group (Australia), 250 Camberwell Road, Camberwell, Victoria 3124, Australia
(a division of Pearson Australia Group Pty. Ltd.)
Penguin Books India Pvt. Ltd., 11 Community Centre, Panchsheel Park, New Delhi—110 017, India
Penguin Group (NZ), Cnr. Airborne and Rosedale Roads, Albany, Auckland 1310, New Zealand
(a division of Pearson New Zealand Ltd.)
Penguin Books (South Africa) (Pty.) Ltd., 24 Sturdee Avenue, Rosebank, Johannesburg 2196,
South Africa

Penguin Books Ltd., Registered Offices: 80 Strand, London WC2R 0RL, England

THE OXFORD ESSENTIAL WRITER'S REFERENCE

A Berkley Book / published by arrangement with Oxford University Press, Inc.

PRINTING HISTORY
Berkley mass-market edition / July 2005

Copyright © 2005 by Oxford University Press, Inc.
Oxford is a registered trademark of Oxford University Press, Inc.
Cover design by Steven Ferlauto.

ISBN: 0-425-20689-0

BERKLEY®
Berkley Books are published by The Berkley Publishing Group,
a division of Penguin Group (USA) Inc.,
375 Hudson Street, New York, New York 10014.
BERKLEY is a registered trademark of Penguin Group (USA) Inc.
The "B" design is a trademark belonging to Penguin Group (USA) Inc.

PRINTED IN THE UNITED STATES OF AMERICA

10 9 8 7 6 5 4 3 2 1

Contents

Prologue

by Richard Goodman

> Knowledge is of two kinds. We know a subject our-
> selves, or we know where we can find it.
>
> —Samuel Johnson

A helpful way to think of this book is as a literary Swiss Army
Knife. Like the array of diversely shaped, providentially useful
parts of that celebrated knife, this book has an array of chapters
for many of the troublesome situations or outright emergencies
you are likely to meet in the writing wilderness. The Swiss knife
constantly surprises and delights with a gizmo we didn't realize
was in the mix. The *Oxford Essential Writer's Reference* has that
eclectic handiness, too. Each chapter is like one of those distinct
miniature tools. We have thought about our own journeys as writers, and recollected those times when we wished we had a certain
tool or guide handy and ready, and instead had to do the best we
could without it.

Like that famous red knife, there's more packed into this book
than you might realize. You may find yourself wondering if you
need a semicolon here, or a period there. Is it important? Milan
Kundera once dismissed an editor over a semicolon. Refer, then,
to Chapter 1, "Grammar, Punctuation, Spelling, and Usage
Guides." You may want to know how to copyright that manuscript
you're struggling with but you'll find all the direction you need in
Chapter 16, "How to Copyright Your Work." Who was it that

stole fire in Greek mythology? The answer is in Chapter 13, "Major Mythological Characters." If you are struggling with an issue in a contract and don't happen to have your own personal lawyer, then consult Chapter 15, "A List of Writers' Advocacy Organizations." And so on.

Before you go anywhere else for the information you seek, be it basic or arcane, open this practical, able book first. The *Oxford Essential Writer's Reference* was created to help you do your job as a writer better, more efficiently, and more confidently, and to help you spend less of your most precious asset: time.

CHAPTER 1

Grammar, Punctuation, Spelling, and Usage Guides

INTRODUCTION

The legendary writing teacher John Gardner put it succinctly and bluntly: "No one can hope to write well if he has not mastered—absolutely mastered—the rudiments: grammar and syntax, punctuation, diction, sentence variety, paragraph structure, and so forth."

Some writing students look upon this as a painful punishment, a severe sentence imposed upon them by some merciless god of literature. But how can anyone expect to be an expert in anything—from brain surgery to bingo—if she or he hasn't mastered the fundamentals of the trade? I've never understood writers who feel that grammar and syntax are somehow irrelevant, or dispensable, aspects of writing. That the *real* writing is in the creativity. As the if the *real* surgery were in how creatively one sliced through brain tissue, and all the "details"—from the meticulous planning to the mundane sewing up—were somehow beneath the great surgeon.

I believe it's a good idea for writers to think about writing more as a craft than as an art. Writing is, in fact, a great deal like carpentry. Much of it involves crafting fine—perhaps even beautiful—sentences, much as a skilled carpenter makes beautiful houses. No carpenter is a natural master. He or she has worked hard to understand and master the tools of his or her trade, and respects them as well. So should you respect the tools of your trade and how they function. Writers often seem less humble then they should be. Marianne Moore cited three things that make for persuasive writing: humility, concentration, and gusto. Notice which she placed first.

So, get these fundamentals under your belt. They will only make you a more confident and more accomplished writer.

Rules of English: Understanding Grammar

Grammar is the system and structure of a language. It embodies all the principles by which the language works. All good writing begins with an understanding of the fundamentals of grammar:

- parts of speech
- parts of sentences
- sentence structures
- sentence functions

PARTS OF SPEECH

Noun

A noun is a word that identifies or names a person, place, thing, action, or quality. There are two types of nouns: proper and common.

PROPER NOUNS

A noun that names a particular person, place, or thing is a **proper noun**. It always begins with a capital letter:

Benito Mussolini	Jell-O
Cairo	Mount Everest
the Chrysler Building	

COMMON NOUNS

A noun that names a type of person, place, or thing is a **common noun**. There are three kinds of common nouns: concrete, abstract, and collective.

A **concrete noun** names someone or something that you can see or touch:

arm   lake
giraffe   stapler
hamburger

An **abstract noun** names something intangible (that is, something that can neither be seen nor touched):

assistance   flavor
bravery   wit
disappointment

A **collective noun** names a group of persons or things:

audience   platoon
colony   set
herd

SINGULAR AND PLURAL NOUNS

A noun that names one person, place, or thing is **singular**. A noun that names more than one person, place, or thing is **plural**. The spelling of a singular noun almost always changes when it becomes a plural. Most plurals can be formed by adding *s* or *es*, but many nouns do not follow this format.

beach/beaches   mouse/mice
bean/beans   party/parties
hairbrush/hairbrushes   school/schools
leaf/leaves   woman/women

If the spelling of a plural noun is in doubt, it is always advisable to consult a dictionary.

APPOSITIVES

An **appositive** is a noun (or a unit of words that acts as a noun) whose meaning is a direct copy or extension of the meaning of the preceding noun in the sentence. In other words, the appositive and the preceding noun refer to the same person, place, or thing. The appositive helps to characterize or elaborate on the preceding noun in a specific way.

The wedding cake, a chocolate <u>masterpiece</u>, was the hit of the reception.

[The noun *cake* and the appositive *masterpiece* are the same thing.]

His primary objective, <u>to write the great American novel</u>, was never realized.
[The noun *objective* and the appositive *to write the great American novel* are the same thing.]

Eleanor's math teacher, <u>Mrs. Kennedy</u>, is retiring next year.
[The noun *teacher* and the appositive *Mrs. Kennedy* are the same person.]

POSSESSIVES

A **possessive** is a noun whose form has changed in order to show possession. Certain rules can be followed to determine how the form should change for any given noun. In the case of a singular noun, add an apostrophe and an *s*:

<u>Lincoln's</u> inaugural address
the <u>baby's</u> favorite blanket

Exception: Most singular nouns that end in *s* follow the preceding rule with no difficulty (e.g., *Chris's*, *Dickens's*), but some singular nouns that end in *s* may be exempted from the rule because the pronunciation of the plural is less awkward with just an apostrophe and no final *s*:

<u>Ramses</u>' dynasty
<u>Aristophanes</u>' great comedic works

In the case of a plural noun that ends in *s*, add just an apostrophe:

the <u>Lincolns</u>' summer home
our <u>babies</u>' double stroller

In the case of a plural noun that does not end in *s*, add an apostrophe and an *s*:

<u>men's</u> footwear
the <u>fungi's</u> rapid reproduction

In the case of a compound noun (a noun made of more than one word), only the last word takes the possessive form:

> my <u>sister-in-law's</u> house
> the <u>commander in chief 's</u> personal staff

In the case of joint possession (that is, two or more nouns possess the same thing together), only the last of the possessing nouns takes the possessive form:

> <u>Ryan and Saul's</u> nickel collection
> [There is only one nickel collection, and *both* Ryan and Saul own it *together*.]

> <u>Gramma and Grampa's</u> photo albums
> [However many photo albums there may be, they all belong to *both* Gramma and Grampa *together*.]

In the case of individual possession by two or more nouns (that is, two or more nouns possess the same type of thing, but separately and distinctly), each of the possessing nouns takes the possessive form:

> <u>Lenny's and Suzanne's</u> footprints on the beach
> [Lenny and Suzanne *each* left *their own distinct* footprints on the beach.]

> <u>Strauss's and Khachaturian's</u> waltzes
> [Strauss and Khachaturian *each* composed *their own distinct* waltzes.]

Pronoun

A pronoun is a word that represents a person or thing without giving the specific name of the person or thing. There are five classes of pronouns: personal, relative, demonstrative, indefinite, and interrogative.

A personal pronoun is used to refer to the person speaking (first person), the person spoken to (second person), or the person or thing spoken about (third person). A pronoun formed from certain personal pronouns by adding the suffix *-self* (singular) or *-selves* (plural) is called "reflexive."

PERSON	SINGULAR	PLURAL	REFLEXIVE SINGULAR	REFLEXIVE PLURAL
first person	*I*	*we*	—	—
	my	*our*	*myself*	*ourselves*
	mine	*ours*	—	—
	me	*us*	—	—
second person	*you*	*you*	—	—
	your	*your*	*yourself*	*yourselves*
	yours	*yours*	—	—
	you	*you*	—	—
third person masculine	*he*	*they*	—	—
	his	*their*	—	—
	his	*theirs*	—	—
	him	*them*	*himself*	*themselves*
third person feminine	*she*	*they*	—	—
	her	*their*	—	—
	hers	*theirs*	—	—
	her	*them*	*herself*	*themselves*
third person neuter	*it*	*they*	—	—
	its	*their*	—	—
	its	*theirs*	—	—
	it	*them*	*itself*	*themselves*

Note that the gender designations of masculine, feminine, and neuter apply only to the third person singular.

Reflexive personal pronouns are so called because they reflect the action of the verb back to the subject. It is incorrect to use a reflexive pronoun by itself; there must be a subject to which it refers.

incorrect:	Denise and <u>myself</u> will fix the car.
	[The reflexive pronoun *myself* has no subject to refer to; the wording should be "Denise and I."]
correct:	I will fix the car <u>myself</u>.
	[The reflexive pronoun *myself* refers to the subject *I*.]

A **reflexive pronoun** that adds force or emphasis to a noun or another pronoun is called "intensive":

You <u>yourself</u> must return the ladder.
Terri and Phil want to wallpaper the kitchen <u>themselves</u>.

A **relative pronoun** introduces a descriptive clause. The relative pronouns are *which, that, who, whoever, whose, whom,* and *whomever.*

Wendy was the pianist <u>who</u> won the scholarship.
Is Mr. Leonard the teacher <u>whose</u> book was just published?
<u>Whoever</u> wrote the speech is a genius.
I attended the morning meeting, <u>which</u> lasted for three hours.

A **demonstrative pronoun** is specific. It is used to point out particular persons, places, or things. The demonstrative pronouns are *this, that, these,* and *those.*

These are the finest fabrics available.
I'll look at those first.
What is this?

An **indefinite pronoun** is nonspecific. It is used to refer to persons, places, or things without particular identification. There are numerous indefinite pronouns, including the following:

all	everyone	none
any	everything	no one
anybody	few	other
anyone	little	others
anything	many	several
both	most	some
each	much	somebody
either	neither	someone
everybody	nobody	something

George brought two desserts, but I didn't try <u>either</u>.
<u>Many</u> are called, but <u>few</u> are chosen.
Can <u>somebody</u> please answer the phone?

An **interrogative pronoun** is used to ask a question. The interrogative pronouns are *who, which,* and *what.*

<u>Who</u> wants to buy a raffle ticket?
<u>Which</u> of the two applicants has more practical experience?
<u>What</u> is the purpose of another debate?

PRONOUN CASES

The case of a pronoun is what determines its relation to the other words in the sentence. There are three pronoun cases: nominative, objective, and possessive.

Nominative case

The nominative pronouns are *I, we, you, he, she, it, they, who*, and *whoever*.

A pronoun that is the subject (or part of the subject) of a sentence is in the nominative case:

> <u>They</u> loved the movie.
> Mark and <u>I</u> are going to the Bahamas.

A pronoun that is a predicate is in the nominative case:

> It was <u>she</u> who wrote the poem.
> The winner will probably be <u>you</u>.

Objective case

The objective pronouns are *me, us, you, him, her, it, them, whom*, and *whomever*.

A pronoun that is the direct object of a verb is in the objective case:

> Stephen already invited <u>them.</u>
> Should we keep <u>it</u>?

A pronoun that is the indirect object of a verb is in the objective case:

> Captain Mackenzie told <u>us</u> many seafaring tales.
> I'll give <u>you</u> the recipe tomorrow.

A pronoun that is the object of a preposition is in the objective case:

> Does she think this job is beneath <u>her</u>?
> To <u>whom</u> was it addressed?

Possessive case

A possessive pronoun shows ownership.

The possessive pronouns used as predicate nominatives are *mine, ours, yours, his, hers, its, theirs*, and *whose*.

The blue station wagon is <u>mine</u>.
None of the cash was <u>theirs</u>.

The possessive pronouns used as adjectives are *my*, *our*, *your*, *his*, *her*, *its*, *their*, and *whose*.

<u>Whose</u> test scores were the highest?
I believe this is <u>your</u> package.

TIP

A possessive pronoun never has an apostrophe. Remember, the word *it's* is the contraction of *it is* or *it has*—not the possessive form of *it*.

- possessive: Life has its ups and downs.
- contraction: It's good to see you.

SINGULAR AND PLURAL AGREEMENT

It is important to identify a pronoun as singular or plural and to make certain that the associated verb form is in agreement. The pronouns that tend to cause the most problems for writers and speakers are the indefinite pronouns.

Some indefinite pronouns are always singular and therefore always require a singular verb. These include *everybody*, *everyone*, *somebody*, *someone*, *nobody*, *one*, *either*, and *neither*.

<u>Nobody</u> <u>wants</u> to leave.
Don't get up unless <u>someone</u> <u>knocks</u> on the door.
<u>Either</u> of these two colors <u>is</u> fine.

Other indefinite pronouns may be singular or plural, depending on the particular reference. These include *any*, *all*, *some*, *most*, and *none*.

If <u>any</u> of these marbles are yours, let me know.
[The noun *marbles* is plural.]

If <u>any</u> of this cake is yours, let me know.
[The noun *cake* is singular.]

Most of the potatoes are already gone.
[The noun *potatoes* is plural.]

Most of the evening is already gone.
[The noun *evening* is singular.]

Verb

A **verb** is a word that expresses an action or a state of being.
An **action verb** expresses a physical or mental action:

break	operate
eat	unveil
intercept	wish

A **state of being verb** expresses a condition or state of being:

be	lack
become	seem
is	smell

TRANSITIVE VERBS

A **transitive verb** expresses an action that is performed on someone or something. The someone or something is the **direct object**. Notice in each of the following examples that the direct object receives the action of the verb.

Ingrid restores antique furniture.
[transitive verb: *restores*; direct object: *furniture*]

Hernandez pitched the ball.
[transitive verb: *pitched*; direct object: *ball*]

Did you feed the animals?
[transitive verb: *feed*; direct object: *animals*]

Sometimes a transitive verb has both a direct object and an indirect object. An **indirect object** is the person or thing to whom or for whom the verb's action is being performed. Notice in each of the following examples that the direct object receives the action of the verb, while the indirect object identifies who or what the action affected.

The captain <u>handed</u> <u>us</u> our <u>orders</u>.
[transitive verb: *handed*; direct object: *orders*; indirect object: *us*]

Did you <u>give</u> the <u>plants</u> some <u>water</u>?
[transitive verb: *give*; direct object: *water*; indirect object: *plants*]

I <u>tossed</u> a <u>pen</u> to <u>Herman</u>.
[transitive verb: *tossed*; direct object: *pen*; indirect object: *Herman*]

TIP

Remember: A direct object answers *what?* An indirect object answers *to whom?* (or *to what?*) or *for whom?* (or *for what?*).

direct objects:	*What* does Ingrid restore?	furniture
	What did Hernandez pitch?	ball
	Did you feed *what*?	animals
	What did the captain hand?	orders
	Did you give *what*?	water
	What did I toss?	pen
indirect objects:	*To whom* did the captain hand orders?	us
	Did you give water *to what*?	plants
	To whom did I toss a pen?	Herman

INTRANSITIVE VERBS

An **intransitive verb** does not have an object. Notice in each of the following examples that the verb expresses an action that occurs without needing to be received.

We <u>marched</u> in the parade.
The tea kettle <u>whistled</u>.
Heidi <u>sleeps</u> on the third floor.

LINKING VERBS

A **linking verb** joins a word (or unit of words) that names a person or thing to another word (or unit of words) that renames or describes the person or thing. It is always intransitive and always expresses a state of being. The most common linking verbs are *to be* and all the forms of *to be*, which include *am*, *are*, *is*, *was*, and *were*. Other common linking verbs include the following:

act	feel	remain	sound
appear	grow	seem	taste
become	look	smell	turn

The air <u>seemed</u> humid yesterday.
What <u>smells</u> so good?
The days <u>grow</u> shorter.
I <u>am</u> a registered voter.
Kim <u>remains</u> a devout Catholic.
Butch and Sundance <u>were</u> the title characters.

TIP

Remember: Because an intransitive verb does not have an object, the question *what?* will be unanswerable.

> *What* did we march?
> *What* did the kettle whistle?
> *What* does Heidi sleep?

These questions simply cannot be answered; therefore the verbs are intransitive.

Predicate adjectives and nominatives

The word (or unit of words) that a linking verb joins to the subject can be either an adjective or a noun, but its function is always the same: to tell something about the subject. An adjective that follows a linking verb is a **predicate adjective**. A noun that follows a linking verb is a **predicate nominative**.

predicate adjective: The air seemed <u>humid</u> yesterday.
                        What <u>smells</u> so good?
                        The days grow <u>shorter</u>.

predicate nominative: I am a registered <u>voter</u>.
                        Kim remains a devout <u>Catholic</u>.

Butch and Sundance were the
title <u>characters</u>.

VOICE

The subject of a transitive verb either performs or receives the action. A verb whose subject performs is said to be in the **active voice**. A verb whose subject receives is said to be in the **passive voice**.

active voice: Brainerd & Sons <u>built</u> the storage shed.
[The subject *Brainerd & Sons* performed the action of building.]

Lydia <u>will curry</u> the horses.
[The subject *Lydia* will perform the action of currying.]

passive voice: The storage shed <u>was built</u> by Brainerd & Sons.
[The subject *shed* received the action of building.]
The horses <u>will be curried</u> by Lydia.
[The subject *horses* will receive the action of currying.]

MOOD

Verbs have a quality that shows the attitude or purpose of the speaker. This quality is called the **mood**. There are three verb moods: indicative, imperative, and subjunctive.

The **indicative mood** shows a statement or question of fact:

Does Paula <u>know</u> the combination to the safe?
Dr. Sliva <u>is</u> my dentist.

The **imperative mood** shows a command or request:

<u>Make</u> the most of your situation.
<u>Proceed</u> to the third traffic light.

The **subjunctive mood** shows a condition of doubtfulness, possibility, desirability, improbability, or unreality:

<u>Should</u> you <u>decide</u> to return the blouse, you will need the receipt.

If <u>I were rich</u>, I'd quit my job.

PERSON AND NUMBER

The **person** (first, second, or third) of a verb depends on to whom or to what the verb refers: the person speaking (first person), the person spoken to (second person), or the person or thing spoken about (third person).

The **number** (singular or plural) of a verb depends on whether the verb refers to a singular subject or a plural subject.

For nearly all verbs, the form of the verb changes only in the third person singular.

PERSON	SINGULAR	PLURAL
first person	I *know*	we *know*
second person	you *know*	you *know*
third person	he *knows*	they *know*
	she *knows*	they *know*
	it *knows*	they *know*
	Chris *knows*	Chris and Pat *know*
	Mrs. Hansen *knows*	the Hansens *know*
	God *knows*	the gods *know*
	the teacher *knows*	the teachers *know*
	the heart *knows*	our hearts *know*

TENSE

The **tense** of a verb shows the time of the verb's action. There are six verb tenses: present, present perfect, past, past perfect, future, and future perfect.

The **present tense** shows action occurring in the present:

I smell fresh coffee.

The present tense can also show the following:

action that is typical or habitual:	I <u>design</u> greenhouses. Stuart <u>daydreams</u> during math class.

action that will occur: Lynne <u>retires</u> in six months.
Our plane <u>lands</u> at midnight.

facts and beliefs: March <u>follows</u> February.
Greed <u>destroys</u> the spirit.

TIP

Yet another function of the present tense is what is called the historical present. This usage allows the writer or speaker to relate past actions in a present tone, which may enhance the descriptive flow of the text.

The United States <u>acquires</u> the Oklahoma Territory from France in 1803 as part of the Louisiana Purchase. Following the War of 1812, the U.S. government <u>begins</u> a relocation program, forcing Indian tribes from the eastern United States to move into certain unsettled western areas, including Oklahoma. Because of their opposition to the U.S. government, most of these native people lend their support to the Confederate South during the American Civil War. In 1865, the war ends in utter defeat for the Confederacy, and all of the Oklahoma Territory soon <u>falls</u> under U.S. military rule.

When using the historical present, writers and speakers must be careful not to lapse into the past tense. For example, it would be an incorrect mix of tenses to say, "In 1865, the war <u>ended</u> in utter defeat for the Confederacy, and all of the Oklahoma Territory soon <u>falls</u> under U.S. military rule."

The **present perfect tense** is formed with the word *has* or *have*. It shows action begun in the past and completed by the time of the present:

James <u>has checked</u> the air in the tires at least three times.

I <u>have read</u> the book you're talking about.

The **past tense** shows action that occurred in the past:

Greg <u>memorized</u> his speech.
The mouse <u>scurried</u> across the room.

The **past perfect tense** is formed with the word *had*. It shows action that occurred in the past, prior to another past action:

> Eugene <u>had finished</u> his story by the time we got to the airport.
> The parrot <u>had flown</u> into another room long before we noticed an empty cage.

The **future tense** is formed with the word *will*. It shows action that is expected to occur in the future:

> The president <u>will address</u> the nation this evening.
> Tempers <u>will flare</u> when the truth comes out.

The **future perfect tense** is formed with the words *will have*. It shows action that is expected to occur in the future, prior to another future or expected action:

> Noreen <u>will have finished</u> painting by the time we're ready to lay the carpet.
> The candidates <u>will have traveled</u> thousands of miles before this campaign is over.

VERBALS

A verb form that acts as a part of speech other than a verb is a **verbal**. There are three types of verbals: infinitives, participles, and gerunds.

An **infinitive** is a verb form that can act as a noun, an adjective, or an adverb. It is preceded by the preposition *to*.

noun:	<u>To steal</u> is a crime.
	[The infinitive *to steal* is the subject.]
	Our original plan, <u>to elope</u>, was never discovered.
	[The infinitive *to elope* is an appositive.]
adjective:	Those are words <u>to remember</u>.
	[The infinitive *to remember* modifies the noun *words*.]
adverb:	The hill was too icy <u>to climb</u>.
	[The infinitive *to climb* modifies the predicate adjective *icy*.]

He lived <u>to golf</u>.
[The infinitive *to golf* modifies the verb *lived*.]

A **participle** is a verb form that has one of two uses: to make a verb phrase ("<u>they were trying</u>"; "the car <u>has died</u>") or to act as an adjective. A participle is a verbal only when it acts as an adjective.

A **present participle** always ends in *-ing*:

catching   winding
laughing

A **past participle** usually ends in *-ed*, *-en*, or *-t*:

given   toasted
lost

In the following examples, each participle acts as an adjective and is therefore a verbal:

Does the zoo have a <u>laughing</u> hyena?
We live on a <u>winding</u> road.
It was a <u>lost</u> opportunity.
Add a cup of <u>toasted</u> coconut.

TIP

Remember: Both gerunds and present participles always end in *-ing*, but their functions are quite distinct. Also remember that a present participle is only a verbal when it acts as an adjective, *not* when it acts as a verb phrase.

verbal:	Her singing has improved this year. [Used as a noun, *singing* is a gerund, which is always a verbal.]
	Peterson hired the singing cowboys. [Used as an adjective, *singing* is a present participle that is also a verbal.]
not a verbal:	The birds are singing. [Used to form a verb phrase, *singing* is a present participle, but not a verbal]

A **gerund** is a verb form that acts as a noun. It always ends in *-ing*:

> <u>Reading</u> is my favorite pastime.
> The next step, <u>varnishing</u>, should be done in a well-ventilated area.
> The doctor suggested guidelines for sensible <u>dieting</u>.

Adjective

An **adjective** is a word that modifies a noun. There are two basic types of adjectives: descriptive and limiting.

DESCRIPTIVE ADJECTIVES

A **descriptive adjective** describes a noun. That is, it shows a quality or condition of a noun:

> She is an <u>upstanding</u> citizen.
> Josh has invited his <u>zany</u> friends.
> That was a <u>mighty</u> clap of thunder.
> I prefer the <u>white</u> shirt with the <u>long</u> sleeves.

LIMITING ADJECTIVES

A **limiting adjective** shows the limits of a noun. That is, it indicates the number or quantity of a noun, or it points out a certain specificity of a noun. There are three types of limiting adjectives: numerical adjectives, pronominal adjectives, and articles.

A **numerical adjective** is a number. It may be cardinal ("how many") or ordinal ("in what order"):

cardinal: We have served <u>one million</u> customers.
             There are <u>three</u> prizes.
             After Arizona was admitted, there were <u>forty-eight</u> states.

ordinal: You are the <u>one millionth</u> customer.
             We won <u>third</u> prize.
             Arizona was the <u>forty-eighth</u> state to be admitted.

A **pronominal adjective** is a pronoun that acts as an adjective. A pronominal adjective may be personal (*my, our, your, his, her, their, its*), demonstrative (*this, that, these, those*), indefinite (*all, any, few, other, several, some*), or interrogative (*which, what*).

personal:	We loved <u>her</u> goulash.
	The squirrel returned to <u>its</u> nest.
demonstrative:	<u>Those</u> directions are too complicated.
	<u>This</u> window is broken.
indefinite:	Pick <u>any</u> card from the deck.
	<u>All</u> luggage will be inspected.
interrogative:	<u>Which</u> radios are on sale?
	<u>What</u> color is the upholstery?

There are three **articles** in English: *a*, *an*, and *the*. Articles are classified as either indefinite (*a, an*) or definite (*the*).

indefinite:	At dawn, <u>a</u> helicopter broke the silence.
	<u>An</u> usher seated us.
definite:	<u>The</u> paintings lacked imagination.

Comparison of adjectives

Descriptive adjectives are able to indicate qualities and conditions by three degrees of comparison: positive, comparative, and superlative. Adjectives may be compared in downward or upward order.

For **downward comparisons**, most adjectives use the words *less* (comparative) and *least* (superlative).

DOWNWARD COMPARISONS

positive	comparative	superlative
(the quality or condition)	(a degree lower than the positive)	(the lowest degree of the positive)
intelligent	less intelligent	least intelligent
kind	less kind	least kind
salty	less salty	least salty

For **upward comparisons**, there are three different formats:

UPWARD COMPARISONS

positive (the quality or condition)	comparative (a degree higher than the positive)	superlative (the highest degree of the positive)

1. Almost all one-syllable adjectives use the endings *–er* (comparative) and *–est* (superlative). Some adjectives with two or more syllables follow this format as well.

kind	kinder	kindest
straight	straighter	straightest
salty	saltier	saltiest

2. Most adjectives with two or more syllables use the words *more* (comparative) and *most* (superlative). Most one-syllable adjectives may use this format as an optional alternative to using *–er* and *–est*.

harmonious	more harmonious	most harmonious
impatient	more impatient	most impatient
talkative	more talkative	most talkative
kind	more kind	most kind

TIP

Never "double compare" an adjective. Remember:

- Sometimes a descriptive adjective may use either -*er* or *more*, but it never uses both.

    correct: The red grapes are <u>sweeter</u> than the green ones.
    The red grapes are <u>more sweet</u> than the green ones.

    incorrect: The red grapes are <u>more sweeter</u> than the green ones.

- Sometimes a descriptive adjective may use either -*est* or *most*, but it never uses both.

    correct: Samson is the <u>friendliest</u> dog in the building.
    Samson is the <u>most friendly</u> dog in the building.

    incorrect: Samson is the <u>most friendliest</u> dog in the building.

---

3. Some adjectives have irregular forms.

bad/ill	worse	worst
good/well	better	best
far	farther/further	farthest/furthest
little	less	least
many	more	most

Adverb

An **adverb** is a word that modifies a verb, an adjective, or another adverb.

Adverb meanings

An adverb usually describes how, where, when, or to what extent something happens.

An **adverb of manner** describes *how*:

They argued loudly.

An **adverb of place** describes *where*:

Please sit near me.

An **adverb of time** describes *when*:

I'll call you later.

An **adverb of degree** describes *to what extent*:

The laundry is somewhat damp.

Adverb functions

A **relative adverb** introduces a subordinate clause:

I'll be out on the veranda when the clock strikes twelve.

A **conjunctive adverb** (also called a **transitional adverb**) joins two independent clauses:

Dinner is ready; however, you may have to heat it up.

An **interrogative adverb** introduces a question:

Where did Lisa go?

TIP

A great number of adverbs are created by adding the suffix *-ly* to an adjective:

hesitant + *-ly* = hesitantly

strong + *-ly* = strongly

This does not mean, however, that all adverbs end in *-ly*.

adverbs: fast, seldom, now

Nor does it mean that all words ending in *-ly* are adverbs.

adjectives: friendly, homely, dastardly

The way to determine if a word is an adverb or an adjective is to see how it is used in the sentence:

- If it modifies a noun, it is an adjective.
- If it modifies a verb, an adjective, or another adverb, it is an adverb.

An **independent adverb** functions independently from the rest of the sentence. That is, the meaning and grammatical correctness of the sentence would not change if the independent adverb were removed:

Besides, I never liked living in the city.

COMPARISON OF ADVERBS

Like adjectives, adverbs of manner may be compared in three degrees: positive, comparative, and superlative.

Most adverbs, especially those that end in *-ly*, take on the upward comparing words *more* and *most*.

positive	comparative	superlative
nicely	more nicely	most nicely
diligently	more diligently	most diligently

Some adverbs take on the upward comparing suffixes *-er* and *-est*:

positive	comparative	superlative
early	earlier	earliest
soon	sooner	soonest
close	closer	closest

Some adverbs have irregular upward comparisons.

positive	comparative	superlative
much	more	most
well	better	best
far	farther	farthest
far	further	furthest

Almost all adverbs take on the downward comparing words *less* and *least*:

positive	comparative	superlative
nicely	less nicely	least nicely
diligently	less diligently	least diligently
early	less early	least early
soon	less soon	least soon
close	less close	least close

Preposition

A **preposition** is a word or group of words that governs a noun or pronoun by expressing its relationship to another word in the clause.

The suspects landed *in* jail.
[The relationship between the noun *jail* and the verb *landed* is shown by the preposition *in*.]

Please hide the packages <u>under</u> the bed.
[The relationship between the noun *bed* and the noun *packages* is shown by the preposition *under*.]

The guitarist playing <u>with</u> our band is Samantha's uncle.
[The relationship between the noun *band* and the participle *playing* is shown by the preposition *with*.]

I already knew <u>about</u> it.
[The relationship between the pronoun *it* and the verb *knew* is shown by the preposition *about*.]

TIP

Many words used as prepositions may be used as other parts of speech as well.

The closest village is <u>over</u> that hill.	[preposition]
He leaned <u>over</u> and whispered in my ear.	[adverb]
I told no one <u>but</u> Corinne.	[preposition]
We played our best, <u>but</u> the other team won.	[conjunction]
She is <u>but</u> a shadow of her former self.	[adverb]

Common prepositions

aboard	beneath	in front of	past
about	beside	in lieu of	per
above	besides	in place of	prior to
according to	between	in regard to	regarding
across	beyond	in spite of	round
after	but	inside	since
against	but for	instead of	thanks to
ahead	by	into	through
along	by means of	like	throughout
along with	by way of	near	till
amid	concerning	next to	to
around	contrary to	of	toward
as	despite	off	under
as far as	down	on	underneath
as for	during	on account of	unlike
as to	except	on behalf of	until
aside from	for	onto	up
at	from	opposite	upon
because of	in	out	up to
before	in addition to	out of	with
behind	in back of	outside	within
below	in case of	over	without

Conjunction

A **conjunction** is a word (or unit of words) that connects words, phrases, clauses, or sentences. There are three kinds of conjunctions: coordinating, subordinating, and correlative.

COORDINATING CONJUNCTIONS

A **coordinating conjunction** connects elements that have the same grammatical rank—that is, it connects words to words (nouns to nouns, verbs to verbs, etc.), phrases to phrases, clauses to clauses, sentences to sentences. A coordinating conjunction is almost always one of these seven words: *and, but, for, nor, or, so, yet.*

Would you prefer rice <u>or</u> potatoes?
[The coordinating conjunction *or* connects the two nouns *rice* and *potatoes.*]

I have seen <u>and</u> heard enough.
[The coordinating conjunction *and* connects the two verbs *seen* and *heard.*]

Vinnie's cat lay on the chair purring softly <u>yet</u> twitching its tail.
[The coordinating conjunction *yet* connects the two participial phrases *purring softly* and *twitching its tail.*]

O'Donnell is the reporter whose name is on the story <u>but</u> who denies having written it.
[The coordinating conjunction *but* connects the two subordinate clauses *whose name is on the story* and *who denies having written it.*]

We wanted to see batting practice, <u>so</u> we got to the stadium early.
[The coordinating conjunction *so* connects the two sentences *We wanted to see batting practice* and *We got to the stadium early*, creating one sentence. Notice that a comma precedes the conjunction when two sentences are joined.]

SUBORDINATING CONJUNCTIONS

A **subordinating conjunction** belongs to a subordinate clause. It connects the subordinate clause to a main clause.

> I could get there on time if only the ferry were still running.
> [The subordinating conjunction *if only* connects the subordinate clause *if only the ferry were still running* to the main clause *I could get there on time*.]

TIP

A noun clause or an adjective clause may or may not be introduced by a subordinating conjunction, but an adverb clause is always introduced by a subordinating conjunction.

- noun clause introduced by subordinating conjunction:
  Jack asked the question <u>even though he knew the answer</u>.

- noun clause with no subordinating conjunction:
  We gave <u>every single detail</u> our fullest attention.

- adjective clause introduced by subordinating conjunction:
  This is the farm <u>where we boarded our horses</u>.

- adjective clause with no subordinating conjunction:
  The people <u>we met last night</u> are Hungarian.

- adverb clause with subordinating conjunction (as is always the case):
  I will speak <u>as soon</u> as the crowd quiets down.

Common subordinating conjunctions

after	but	since	until
although	even if	so	when
as	even though	so that	whenever
as if	how	than	where
as long as	if	that	whereas
as though	if only	though	wherever
because	in order that	till	while
before	rather than	unless	why

CORRELATIVE CONJUNCTIONS

Two coordinating conjunctions that function together are called a pair of **correlative conjunctions**. These are the most common pairs of correlative conjunctions:

both . . . and
either . . . or
neither . . . nor

not only . . . but
not only . . . but also
whether . . . or

The site in Denver offers the potential for both security and expansion.
[The pair of correlative conjunctions *both . . . and* connects the two nouns *security* and *expansion*.]

I'm running in tomorrow's race whether it is sunny or rainy.
[The pair of correlative conjunctions *whether . . . or* connects the two adjectives *sunny* and *rainy*.]

TIP

It would be incorrect to say:

Their dog is <u>neither</u> quiet <u>nor</u> obeys simple commands.

Why? Because the pair of correlative conjunctions *neither . . . nor* is being used to connect the adjective *quiet* to the verb phrase *obeys simple commands*. This is not a grammatically valid connection.

Remember: A pair of correlative conjunctions is comprised of two coordinating conjunctions, and a coordinating conjunction must connect elements that have the same grammatical rank—that is, it must connect words to words (nouns to nouns, verbs to verbs, etc.), phrases to phrases, clauses to clauses, sentences to sentences.

Therefore, the sentence must be reworded to make the grammatical ranks match. Here are two such corrected versions:

Their dog is <u>neither</u> quiet <u>nor</u> obedient.
[The adjective *quiet* is connected to the adjective *obedient*.]

Their dog <u>neither</u> stays quiet <u>nor</u> obeys simple commands.
[The verb phrase *stays quiet* is connected to the verb phrase *obeys simple commands*.]

Interjection

An interjection is a word or phrase that expresses emotion, typically in an abrupt or emphatic way. It is not connected grammatically to the rest of the sentence. When the emotion expressed is very strong, the interjection is followed by an exclamation point. Otherwise it is followed by a comma:

> <u>Stop</u>! I can't let you in here.
> <u>Yeah!</u> Dempsey has won another fight.
>
> <u>Ah</u>, that was a wonderful meal.
> <u>Oh no</u>, I left my sweater on the train.

TIP

Interjections occur more often in speech than in writing. It is not wrong to use interjections in writing, but writers should do so sparingly. Remember, an interjection is essentially an interruption, and too many may disrupt the flow of the text.

PHRASES, CLAUSES, SENTENCES, AND PARAGRAPHS

Phrases

A **phrase** is a unit of words that acts as a single part of speech.

NOUN PHRASES

A phrase made up of a noun and its modifiers is a **noun phrase**:

> <u>The biggest pumpkin</u> won <u>a blue ribbon</u>.
> <u>A magnificent whooping crane</u> flew overhead.

Most noun phrases can be replaced with a pronoun:

> Give the tickets to <u>the tall, dark-haired gentleman</u>.
> Give the tickets to <u>him</u>.

VERB PHRASES

A phrase made up of a main verb and its auxiliaries is a **verb phrase** (also called a **complete verb**):

We <u>have been waiting</u> for three hours.
What type of music <u>do you prefer</u>?

ADJECTIVE PHRASES

A phrase made up of a participle and its related words is an **adjective phrase** (also called an **adjectival phrase** or a **participial phrase**). Acting as a single adjective, it modifies a noun or pronoun:

<u>Awakened by the siren</u>, we escaped to safety.
[The adjective phrase *Awakened by the siren* modifies the pronoun *we*.]

<u>Following his grandmother's directions</u>, Harry baked a beautiful apple pie.
[The adjective phrase *Following his grandmother's directions* modifies the noun *Harry*.]

PREPOSITIONAL PHRASES

A phrase that begins with a preposition is a **prepositional phrase**. It can act as an adjective or an adverb:

adjective: The car <u>with the sunroof</u> is mine.
[The noun *car* is modified by the prepositional phrase *with the sunroof*.]

adverb: <u>After the storm</u>, we gathered the fallen branches.
[The verb *gathered* is modified by the prepositional phrase *After the storm*.]

Clauses

A clause is a unit of words that contains a subject and a predicate.

INDEPENDENT CLAUSES

A clause that can stand by itself as a complete thought is an **independent clause**. Any independent clause can stand alone as a complete sentence:

<u>The Milwaukee Brewers joined the National League in November 1997.</u>

It is snowing.
Vitus is the patron saint of actors.
Bob called.
The Celts were highly ritualistic.
Read what child development experts have to say.

SUBORDINATE CLAUSES

A clause that cannot stand by itself as a complete thought is a **subordinate clause** (also called a **dependent clause**). It cannot be a part of a sentence unless it is related by meaning to the independent clause. Essentially, it exists to build upon the information conveyed by the independent clause. A subordinate clause can relate to the independent clause as an adjective, an adverb, or a noun:

adjective: The Milwaukee Brewers, who play at Miller Park, joined the National League in November 1997.

adverb: Bob called when you were at the store.

noun: Read what child development experts have to say about the virtues and drawbacks of home-schooling.

ELLIPTICAL CLAUSES

An **elliptical clause** deviates from the rule that states "a clause contains a subject and a predicate." What an elliptical clause does is *imply* both a subject and a predicate, even though both elements do not in fact appear in the clause:

While vacationing in Spain, Jo received word of her promotion.
[The elliptical clause implies the subject "she" and the predicate "was vacationing"—that is, it implies "While she was vacationing in Spain."]

Myers arrived on Saturday the 12th; Anderson, the following Monday.
[The elliptical clause implies the predicate "arrived the following Monday"—that is it implies "Anderson arrived the following Monday."]

Elliptical clauses are valuable devices, as they allow the writer to avoid excessive wordiness, preserve a sense of variety, and enhance the rhythm of the text.

RESTRICTIVE CLAUSES

A clause that is essential to the meaning of the sentence—that is, it *restricts* the meaning of the sentence—is a **restrictive clause**. The content of a restrictive clause identifies a particular person, place, or thing. If the restrictive clause were to be removed, the meaning of the sentence would change. A restrictive clause begins with the relative pronoun *that*, *who*, or *whom*. It should never be set off with commas.

I'm returning the coat <u>that I bought last week</u>.
[The identification of the coat is important. It's not just any coat. It's specifically the one and only coat "that I bought last week." Without the restrictive clause, the identification would be lost.]

The president <u>who authorized the Louisiana Purchase</u> was Thomas Jefferson.
[The point of this sentence is to identify specifically the one and only president responsible for the Louisiana Purchase. Without the restrictive clause, the point of the sentence would be lost.]

NONRESTRICTIVE CLAUSES

A clause that is not essential to the meaning of the sentence—that is, it does *not restrict* the meaning of the sen-tence—is a **nonrestrictive clause**. The content of a nonrestrictive clause adds information to what has already been identified. If the nonrestrictive clause were to be removed, the meaning of the sentence would not change. A non-restrictive clause begins with the relative pronoun *which*, *who*, or *whom*. It should always be set off with commas.

I'm returning my new coat, <u>which doesn't fit</u>.

President Jefferson, <u>who authorized the Louisiana Purchase</u>, was the third U.S. president.

[The clauses *which doesn't fit* and *who authorized the Louisiana Purchase* are informative but not necessary. Without them, the meaning of each sentence is still clear.]

Sentences

Properly constructed sentences are integral to good communication. By definition, a sentence is "a set of words that is complete in itself, typically containing a subject and predicate, conveying a statement, question, exclamation, or command, and consisting of a main clause and sometimes one or more subordinate clauses." Simply put, a sentence is a group of words that expresses a complete thought.

SUBJECT AND PREDICATE

The primary building blocks of a sentence are the subject and the predicate.

The **subject** (usually a noun or pronoun) is the part that the sentence is telling about. A **simple subject** is simply the person, place, or thing being discussed. A **complete subject** is the simple subject along with all the words directly associated with it:

The large tropical plant in my office has bloomed every summer.
[Here, the simple subject is *plant*. The complete subject is *The large tropical plant in my office*.]

Two or more subjects that belong to the same verb comprise what is called a **compound subject**:

Stan Garrison and the rest of the department are relocating next week.
[Here, the compound subject consists of *Stan Garrison* and *the rest of the department*. They share the verb phrase *are relocating*.]

The **predicate** (a verb) is the "action" or "being" part of the sentence—the part that tells something about the subject. A **simple predicate** is simply the main verb and its auxiliaries. A **complete predicate** is the simple predicate along with all the words directly associated with it:

The setting sun <u>has cast a scarlet glow across the skyline</u>.
[Here, the simple predicate is *has cast*. The complete predicate is *has cast a scarlet glow across the skyline*.]

Two or more predicates that have the same subject comprise what is called a **compound predicate**:

I <u>wanted to buy some art</u> but *left empty-handed*.
[Here, the compound predicate consists of *wanted to buy some art* and *left empty-handed*. They share the subject *I*.]

FOUR SENTENCE STRUCTURES

A **simple sentence** contains one independent clause. Its subject and/or predicate may or may not be compound, but its one and only clause is always independent:

Paula rode her bicycle.
[subject + predicate]

Honus Wagner and Nap Lajoie are enshrined in the Baseball Hall of Fame.
[compound subject + predicate]

The correspondents traveled across the desert and slept in makeshift shelters.
[subject + compound predicate]

Lunch and dinner are discounted on Sunday but are full price on Monday.
[compound subject + compound predicate]

A **compound sentence** contains two or more independent clauses. The following examples show the various ways that coordinating conjunctions (e.g., *and*, *but*, *yet*), conjunctive adverbs (e.g., *however*, *therefore*), and punctuation may be used to join the clauses in a compound sentence:

Ken made the phone calls and Maria addressed the envelopes.

The war lasted for two years, but the effects of its devastation will last for decades.

Judges and other officials should sign in by noon; exhibitors will start arriving at 2:00.

I have decided to remain on the East Coast; however, I am willing to attend the monthly meetings in Dallas.

FDR initiated the New Deal, JFK embraced the New Frontier, and LBJ envisioned the Great Society.

A **complex sentence** contains one independent clause and one or more subordinate clauses:

Even though I majored in English, I was hired to teach applied physics.

We can have the party indoors if it gets too windy.

Before I agree, I have to read the final report that you drafted.

[The independent clauses are *I was hired to teach applied physics; We can have the party indoors; I have to read the final report.* The subordinate clauses are *Even though I majored in English; if it gets too windy; Before I agree; that you drafted.*]

A **compound-complex sentence** contains two or more independent clauses and one or more subordinate clauses:

Because the candidates have been so argumentative, some voters are confused and many have become disinterested.

We will begin painting tomorrow if the weather's nice; if it rains, we will start on Thursday.
[The independent clauses are *some voters are confused; many have become disinterested; We will begin painting tomorrow, we will start on Thursday.* The subordinate clauses are *Because the candidates have been so argumentative; if the weather's nice; if it rains.*]

FOUR SENTENCE FUNCTIONS

A **declarative sentence** states a fact, an assertion, an impression, or a feeling. It ends with a period:

Florence is a beautiful city.

Lewis Carroll died in 1898.
I'm sorry I missed the end of your speech.

An **interrogative sentence** asks a question. It ends with a question mark:

Did you read the article about migrating geese patterns?
How do spell your last name?
Mr. Young owns a kennel?

An **imperative sentence** makes a request or gives an order. It typically ends with a period but occasionally may end with an exclamation point:

Please lock the doors.
Do not throw trash in the recycling bins.
Think before you speak!

An **exclamatory sentence** expresses surprise, shock, or strong feeling. It ends with an exclamation point:

Look at this mess!
I can't believe how great this is!
I lost my purse!

Paragraphs

A paragraph is a series of sentences that conveys a single theme. Paragraphs help writers organize thoughts, actions, and descriptions into readable units of information. The paragraph, as a unit of text, may have one of several functions. It may be descriptive, giving certain details or impressions about a person, thing, or event. It may be instructive, explaining a method or procedure. It may be conceptual, stating thoughts, feelings, or opinions.

Every paragraph should contain a sentence that states the main idea of the paragraph. This is called the **topic sentence**. The other sentences in the paragraph are the **supporting sentences**, and their function is just that—to support or elaborate on the idea set forth in the topic sentence. Most paragraphs begin with the topic sentence, as in the following example:

Each Thanksgiving we make place cards decorated with pressed autumn leaves. After gathering the smallest and most colorful leaves from the maples and oaks in our backyard, we place the leaves between sheets of blotter paper, which we then cover with a large, heavy book. In just a day or two, the leaves are ready to be mounted on cards. We use plain index cards, folded in half. Using clear adhesive paper, we put one leaf on each card, leaving room for the guest's name.

Try reading the preceding paragraph without the topic sentence (the first sentence). The supporting information becomes less unified because it has no main idea to support. Now imagine adding to the paragraph the following sentence:

Last year, three of our guests were snowed in at the airport.

This would be a misplaced addition to the paragraph, as it is unrelated to the topic sentence (that is, it has nothing to do with making Thanksgiving place cards). Because it introduces a new and distinct idea, it should become the topic sentence for a new and distinct paragraph.

SENTENCE DEVELOPMENT: AVOIDING PROBLEMS

Sentence style

Getting one's ideas across in words is the core of communication. Sentences provide the means to arrange ideas in a coherent way. Certainly, the rules of grammar should be observed when constructing a sentence, but the general rhythm of the sentence is also important. Sentences may be categorized into three general types: loose, periodic, and balanced. Good writers typically use a combination of these styles in order to create a flow of ideas that will hold the reader's interest.

A loose sentence gets to the main point quickly. It begins with a basic and complete statement, which is followed by additional information:

The power went out, plunging us into darkness, silencing the drone of the television, leaving our dinner half-cooked.

[The basic statement is *The power went out*. Everything that follows is additional information.]

A **periodic sentence** ends with the main point. It begins with additional information, thus imposing a delay before the basic statement is given:

> With no warning, like a herd of stampeding bison, a mob of fans crashed through the gate.
> The basic statement is *a mob of fans crashed through the gate*. Everything that precedes is additional information.

A **balanced sentence** is comprised of grammatically equal or similar structures. The ideas in the sentence are linked by comparison or contrast:

> To visit their island villa is to sample nirvana.

As writers become more comfortable with the basic rules of grammar and the general patterns of sentence structure, they are able to remain compliant with the rules while getting more creative with the patterns. Many well-constructed sentences will not agree precisely with any of the three preceding examples, but they should always evoke an answer of "yes" to two fundamental questions:

- Is the sentence grammatically correct?
- Will the meaning of the sentence be clear to the reader?

Flawed sentences

Three types of "flawed sentences" are sentence fragments, run-on sentences, and sentences with improperly positioned modifiers.

SENTENCE FRAGMENTS

A **sentence fragment** is simply an incomplete sentence. Fundamental to every sentence is a complete thought that is able to stand on its own. Because a phrase or subordinate clause is not an independent thought, it cannot stand on its own as a sentence. To be a part of a sentence, it must either be connected to an independent clause or be reworded to become an independent clause. Consider this sentence fragment:

> My English guest who stayed on for Christmas.

Here are three possible ways to create a proper sentence from that fragment:

> Everyone left on Tuesday except Dan, my English guest who stayed on for Christmas.
> [The fragment is added to the independent clause *Everyone left on Tuesday except Dan.*]

> My English guest stayed on for Christmas.
> [The fragment becomes an independent clause by removing the word *who*.]

> Dan was my English guest who stayed on for Christmas.
> [The fragment becomes an independent clause by adding the words *Dan was*.]

RUN-ON SENTENCES

A **run-on sentence** results when two or more sentences are improperly united into one sentence. Characteristic of a run-on sentence is the absence of punctuation between the independent clauses or the use of incorrect punctuation (typically a comma) between the independent clauses:

> Our flight was canceled we had to spend the night in Boston.
> Our flight was canceled, we had to spend the night in Boston.

Here are three possible ways to correct the preceding run-on sentences:

> Our flight was canceled; we had to spend the night in Boston.
> [A semicolon provides a properly punctuated separation of the two independent clauses.]

> Our flight was canceled, so we had to spend the night in Boston.
> [A comma followed by a conjunction (*so*) provides a properly worded and punctuated separation of the two independent clauses.]

> Our flight was canceled. We had to spend the night in Boston.
> [The creation of two distinct sentences provides an absolute separation of the two independent clauses.]

MODIFIER PROBLEMS

The improper placement of modifying words, phrases, and clauses is a common mistake. The result is a sentence in which the modifier unintentionally refers to the wrong person or thing. The three principal culprits are dangling modifiers, misplaced modifiers, and squinting modifiers. Writers must be careful to avoid these troublesome errors in sentence construction. Review the following examples to see how an improperly placed modifier can be confusing to the reader. It is important to recognize the subtle differences between the incorrect sentences and their corrected versions.

A **dangling modifier** is an adjectival phrase or clause that lacks a proper connection because the word it is supposed to modify is missing.

dangling: While waiting for my son, a cat jumped onto the hood of my car.
[This wrongly implies that "a cat was waiting for my son."]

correct: While I was waiting for my son, a cat jumped onto the hood of my car.
While waiting for my son, I saw a cat jump onto the hood of my car.

A cat jumped onto the hood of my car while I was waiting for my son.
[The word that was missing is "I."]

dangling: At age seven, her grandfather died of diphtheria.
[This wrongly implies that "her grandfather died when he was seven."]

correct: When she was seven, her grandfather died of diphtheria.
Her grandfather died of diphtheria when she was seven.
At age seven, she lost her grandfather when he died of diphtheria.
[The word that was missing is "she."]

A **misplaced modifier** is a phrase or clause that is not positioned close enough to the word it is supposed to modify. It will seem to the reader that a different word is being modified.

misplaced: There was an outbreak in our school of chicken pox.
             [This wrongly implies that there is "a school of chicken pox."]

correct: There was an outbreak of chicken pox in our school.
             In our school there was an outbreak of chicken pox.
             Our school experienced an outbreak of chicken pox.

misplaced: I was stopped by a policeman without a driver's license.
             [This wrongly implies that there was "a policeman without a driver's license."]

correct: Driving without a license, I was stopped by a policeman.
             I was stopped by a policeman, and I did not have a driver's license.

A **squinting modifier** is an adverb placed between two verbs. For the reader, it is often difficult to determine which verb the adverb is supposed to modify.

squinting: The stack of chairs she had arranged carefully collapsed in the wind.
             [Was the stack of chairs "arranged carefully" or did it "carefully collapse"?]

correct: The stack of chairs she had carefully arranged collapsed in the wind.
             [Of the two possible meanings, this is only one that makes sense.]

squinting: The stack of chairs she had arranged quickly collapsed in the wind.
             [Was the stack of chairs "arranged quickly" or did it "quickly collapse"?]

correct: The stack of chairs she had quickly arranged collapsed in the wind.

The stack of chairs she had arranged collapsed quickly in the wind.

[Either meaning could make sense, so only the writer would know which version is correct.]

Guide to Spelling

Any reader or writer knows that spelling is an important component of writing. Some individuals seem to have little or no trouble spelling words correctly, while others seem to struggle with spelling, often misspelling the same words over and over.

For those who have experienced the struggle, it is important to remember that spelling is a skill that improves with practice. Regular reading and writing, accompanied by a dictionary for consultation, are the best methods for improving one's spelling. Anyone who has encountered trouble with spelling knows that the English language contains numerous irregularities. Even so, there are basic spelling rules that can be followed in most cases.

[For spelling guidelines for plural nouns and possessive nouns, refer to the "Noun" section under "Parts of Speech."]

TIP

Keep a list of words that you find difficult to spell. Use a dictionary to confirm the correct spellings. Add to your list whenever you encounter a troublesome word. Refer to your list often, and quiz yourself. Make up sentences that include words from the list, writing them without going back and forth to double-check the spelling. Compare the words in your sentences to the words on your list. Make a note of the words that continue to give you trouble, and write these words in sentences every day until you have learned to spell them.

COMPOUND ADJECTIVES AND NOUNS

A compound adjective or noun is a single term formed from two or more distinct words. There are three spelling formats for compounds: open, hyphenated, and closed.

In an **open compound**, the component words are separate, with no hyphen (*well fed; wagon train*).
In a **hyphenated compound**, the component words are joined by a hyphen (*half-baked; city-state*).
In a **closed compound**, the component words are joined into a single word (*hardheaded; campfire*).

Compound Adjectives

For most cases of open compound adjectives, there is a general rule of thumb: the compound is left open when it is not followed by the modified noun; the compound is hyphenated when it is followed by the modified noun:

<u>She</u> was <u>well known</u> in the South for her poetry.
[The compound *well known* is open because it is not followed by the modified noun *She*.]

In the South, she was a <u>well-known poet</u>.
[The compound *well-known* is hyphenated because it is followed by the modified noun *poet*.]

A notable exception occurs when the first part of the compound adjective is an adverb that ends in *–ly*. In this case, the compound remains open, even when it is followed by the noun:

The <u>woman</u> who met us in the lobby was <u>beautifully dressed</u>.
A <u>beautifully dressed woman</u> met us in the lobby.

Compound Nouns

For spellers, the least troublesome compound nouns are familiar closed compounds:

briefcase	downstairs
cupcake	fireplace

Other compound nouns can be troublesome. Although certain ones, such as *mother-in-law*, are always hyphenated, many compound nouns commonly occur in more than one acceptable format, such as *ice cap* or *icecap* and *vice president* or *vice-president*. For most spelling questions, the best resource is a dictionary; for questions pertaining specifically to compounds, an unabridged edition is recommended.

TIP

Different dictionaries often disagree on the preferred spelling formats for a number of compounds, so writers are well advised to consult just one dictionary when establishing a spelling style.

PREFIXES

A prefix is a group of letters added to the beginning of a word to adjust its meaning.

In most cases, prefixes are affixed to the root word without hyphenation:

antibacterial	semicircle
postwar	

Often, however, a hyphen is customary, necessary, or preferable.

Certain prefixes almost always take a hyphen: *all-*, *ex-*, *full-*, *quasi-*, *self-*:

all-encompassing	quasi-liberal
ex-partner	self-confidence
full-bodied	

When the root word begins with a capital letter, the prefix takes a hyphen:

anti-American
pre-Conquest

Sometimes, without a hyphen, a word could be easily confused with another:

We <u>recovered</u> our furniture.

Does this mean we *found* our *missing* furniture? Or did we *put new coverings on* our furniture? If the latter is meant, a hyphen would have avoided confusion:

We <u>re-covered</u> our furniture.

Sometimes, a hyphen is not necessary but preferable. Without it, the word may look awkward. One such circumstance is when the last letter of the prefix and the first letter of the root word are both vowels, or when an awkward double consonant is created. For each of the following pairs of words, either spelling is acceptable:

antiknock / anti-knock	semiindependent / semi-independent
preadapt / pre-adapt	nonnegative / non-negative

TIP

Regarding the use of optional hyphens, the writer should establish a preferred style. Keeping a running list of hyphenated terms can help writers keep track of which spellings they have already used in their text, thus making the style consistent.

SUFFIXES

A suffix is a group of letters added to the end of a word to create a derivative of the word. There are exceptions to the following guidelines on how to spell with suffixes, but in most cases these rules apply:

A root word that ends in *e* drops the *e* when the suffix begins with a vowel:

rehearse / rehearsing

However, most words that end in *ce* or *ge* keep the *e* when the suffix begins with *a* or *o*:

service / serviceable
advantage / advantageous

A root word that ends in *e* keeps the *e* when the suffix begins with a consonant:

wise / wisely

A root word that ends in a *y* preceded by a consonant changes the *y* to *i* when the suffix begins with any letter other than *i*:

satisfy / satisfies / satisfying

A root word that ends in *ie* changes the *ie* to *y* when the suffix is –*ing*:

lie / lying

A root word that ends in *oe* keeps the *e* when the suffix begins with a vowel, unless the vowel is *e*:

toe / toeing / toed

A one-syllable root word that ends in a single consonant preceded by a single vowel doubles the consonant when the suffix is –*ed*, –*er*, or –*ing*. This rule also applies to root words with two or more syllables if the accent is on the last syllable.

stir / stirred
refer / referring

WORD DIVISION

Sometimes it is necessary to "break" a word when the line on the page has run out of space. Dividing a word at the end of a line is perfectly acceptable, as long as two conditions are met: the word must be divisible, and the division must be made in the right place.

When a word is properly divided, a hyphen is attached to its first part, so that the hyphen is at the end of the line:

At the conclusion of the interview, I had two minutes to summarize my management experiences.

What words are never divisible?	*for example:*
• one-syllable words	catch; flutes; strange; through
• contractions	didn't; doesn't; wouldn't; you're
• abbreviations	Calif.; NASCAR; RSVP; YMCA
• numbers written as numerals	1776; $2, 800; 9:45; 0.137

Where is a correct place to divide a word?	good break:	bad break:
• after a prefix	inter-national	interna-tional
• before a suffix that has more than two letters	govern-ment	gov-ernment
• between the main parts of a closed compound	nut-cracker	nutcrack-er
• at the hyphen of a hyphenated compound	gender-neutral	gen-der-neutral
• after double consonants if the root word ends in the double consonants	address-ing	addres-sing
• otherwise, between double consonants	rib-bon	ribb-on
• in general (for words that don't fall into the previous categories), between syllables	whis-per	whi-sper

Where is an incorrect place to divide a word?	good break:	bad break:
• before a two-letter suffix	——	odd-ly
• after the first syllable if it has only one letter	Ameri-can	A-merican
• before the last syllable if it has only one letter	nu-tria	nutri-a
• before the ending -*ed* if the -*ed* is not pronounced as a separate syllable	——	abash-ed

---

TIP

When dividing a word at the end of a line, it is always a good idea to use a dictionary to verify the word's proper syllabification.

NUMBERS

Numbers are an important part of everyday communication, yet they often cause a writer to stumble, particularly over questions of spelling and style. The guidelines on *how* to spell out a number are fairly straightforward. The guidelines on *when* to spell out a number are not so precise.

How to Spell Out Numbers

CARDINAL NUMBERS

The most common problem associated with the spelling of whole cardinal numbers is punctuation. The rules are actually quite simple: Numeric amounts that fall between twenty and one hundred are always hyphenated. No other punctuation should appear in a spelled-out whole number, regardless of its size.

26	twenty-six
411	four hundred eleven
758	seven hundred fifty-eight
6,500	six thousand five hundred
33,003	thirty-three thousand three
972,923	nine hundred seventy-two thousand nine hundred twenty-three

Note: The word *and* does not belong in the spelling of a number. For example, "758" should not be spelled "seven hundred and fifty-eight."

ORDINAL NUMBERS

The punctuation of spelled-out ordinal numbers typically follows the rules for cardinal numbers.

What should we do for their <u>fifty-fifth</u> anniversary?
He graduated <u>two hundred twenty-ninth</u> out of a class of two hundred thirty.

When ordinal numbers appear as numerals, they are affixed with *-th*, with the exception of those ending with the ordinal *first*, *second*, or *third*.

1st	581st
2nd	32nd
3rd	73rd
4th	907th

Note: Sometimes 2nd is written as 2d, and 3rd as 3d.

FRACTIONS

A fraction can appear in a number of formats, as shown here:

⅜	case fraction (or split fraction)
3/8	fraction with solidus
0.375	decimal fraction
three-eighths	spelled-out fraction

When acting as an adjective, a spelled-out fraction should always be hyphenated.

The Serbian democrats have won a <u>two-thirds</u> majority.

When acting as a noun, a spelled-out fraction may or may not be hyphenated, according to the writer's or publisher's preferred style.

At least <u>four-fifths</u> of the supply has been depleted.

> *or*

At least <u>four fifths</u> of the supply has been depleted.

When to Spell Out Numbers

When to spell out a number, whole or fractional, is as much a matter of sense as of style. Text that is heavy with numbers, such as scientific or statistical material, could become virtually unreadable if the numbers were all spelled out. Conversely, conventional prose that occasionally makes mention of a quantity may look unbalanced with an occasional numeral here and there.

Often, the decision to spell or not to spell comes down to simple clarity:

Our standard paper size is 8½ by 11.
Our standard paper size is 8 1/2 by 11.
Our standard paper size is eight and a half by eleven.
Our standard paper size is eight and one-half by eleven.

The preceding four sentences say exactly the same thing, but the best choice for readability is the first.

Even the most comprehensive books of style and usage do not dictate absolute rules regarding the style of numbers in text. When

---

TIP

Numerals and other symbols should never begin a sentence. If the symbol should not or cannot be spelled out, the sentence needs to be reworded.

19 students have become mentors.
should be:
Nineteen students have become mentors.

2006 is the year we plan to get married.
should be:
We plan to get married in 2006.

$10 was found on the stairs.
should be:
Ten dollars was found on the stairs.

6:00 is the earliest I can leave.
should be:
Six o'clock is the earliest I can leave.
or:
The earliest I can leave is 6:00.

$y = 2x + 1$ is a line with a slope of 2.
should be:
The line $y = 2x + 1$ has a slope of 2.

---

writing, it is most important to be as consistent as possible with a style once one has been established. For example, some writers or publishers may adopt a policy of spelling out the numbers zero through ten. Others may prefer to spell out the numbers zero through ninety-nine. Either style is perfectly acceptable, as long as the style is followed throughout the written work.

Sometimes, even after adopting a basic number style, the writer may wish to incorporate certain style allowances and exceptions. Perhaps the decision has been made by the writer to spell out only the numbers zero though ninety-nine. But in one paragraph, a sentence reads, "There must have been more than 1,000,000 people there." In this case, it may be better to write, "There must have been more than a million people there."

SYMBOLS

In most contexts of formal writing, the use of symbols should be strictly limited, but there are occasions when a symbol may be a better choice than a word. Text that deals largely with commerce, for instance, may rely on the use of various monetary symbols to keep the text organized and readable. In any text, mathematical equations and scientific formulas are much easier to read if written with symbols rather than words. Also, it is usually appropriate to use symbols within tables and charts; as symbols conserve space, they prevent a "cluttered look." Here are some of the most common symbols found in print:

@	at	/	per or solidus
c/o	care of	%	percent
$	dollar	°	degree
¢	cent	+	plus
Can$	Canadian dollar	–	minus
£	pound sterling	÷	divided by
¥	yen	×	times
#	number or pound	±	plus or minus
=	equals	©	copyright
≈	is approximately equal to	®	registered
•	is not equal to	™	trademark
<	is less than	¶	paragraph
>	is greater than	§	section
≤	is less than or equal to	*	asterisk
≥	is greater than or equal to	†	dagger
√	square root	‡	double dagger
∞	infinity	‖	parallels or pipes

Symbols are sometimes used to point out note references to the reader. In a table or chart, for instance, the writer may wish to indicate that an item is further explained or identified elsewhere on the page. A symbol placed with the item signals the reader to look for an identical symbol, which precedes the additional information. Sometimes, numerals are the symbols of choice, but if the material within the table or chart consists of numerals, it is probably better to use non-numeric symbols for the note references. The conventional set of symbols used for this purpose, in the conventional sequence in which to use them, is *, †, ‡, §, ‖, #.

COMMONLY MISSPELLED WORDS

abbreviated	angel	benefited
absence	angle	bicycle
absolutely	annihilation	bouillon
acceptance	annually	boundary
accessible	answer	bulletin
accidentally	anticipate	bureau
accommodate	anxiety	buried
accompany	apartheid	business
accuracy	aperitif	cafeteria
ache	apology	calendar
achieve	apparatus	campaign
achievement	apparent	cancellation
acquaintance	appearance	captain
acquire	appetite	carburetor
acre	appreciate	career
across	approach	ceiling
actually	appropriate	cemetery
administration	approximately	census
admittance	argue	certificate
adolescent	argument	chamois
advantageous	arithmetic	changeable
advertisement	arrangement	character
advisable	ascend	characteristic
affectionate	ascertain	chauffeur
affidavit	assistant	chic
aficionado	athletic	chief
afraid	attendance	chocolate
again	authority	choice
aggravate	auxiliary	choose
aghast	available	chose
aisle	awkward	Christian
allege	bachelor	clothes
allotment	because	collateral
ally	beggar	colonel
amateur	beginning	color
analysis	behavior	column
analyze	believe	commercial
anesthetic	benefit	commission

committee	desperate	excellent
community	despise	exciting
compel	develop	exercise
competitor	difference	exhilarating
completely	dilemma	exhort
conceivable	diphthong	existence
concentrate	disappearance	expense
condemn	disappoint	experience
confidence	disastrous	experiment
confidential	discipline	extraordinary
confusion	discrepancy	extremely
connoisseur	disease	facsimile
conscience	diuretic	familiar
conscious	doctor	fantasy
continuous	duplicate	fascinate
controlled	easily	fashionable
controversial	ecclesiastical	fasten
conversant	ecstasy	fatal
convertible	effect	favorite
cooperate	efficient	February
copyright	eighth	field
corps	elementary	fiery
correspondence	eligible	finally
counterfeit	embarrass	financial
courageous	eminent	fluorescent
courteous	emphasize	forehead
criticism	encouragement	foreign
criticize	encumbrances	forfeit
cruelly	enforceable	fortunately
curiosity	entirely	forty
curious	entourage	forward
cylinder	envelope	fourth
dealt	environment	freight
debtor	equipped	friend
deceive	escape	fulfill
decision	especially	further
definite	essential	gauge
dependent	et cetera	genius
describe	(*abbreviated* etc.)	gourmet
despair	exaggerate	government

governor	individually	manufacturer
gracious	inevitable	marriage
grammar	influence	marvelous
guarantee	ingredient	Massachusetts
guerrilla	innocence	mathematics
guess	inoculate	meant
guidance	insurance	mechanic
gymnasium	intelligence	medical
gypsy	intelligent	medicine
handsome	interference	melancholy
hangar	interrupt	merchandise
hanger	iridescent	millionaire
happened	irrelevant	miniature
happiness	itinerary	minimum
harass	jealous	minuscule
Hawaii	jewelry	minute
heavily	knowledge	miscellaneous
height	laboratory	mischief
heinous	laborer	mischievous
heroine	laid	misspell
hors d'oeuvre	legitimate	mortgage
hospital	leisure	muscle
humor	liaison	mysterious
humorous	library	narrative
hungrily	license	naturally
hygiene	lieutenant	necessary
hypocrisy	lightning	nickel
hypocrite	likely	niece
hysterical	liquefy	ninety
ignorance	liquidate	noisily
illiterate	listener	non sequitur
imagine	literature	noticeable
immediately	livelihood	obstacle
impossible	lively	occasionally
incidentally	loneliness	occurrence
increase	luxury	offensive
indefinite	magazine	official
independent	magnificent	often
indictment	maintenance	omission
indispensable	maneuver	omit

omitted	practice	relieve
once	prairie	religious
operate	preferred	removal
opponent	prejudice	rendezvous
opportunity	preparation	repertoire
optimistic	presence	repetition
orchestra	pressure	rescind
ordinarily	pretension	reservoir
organization	privilege	resistance
originally	probably	resource
outrageous	procedure	responsibility
pageant	proceed	restaurant
paid	procure	rheumatism
parallel	professor	rhythm
paralleled	proffered	ridiculous
paralyze	promissory	roommate
parliament	pronunciation	sachet
particular	propaganda	sacrifice
pastime	psychic	sacrilegious
peaceful	psychology	safety
peculiar	pumpkin	satisfied
performance	punctual	scarcely
permanent	punctuation	scarcity
perseverance	pursuit	scene
personality	questionnaire	schedule
personnel	quiet	scholar
perspiration	quite	scissors
persuade	quotient	scurrilous
pessimistic	raspberry	seance
phenomenal	realize	secretary
Philippines	really	seize
philosophy	realtor	semester
physical	realty	separate
picnicking	receipt	sergeant
pleasant	recipe	shepherd
politician	recognize	siege
Portuguese	recommend	similar
possession	referred	sincerely
possibility	reign	skein
practically	relevant	skiing

skillful	supersede	unanimous
sophomore	surgeon	unnecessary
soufflé	surprise	useful
source	susceptible	useless
souvenir	suspense	usually
specialty	swimming	vacillate
specifically	sympathetic	vacuum
specimen	synonym	vague
sponsor	temperamental	valuable
statistics	temperature	variety
straight	tendency	various
strength	therefore	vegetable
stretch	thorough	vengeance
strictly	though	vilify
stubborn	thoughtful	villain
substitute	tomorrow	warrant
subtle	tragedy	weather
succeed	transferred	Wednesday
successful	traveled	weird
suede	tremendous	whether
sufficient	truly	whole
summary	twelfth	yacht
superintendent	typical	yield

Guide to Capitalization and Punctuation

CAPITALIZATION

Beginnings

The first word in a sentence is capitalized:

Dozens of spectators lined the street.

The first word in a direct quotation is capitalized:

Andy stood by the window and remarked, "The view from here is spectacular."

If a colon introduces more than one sentence, the first word after the colon is capitalized:

We went over our findings, one piece of evidence at a time: <u>The</u> custodian had discovered the body just before midnight. The keys to the victim's office were found in the stairwell. In the adjoining office, three file cabinets had been overturned.

If a colon introduces a formal and distinct statement, the first word after the colon is capitalized:

All my years on the basketball court have taught me one thing: <u>Winning</u> is more of a process than an outcome.

If a colon introduces a complete statement that is merely an extension of the statement preceding the colon, the first word after the colon is usually lowercased:

Everything in the house was a shade of pink: the sofa was carnation blush, the tiles were misty mauve, and the carpet was dusty rose.

If a colon introduces an incomplete statement, the first word after the colon is lowercased:

The caterer provided three choices: <u>chicken</u>, beef, and shrimp.

Proper Names

Proper names are capitalized. This is true of all proper names, including those of persons, places, structures, organizations, vessels, vehicles, brands, etc. Notice from the following examples that when a properly named entity is referred to in a "non-named" general sense, the general sense is almost always lowercased:

Eleanor Roosevelt
J. D. Salinger
Carson City / a city in Nevada
Ural Mountains / a view of the mountains
New York Public Library / borrowing books from the public library
Washington Monument / our photos of the monument
Calvin Leete Elementary School / the rear entrance of the school
Amherst Historical Society / when the society last met
Boeing 747

USS *Missouri* [note that the names of specific ships, aircraft, spacecraft, etc., are italicized]
Chevy Malibu
Slinky

Titles

The titles of works are capitalized. Titled works include:

- written material (books, periodicals, screenplays, etc.)
- components of written material (chapters, sections, etc.)
- filmed and/or broadcast works (movies, television shows, radio programs, etc.)
- works of art (paintings, sculptures, etc.)
- musical compositions (songs, operas, oratorios, etc.)

There are certain rules of convention regarding which words in the titles are capitalized.
Capitalize:

- first word in the title
- last word in the title
- nouns and pronouns
- adjectives
- verbs
- adverbs
- subordinating conjunctions (*although, as, because, if, since, that, whenever*, etc.)

Do not capitalize (unless they are first or last words in the title):

- articles (*a, an, the*)
- coordinating conjunctions (*and, but, for, nor, or, so, yet*)
- prepositions (although some guides suggest capitalizing prepositions of more than four letters)
- the word *to* in infinitives

The King, the Sword, and the Golden Lantern
A Room within a Room (*or* A Room Within a Room)
Seventy Ways to Make Easy Money from Your Home
The Stars Will Shine Because You Are Mine

If a subtitle is included, it typically follows a colon. It follows the capitalization rules of the main title, thus its first word is always capitalized:

> Aftermath Explored: The Confessions of a Nuclear
> Physicist

The first element in a hyphenated compound is always capitalized. The subsequent elements are capitalized unless they are articles, prepositions, or coordinating conjunctions. But if the compound is the last word in the title, its final element is always capitalized, regardless of its part of speech:

> Nineteenth-Century Poets
> Over-the-Top Desserts
> The Love-in of a Lifetime
> The Year of the Love-In

An element that follows a hyphenated prefix is capitalized only if it is a proper noun or adjective:

> Pre-Columbian Artifacts
> Memoirs of a Semi-independent Child

Education

An academic title is capitalized (whether it is spelled out or abbreviated) when it directly accompanies a personal name. Otherwise, it is lowercased:

> Professor Sarah McDonald
> Assoc. Prof. Brown
> my chemistry professor

An academic degree or honor is capitalized (whether it is spelled out or abbreviated) when it directly accompanies a personal name. Otherwise, it is lowercased:

> Harold L. Fox, Ph.D.
> Charles Gustafson, Fellow of the Geological Society
> working toward her master's degree

Academic years are lowercased:

> the senior prom
> he's a sophomore
> the fourth grade

The course name of a particular school subject is capitalized. A general field of study is lowercased (unless the word is normally capitalized, such as "English"):

> Astronomy 101
> Algebra II
> taking classes in psychology, French literature, and chemistry

Calendar Terms and Time

The names of the days of the week and months of the year are capitalized:

Sunday	September
Monday	October
Tuesday	November

The names of the four seasons are lowercased:

winter	summer
spring	fall or autumn

The names of holidays (religious and secular) and periods of religious observance are capitalized:

Arbor Day	Lent
Easter	Memorial Day
Halloween	Ramadan

The names of time zones and the time systems they designate are lowercased (except for any words that are proper names). Their abbreviations are capitalized:

> eastern daylight time (EDT)
> Greenwich mean time (GMT)
> Pacific standard time (PST)

Legislation, Treaties, etc.

The formal name of a policy, treaty, piece of legislation, or similar agreement is capitalized. A general reference to such is lowercased:

> Volstead Act
> the act sponsored by Congressman Volstead
> Treaty of Versailles
> the treaty at Versailles
> Bottle Bill
> Articles of Confederation
> Connecticut Constitution
> Connecticut's constitution
> North American Free Trade Agreement

TIP

Which titles should be set in italics, and which should be set off by quotation marks? In printed material, the distinction can be significant. Here's a handy list of the most common categories of titles and their standard treatments in type:

italics:

- books
  Crossroads of Freedom: Antietam, by James M. McPherson
- pamphlets
  Thomas Paine's *Common Sense*
- magazines
  Popular Mechanics
- newspapers
  USA Today
- movies
  One Flew Over the Cuckoo's Nest
- television or radio series
  This Week in Baseball
- plays
  Neil Simon's *Lost in Yonkers*
- long poems
  Beowulf

- collections of poems and other anthologies
  The Collected Poems of Emily Dickinson
- operas, oratorios, and other long musical compositions
  Madame Butterfly
- painting, sculptures, and other works of art
  Thomas Cole's *Mount Etna from Taormina*

quotation marks:

- articles
  "*How to Remove Wallpaper*"
- chapters
  "Betsy Saves the Day"
- short stories
  "The Pit and the Pendulum, " by Edgar Allan Poe
- short poems
  "Tree at My Window, " by Robert Frost
- essays
  Emerson's "Spiritual Laws"
- television or radio episodes
  "Lucy Does a TV Commercial"
- songs and other short musical compositions
  "Are You Lonesome Tonight?"

Military Service

A military title or rank is capitalized (whether it is spelled out or abbreviated) when it directly accompanies a personal name. Otherwise, it is lowercased:

Gen. George Patton
Ensign Irene Mahoney
promoted to admiral
James Kirk, captain of the *USS Enterprise*

There are two significant exceptions to the preceding rule: the U.S. military titles "Fleet Admiral" and "General of the Army" should always be capitalized, even when not directly accompanying a personal name:

became General of the Army in 1950
a visit from the Fleet Admiral

The full official name of a military group or force is capitalized. A general reference to a military group or force is lowercased:

the Royal Air Force
the British air force
the Army Corps of Engineers
the Third Battalion
our battalion
the U.S. Navy
joined the navy

The full name of a battle or war is capitalized. A general reference to a battle or war is lowercased:

the Russian Revolution
fought in the revolution
the Spanish-American War
the war in Vietnam
the Battle of the Bulge
the first battle of the campaign
the Norman Conquest

The official name of a military award or medal is capitalized:

the Purple Heart
the Silver Star
the Victoria Cross
the Congressional Medal of Honor

Science

The capitalization rules governing scientific terminology cover a wide range of categories and applications. Some of the basic rules are discussed here.

Taxonomic nomenclature—that is, the scientific classification of plants and animals—follows specific rules for both capitalization and italics.

The names of the phylum, class, order, and family of a plant or animal are capitalized and set in roman type. This format also applies to the intermediate groupings (suborder, subfamily, etc.) within these divisions:

> The North American river otter belongs to the phylum Chordata, the subphylum Vertebrata, the class Mammalia, the order Carnivora, and the family Mustelidae.

The divisions lower than family—that is, genus, species, and subspecies—are set in italic type. Of these, only the genus is capitalized. When a plant or animal is identified by its "scientific name" or "Latin name, " the name given is the genus and species (and, when applicable, the subspecies):

> The scientific name of the river otter is *Lutra canadensis*.
> The Manitoban elk (*Cervus elaphus manitobensis*) is a subspecies of the North American elk.

The common names of plants and animals, as well as their hybrids, varieties, and breeds, are lowercased and set in roman type. A part of the name may be capitalized if that part is a term normally capitalized (that is, a proper name). If there is doubt, a dictionary should be consulted.

Alaskan malamute	rainbow trout
Christmas cactus	rose-breasted grosbeak
Johnny-jump-up	Swainson's hawk
maidenhair fern	Vietnamese potbellied pig

The names of astronomical entities, such as planets, stars, constellations, and galaxies, are capitalized:

Alpha Centauri	Mercury
Canis Major	Milky Way
Crab Nebula	Orion
Ganymede	Sirius

The names of geological eras, periods, epochs, etc., are capitalized. When included with the name, the words *era, period, epoch*, etc., are lowercased.

TIP

The names *sun, moon,* and *earth* are frequently lowercased. It is customary to capitalize them only when they are being referred to as components of the solar system. Also noteworthy is the fact that, in any context, the words *sun* and *moon* typically are preceded by the definite article, *the.* In non-astronomical contexts, the word *earth* often is preceded by *the*, but it is never preceded by *the* when used specifically as the name of a planet. Hence, *the Earth* would not be an appropriate use of capitalization.

> We enjoyed the warmth of <u>the sun</u>.
> The glow of <u>the moon</u> has inspired poets for centuries.
> Countless species inhabit <u>the earth</u>.
> What on <u>earth</u> are you doing?
> In size, Venus is comparable to <u>Earth</u>.
> The eclipse of <u>the Moon</u> will be visible from the night side of <u>Earth</u>.
> They made observations of Neptune's orbit around <u>the Sun</u>.

Mesozoic era	Oligocene epoch
Quaternary period	Upper Jurassic

Abbreviations

Although the use of abbreviations in formal writing should be limited, abbreviations are legitimate components of the language and deserve the same attention to spelling as do other words. Certain capitalization guidelines for a few types of abbreviations are given below. Because the possible variations are numerous, a standard dictionary should be consulted for more thorough guidance on the spelling, capitalization, and punctuation of a specific abbreviation.

When a capitalized term is abbreviated, the abbreviation is capitalized. If the abbreviation is comprised of initials, all the initials are capitalized:

Professor J. Leggett / Prof. J. Leggett
Sergeant David Potter / Sgt. David Potter
Master of Business Administration / MBA
United States Marine Corps / USMC

When a lowercased term is abbreviated as a simple shortening, the abbreviation is usually lowercased. But if the abbreviation is comprised of initials, all the initials are usually capitalized. When there is a compound word in the term, the initials may include the first letter of the root word:

especially / esp.
teaspoon / tsp.
deoxyribonucleic acid / DNA
monosodium glutamate / MSG
most favored nation / MFN

Usually, an abbreviation that ends in a capital letter is not followed by a period. An abbreviation that ends in a lowercase letter usually is followed by a period, although the period may be optional, depending on the prevailing style of the particular piece of writing.

One group of abbreviations that never ends with a period is the set of chemical symbols. Also, these abbreviations are always initially capitalized even though the terms they represent are lowercased:

Ar	argon	Na	sodium
Dy	dysprosium	Sb	antimony
H	hydrogen	Sn	tin
Kr	krypton	U	uranium
Lr	lawrencium	Xe	xenon

Note that some chemical symbols appear to be straightforward abbreviations (*Ca* for *calcium*) while others seem unrelated to their corresponding terms (*Au* for *gold*). In fact, these symbols are abbreviations of the official scientific, or Latin, names (*Au* for *aurum*, which is Latin for gold).

PUNCTUATION

Punctuation is an essential element of good writing because it makes the author's meaning clear to the reader. Although precise punctuation styles may vary somewhat among published sources, there are a number of fundamental principles worthy of consideration. Discussed below are these punctuation marks used in English:

comma	apostrophe
semicolon	quotation marks
colon	parentheses
period	dash
question mark	hyphen
exclamation point	

Comma

The comma is the most used mark of punctuation in the English language. It signals to the reader a pause, which generally clarifies the author's meaning and establishes a sensible order to the elements of written language. Among the most typical functions of the comma are the following:

1. It can separate the clauses of a compound sentence when there are two independent clauses joined by a conjunction, especially when the clauses are not very short:

    It never occurred to me to look in the attic, and I'm sure it didn't occur to Rachel either.

    The Nelsons wanted to see the Grand Canyon at sunrise, but they overslept that morning.

2. It can separate the clauses of a compound sentence when there is a series of independent clauses, the last two of which are joined by a conjunction:

    The bus ride to the campsite was very uncomfortable, the cabins were not ready for us when we got there, the cook had forgotten to start dinner, and the rain was torrential.

3. It is used to precede or set off, and therefore indicate, a non-restrictive dependent clause (a clause that could be omitted without changing the meaning of the main clause):

I read her autobiography, which was published last July.

They showed up at midnight, after most of the guests had gone home.

The coffee, which is freshly brewed, is in the kitchen.

4. It can follow an introductory phrase:

   Having enjoyed the movie so much, he agreed to see it again.

   Born and raised in Paris, she had never lost her French accent.

   In the beginning, they had very little money to invest.

5. It can set off words used in direct address:

   Listen, people, you have no choice in the matter.

   Yes, Mrs. Greene, I will be happy to feed your cat.

6. It can separate two or more coordinate adjectives (adjectives that could otherwise be joined with and) that modify one noun:

   The cruise turned out to be the most entertaining, fun, and relaxing vacation I've ever had. The horse was tall, lean, and sleek.

   Note that cumulative adjectives (those not able to be joined with *and*) are not separated by a comma:

   She wore bright yellow rubber boots.

7. It is used to separate three or more items in a series or list:

   Charlie, Melissa, Stan, and Mark will be this year's soloists in the spring concert.

   We need furniture, toys, clothes, books, tools, housewares, and other useful merchandise for the benefit auction.

   Note that the comma between the last two items in a series is sometimes omitted in less precise style:

   The most popular foods served in the cafeteria are pizza, hamburgers and nachos.

8. It is used to separate and set off the elements in an address or other geographical designation:

My new house is at 1657 Nighthawk Circle, South Kingsbury, Michigan.

We arrived in Pamplona, Spain, on Thursday.

9. It is used to set off direct quotations (note the placement or absence of commas with other punctuation):

   "Kim forgot her gloves," he said, "but we have a pair she can borrow."

   There was a long silence before Jack blurted out, "This must be the world's ugliest painting." "What are you talking about?" she asked in a puzzled manner.

   "Happy New Year!" everyone shouted.

10. It is used to set off titles after a person's name:

    Katherine Bentley, M.D.

    Martin Luther King, Jr., delivered the sermon.

Semicolon

The semicolon has two basic functions:

1. It can separate two main clauses, particularly when these clauses are of equal importance:

   The crowds gathered outside the museum hours before the doors were opened; this was one exhibit no one wanted to miss.

   She always complained when her relatives stayed for the weekend; even so, she usually was a little sad when they left.

2. It can be used as a comma is used to separate such elements as clauses or items in a series or list, particularly when one or more of the elements already includes a comma:

   The path took us through the deep, dark woods; across a small meadow into a cold, wet cave; and up a hillside overlooking the lake.

   Listed for sale in the ad were two bicycles; a battery-powered, leaf-mulching lawn mower; and a maple bookcase.

Colon

The **colon** has five basic functions:

1. It can introduce something, especially a list of items:

   In the basket were three pieces of mail: a postcard, a catalog, and a wedding invitation.

   Students should have the following items: backpack, loose-leaf notebook, pens and pencils, pencil sharpener, and ruler.

2. It can separate two clauses in a sentence when the second clause is being used to explain or illustrate the first clause:

   We finally understood why she would never go sailing with us: she had a deep fear of the water.

   Most of the dogs in our neighborhood are quite large: two of them are St. Bernards.

3. It can introduce a statement or a quotation:

   His parents say the most important rule is this: Always tell the truth.

   We repeated the final words of his poem: "And such is the plight of fools like me."

4. It can be used to follow the greeting in a formal or business letter:

   Dear Ms. Daniels:

   Dear Sir or Madam:

5. It is used in the United States to separate minutes from hours, and seconds from minutes, in showing time of day and measured length of time:

   Please be at the restaurant before 6:45.

   Her best running time so far has been 00:12:35.

Period

The **period** has two basic functions:

1. It is used to mark the end of a sentence:

It was reported that there is a shortage of nurses at the hospital. Several of the patients have expressed concern about this problem.

2. It is often used at the end of an abbreviation:

On Fri., Sept. 12, Dr. Brophy noted that the patient's weight was 168 lb. and that his height was 6 ft. 2 in.

(Note that another period is not added to the end of the sentence when the last word is an abbreviation.)

Question Mark and Exclamation Point

The only sentences that do not end in a period are those that end in either a question mark or an exclamation point.

Question marks are used to mark the end of a sentence that asks a direct question (generally, a question that expects an answer):

Is there any reason for us to bring more than a few dollars?

Who is your science teacher?

Exclamation points are used to mark the end of a sentence that expresses a strong feeling, typically surprise, joy, or anger:

I want you to leave and never come back!

What a beautiful view this is!

Apostrophe

The apostrophe has two basic functions:

1. It is used to show where a letter or letters are missing in a contraction.

   The directions are cont'd [continued] *on the next page. We've* [we have] *decided that if she can't* [cannot] *go, then we aren't* [are not] *going either.*

2. It can be used to show possession:

   The possessive of a singular noun or an irregular plural noun is created by adding an apostrophe and an s:

the pilot's uniform
Mrs. Mendoza's house
a tomato's bright red color
the oxen's yoke

The possessive of a regular plural noun is created by adding just an apostrophe:

the pilots' uniforms [referring to more than one pilot]
the Mendozas' house [referring to the Mendoza family]
the tomatoes' bright red color [referring to more than one tomato]

Quotation Marks

Quotation marks have two basic functions:

1. They are used to set off direct quotations (an exact rendering of someone's spoken or written words):

   "I think the new library is wonderful, " she remarked to David.

   We were somewhat lost, so we asked, "Are we anywhere near the gallery?"

   In his letter he had written, "The nights here are quiet and starry. It seems like a hundred years since I've been wakened by the noise of city traffic and squabbling neighbors."

   Note that indirect quotes (which often are preceded by *that, if,* or *whether*) are not set off by quotation marks:

   He told me that he went to school in Boston.

   We asked if we could still get tickets to the game.

2. They can be used to set off words or phrases that have specific technical usage, or to set off meanings of words, or to indicate words that are being used in a special way in a sentence:

   The part of the flower that bears the pollen is the "stamen."

   When I said "plain," I meant "flat land," not "ordinary."

> *Oddly enough, in the theater, the statement "break a leg" is meant as an expression of good luck.*
>
> *What you call "hoagies," we call "grinders" or "submarine sandwiches."*
>
> *He will never be a responsible adult until he outgrows his "Peter Pan" behavior.*

Note that sometimes single quotation marks, rather than double quotation marks, may be used to set off words or phrases:

> *The part of the flower that bears the pollen is the 'stamen.'*

What is most important is to be consistent in such usage. Single quotation marks are also used to set off words or phrases within material already in double quotation marks, as:

> *"I want the sign to say 'Ellen's Bed and Breakfast' in large gold letters," she explained.*

Parentheses

Parentheses are used, in pairs, to enclose information that gives extra detail or explanation to the regular text. Parentheses are used in two basic ways:

1. They can separate a word or words in a sentence from the rest of the sentence:

> *On our way to school, we walk past the Turner Farm (the oldest dairy farm in town) and watch the cows being fed.*
>
> *The stores were filled with holiday shoppers (even more so than last year).*

Note that the period goes outside the parentheses, because the words in the parentheses are only part of the sentence.

2. They can form a separate complete sentence:

> *Please bring a dessert to the dinner party. (It can be something very simple.) I look forward to seeing you there.*

Note that the period goes inside the parentheses, because the words in the parentheses are a complete and independent sentence.

Dash

A dash is used most commonly to replace the usage of parentheses within sentences. If the information being set off is in the middle of the sentence, a pair of long (or "em") dashes is used; if it is at the end of the sentence, just one long dash is used:

> *On our way to school, we walk past the Turner Farm—the oldest dairy farm in town—and watch the cows being fed.*

> *The stores were filled with holiday shoppers—even more so than last year.*

Hyphen

A hyphen has three basic functions:

1. It can join two or more words to make a compound, especially when doing so makes the meaning more clear to the reader:

   We met to discuss long-range planning.

   There were six four-month-old piglets at the fair.

   That old stove was quite a coal-burner.

2. It can replace the word "to" when a span or range of data is given. This kind of hyphen is sometimes keyed as a short (or "en") dash:

   John Adams was president of the United States 1797–1801.

   Today we will look for proper nouns in the L–N section of the dictionary.

   The ideal weight for that breed of dog would be 75–85 pounds.

3. It can indicate a word break at the end of a line. The break must always be between syllables:

   It is important for any writer to know that there are numerous punctuation principles that are considered standard and proper, but there is also flexibility regarding acceptable punctuation.

A List of the Most Commonly Used Foreign Words and Phrases

INTRODUCTION

Essentially, "foreign" here means French and Latin words and phrases. Oh, there are some German, Spanish, Italian, and even Hindi contenders, but who are we kidding? The French—and by that we mean the people and their culture—have a particular genius for expressing aspects of our existence with undeniably sophisticated and creative turns of phrase. French phrases can be surprisingly witty, as if they had been minted by Oscar Wilde—and often better, because of their economy. Even the most commonly known and used expressions—*coup d'état*, for example, "a blow to the state"—have an economic, almost world-weary wit to them. I have no idea how many people know what the word "*coup*" means, but I would suspect not everyone does. Still, the genius is in the idea that an overthrow of a government could be called a "blow to the state." The blunt poetry of it!

The Romans—well, they were a commanding presence, and the expressions we still employ from Latin demonstrate that. *Sine qua non*, for instance. "Without which not." That means "an essential condition" for something.

The point is, that these are not merely translated expressions. They *are* translatable, certainly, but what is translated is a little poem, an amusing puzzle. *Roman à clef*, for example. That means "novel with a key." But what does *that* mean? It means that this is a novel in which the characters are based on real people; in other words, it's a "keyed" novel—a novel in which you find the key to who these people are by reading it and discerning the clues. The most infamous of recent examples is *Primary Colors* by Anonymous (aka Joe Klein). There are many others.

There is something wonderfully humbling and exhilarating about a foreign language's ability to express something ours never could—and never will—as well. In an age in which English is sometimes looked upon as the bully of languages, plowing its way through cultures under the holy flag of capitalism, it's good for us to realize there are things that our mother tongue simply cannot do.

Here are some prime examples.

ad hoc: formed, arranged, or done for a particular purpose.

agent provocateur: a person who induces others to break the law so that they can be convicted.

aide-de-camp: a military officer acting as a confidential assistant to a senior officer.

à la: (of a dish) cooked or prepared in a specified style or manner.

à la mode: in fashion; up to date; served with ice cream.

alter ego: a person's secondary or alternative personality; an intimate and trusted friend.

ancien régime: a political or social system that has been displaced, typically by one more modern.

andante: in a moderately slow tempo.

antebellum: occurring or existing before a particular war, esp. the American Civil War.

apartheid: In South Africa, a policy or system of segregation or discrimination on grounds of color.

aperçu: a comment or brief reference which makes an illuminating or entertaining point.

apologia: a formal written defense of one's opinions or conduct.

apparat: the administrative system of a communist party.

a priori: relating to or denoting reasoning or knowledge that proceeds from theoretical deduction rather than from observation or experience.

argot: the jargon or slang of a particular group or class.

aria: a long, accompanied song for a solo voice, typically one in an opera or oratorio.

arpeggio: the notes of a chord played in succession, either ascending or descending.

arrière-pensée: a concealed thought or intention; an ulterior motive.

ashram: a hermitage, monastic community, or other place of religious retreat for Hindus; a place of religious retreat or community life modeled on the Indian ashram.

atelier: a workshop or studio, esp. one used by an artist or designer.

au courant: aware of what is going on; well informed.

au fond: in essence.

auto-da-fé: the burning of a heretic by the Spanish Inquisition; a sentence of such a kind.

avant-garde: new and unusual or experimental ideas, esp. in the arts, or the people introducing them.

baksheesh: In parts of Asia and the Middle East, a small sum of money given as alms, a tip, or a bribe.

barrio: a district of a town in Spain and Spanish-speaking countries; (in the U.S.) the Spanish-speaking quarter of a town or city.

bas-relief: a method of molding, carving, or stamping in which the design stands out from the surface to a lesser extent than might be.

batik: a method (originally used in Java) of producing colored designs on textiles by dyeing them, having first applied wax to the parts to be left undyed.

beau monde: fashionable society.

bel canto: a lyrical style of operatic singing using a full rich broad tone and smooth phrasing.

belle époque: the period of settled and comfortable life preceding World War I.

belles-lettres: essays, particularly of literary and artistic criticism, written and read primarily for their aesthetic effect.

bête noire: a person or thing that one particularly dislikes.

bey: historically, the governor of a district or province in the Ottoman Empire.

Bildungsroman: a novel dealing with one person's formative years or spiritual education.

billet-doux: a love letter.

bon mot: a witty remark.

burka (also burkha): a long, loose garment covering the whole body, worn in public by many Muslim women.

cabana: a cabin, hut, or shelter, esp. one at a beach or swimming pool.

canton: a subdivision of a country established for political or administrative purposes; a state of the Swiss Confederation.

carpe diem: used to urge someone to make the most of the present time and give little thought to the future.

caudillo: in Spanish-speaking regions, a military or political leader.

cause célèbre: a controversial issue that attracts a great deal of public attention.

caveat emptor: the principle that the buyer alone is responsible for checking the quality and suitability of goods before a purchase is made.

chacun à son goût: each to one's own taste.

chador (also chadar or chuddar): a large piece of dark-colored cloth, typically worn by Muslim women, wrapped around the head and upper body to leave only the face exposed.

chanteuse: a female singer of popular songs, esp. in a nightclub.

chef-d'œuvre: a masterpiece.

cinéma-vérité: a style of filmmaking characterized by realistic, typically documentary motion pictures that avoid artificiality and artistic effect and are generally made with simple equipment.

cognoscente: a conoisseur; a discerning expert.

commedia dell'arte: an improvised kind of popular comedy in Italian theaters in the 16th–18th centuries, based on stock characters. Actors adapted their comic dialogue and action according to a few basic plots (commonly love intrigues) and to topical issues.

comme il faut: correct in behavior or etiquette.

compos mentis: having full control of one's mind; sane.

contra (also Contra): a member of a guerrilla force in Nicaragua that opposed the left-wing Sandinista government.

contretemps: an unexpected and unfortunate occurrence.

cordon bleu: cooking of the highest class: a cordon bleu chef; denoting a dish consisting of an escalope of veal or chicken rolled, filled with cheese and ham, and then fried in breadcrumbs.

corpus delicti: the facts and circumstances constituting a breach of a law.

coup de foudre: a sudden unforeseen event, in particular an instance of love at first sight.

coup de grâce: a final blow or shot given to kill a wounded person or animal.

cri de cœur: a passionate appeal, complaint, or protest.

dacha: a country house or cottage in Russia, typically used as a second or vacation home.

danse macabre: a medieval allegorical representation in which a personified Death leads people to the grave, designed to emphasize the equality of all before death.

dashiki: a loose, brightly colored shirt or tunic, originally from West Africa.

de facto: in fact, whether by right or not.

déjà vu: a feeling of having already experienced the present situation.

de rigueur: required by etiquette or current fashion.

dernier cri: the very latest fashion.

détente (also detente): the easing of hostility or strained relations, esp. between countries.

deus ex machina: an unexpected power or event saving a seemingly hopeless situation, esp. as a contrived plot device in a play or novel.

dhow: a lateen-rigged ship with one or two masts, used in the Indian Ocean.

djellaba (also djellabah or jellaba): a loose hooded cloak, typically woolen, of a kind traditionally worn by Arabs.

dolce vita: a life of heedless pleasure and luxury.

doppelgänger: an apparition or double of a living person.

double entendre: a word or phrase open to two interpretations, one of which is usually risqué or indecent.

dramatis personae: the characters of a play, novel, or narrative.

éclat: brilliant display or effect.

élan: energy, style, and enthusiasm.

el Niño: an irregularly occurring and complex series of climatic changes affecting the equatorial Pacific region and beyond every few years, characterized by the appearance of unusually warm, nutrient-poor water off northern Peru and Ecuador, typically in late December.

émigré: a person who has left their own country in order to settle in another, usually for political reasons.

enfant terrible: a person whose unconventional or controversial behavior or ideas shock, embarrass, or annoy others.

ennui: a feeling of listlessness and dissatisfaction arising from a lack of occupation or excitement.

ergo: therefore.

ex post facto: with retroactive effect or force.

fait accompli: a thing that has already happened or been decided before those affected hear about it, leaving them with no option but to accept.

fata Morgana: a mirage.

fatwa: a ruling on a point of Islamic law given by a recognized authority.

faux pas: an embarrassing or tactless act or remark in a social situation.

femme fatale: an attractive and seductive woman, esp. one who will ultimately bring disaster to a man who becomes involved with her.

fin de siècle: relating to or characteristic of the end of a century, esp. the 19th century.

gestalt (also Gestalt): an organized whole that is perceived as more than the sum of its parts.

glasnost: In the former Soviet Union, the policy or practice of more open consultative government and wider dissemination of information, initiated by leader Mikhail Gorbachev from 1985.

Götterdämmerung: In Germanic mythology, the downfall of the gods.

Grand Guignol: a dramatic entertainment of a sensational or horrific nature, originally a sequence of short pieces as performed at the Grand Guignol theater in Paris.

Gulag: a system of labor camps maintained in the Soviet Union from 1930 to 1955 in which many people died.

habeas corpus: a writ requiring a person under arrest to be brought before a judge or into court, esp. to secure the person's release unless lawful grounds are shown for their detention.

hajj: the Muslim pilgrimage to Mecca that takes place in the last month of the year, and that all Muslims are expected to make at least once during their lifetime.

in flagrante delicto: in the very act of wrongdoing, esp. in an act of sexual misconduct:

in loco parentis: in the place of a parent.

jihad: a holy war undertaken by Muslims against unbelievers.

junta: a military or political group that rules a country after taking power by force.

juste milieu: the happy medium; judicious moderation.

Kabbalah (also **Kabbala, Cabala, Cabbala,** or **Qabalah**): the ancient Jewish tradition of mystical interpretation of the Bible, first transmitted orally and using esoteric methods (including ciphers). It reached the height of its influence in the later Middle Ages and remains significant in Hasidism.

karma: In Hinduism and Buddhism, the sum of a person's actions in this and previous states of existence, viewed as deciding their fate in future existences.

kismet: destiny; fate:

laissez-faire: a policy or attitude of leaving things to take their own course, without interfering.

leitmotif (also **leitmotiv**): a recurrent theme throughout a musical or literary composition, associated with a particular person, idea, or situation.

lingua franca: a language that is adopted as a common language between speakers whose native languages are different.

loco: crazy.

magnum opus: a large and important work of art, music, or literature, esp. one regarded as the most important work of an artist or writer.

manqué: having failed to become what one might have been; unfulfilled.

mea culpa: an acknowledgment of one's fault or error.

ménage à trois: an arrangement in which three people share a sexual relationship, typically a domestic situation involving a married couple and the lover of one of them.

mensch: a person of integrity and honor.

meshuga (also **meshugga** or **meshugah**): mad; idiotic.

modus operandi: a particular way or method of doing something, esp. one that is characteristic or well-established.

mot juste: the exact, appropriate word.

mufti: plain clothes worn by a person who wears a uniform for their job, such as a soldier or police officer.

mujahideen (also **mujahedin, mujahidin,** or **mujaheddin**): guerrilla fighters in Islamic countries, esp. those who are Islamic fundamentalists.

mullah (also **mulla**): a Muslim learned in Islamic theology and sacred law.

née: originally called; born (used esp. in adding a woman's maiden name after her married name).

ne plus ultra: the perfect or most extreme example of its kind; the ultimate.

Noh (also **No** or **Nä**): traditional Japanese masked drama with dance and song, evolved from Shinto rites.

nom de plume: a pen name.

nonpareil: having no match or equal; unrivaled.

nouveau riche: people who have recently acquired wealth, typically those perceived as ostentatious or lacking in good taste.

obiter dictum: a judge's incidental expression of opinion, not essential to the decision and not establishing precedent.

outré: unusual and startling.

pas de deux: a dance for two people, typically a man and a woman.

pasha (also **pacha**): the title of a Turkish officer of high rank.

pavé: a setting of precious stones placed so closely together that no metal shows.

Pax Romana: the peace that existed between nationalities within the Roman Empire.

peignoir: a woman's light dressing gown or negligee.

pensée: a thought or reflection put into literary form; an aphorism.

per diem: for each day.

perestroika: In the former Soviet Union, the policy or practice of restructuring or reforming the economic and political system.

persona non grata: an unacceptable or unwelcome person.

pièce de résistance: the most important or remarkable feature.

pied noir: a person of European origin who lived in Algeria during French rule, esp. one who returned to Europe after Algeria was granted independence.

politburo: the principal policymaking committee of a Communist Party.

poste restante: written on a letter as an indication that it should be kept at a specified post office until collected by the addressee.

précis: a summary or abstract of a text or speech.

prêt-à-porter: sold ready-to-wear as opposed to made to measure

prima facie: based on the first impression; accepted as correct until proved otherwise.

pro bono: done without charge or fee.

quid pro quo: something for something; an equal exchange.

raison d'être: the most important reason or purpose for someone or something's existence.

rara avis: rare bird.

risqué: slightly indecent or liable to shock, esp. by being sexually suggestive.

roman à clef: a novel in which real people or events appear with invented names.

sans souci: carefree.

savoir-faire: the ability to say and do the correct thing.

schadenfreude: pleasure at someone else's misfortunes

sic transit gloria mundi: thus passes away the glory of the world.

sine qua non: indispensable element or condition

sotto voce: in a quiet voice, attempting not to be overheard

sui generis: unique, one of a kind.

terra incognita: unknown territory.

tête-à-tête: a private conversation between two people.

touché: in fencing, used as an acknowledgment of a hit by one's opponent; used as an acknowledgment during a discussion of a good or clever point made at one's expense by another person.

tour de force: an impressive performance or achievement that has been accomplished or managed with great skill.

tout le monde: everybody; everyone of importance.

trompe l'oeil: visual illusion in art, esp. as used to trick the eye into perceiving a painted detail as a three-dimensional object.

veni, vidi, vici: I came, I saw, I conquered.

verboten: forbidden, as by law; prohibited.

vis-à-vis: in relation to; with regard to.

voilà (also voila): there it is; there you are.

vox populi: the voice of the people.

Weltanschauung: a world view or philosophy of life.

Weltschmerz: sorrow over the evils of the world

Zeitgeist: the thought or sensibility characteristic of a particular period of time.

CHAPTER 3

100 Tricky Usage Problems and Pitfalls Explained

INTRODUCTION

English may be a wonderful ally for a writer, but it can be a devious one as well. Not consciously, of course. A language doesn't have it in for you—though it may seem so at times. Questions of usage often arise, and they can be slippery ones. Usage is a part of writing that perfectionists and sticklers adore. The definition of usage is "the way in which a word or phrase is normally and correctly used." Of course, the concepts of "normally" and "correctly" go to the heart of the matter (as well as the hearts of the sticklers . . .). It is up to lexicographers—those harmless drudges, as the great Samuel Johnson called them as well as himself—to track and record how words are being used.

Writers should always remember that they are contributors to a language that is in flux. English changes, and continues to change, so as a writer, you are involved in that slow and gradual process. That's a significant responsibility.

[These notes have been adapted from the Usage Notes contributed by Bryan Garner to *The Oxford American Writer's Thesaurus*. Bryan Garner is the editor of *Garner's Modern American Usage, 2e.*]

a   The indefinite article *a* is used before words beginning with a
consonant sound, including /y/ and /w/ sounds. The other
form, *an*, is used before words beginning with a vowel sound.
Since the sound rather than the letter controls, it's not unusual
to find *a* before a vowel or *an* before a consonant. Hence: *a
European country, a one-year term, an FBI agent, an MBA
degree.*The distinction between *a* and *an* was not solidified until
the nineteenth century. Up to that time, *an* preceded most
words beginning with a vowel, regardless of how the first
syllable sounded. The U.S. Constitution, for example, reads:
"The Congress shall have Power . . . [t]o establish an uniform
Rule of Naturalization. But that is no excuse for a twenty-first-
century writer. People worry about whether the correct article is
a or *an* with *historian, historic,* and a few other words. Most
authorities have supported *a* over *an*. The traditional rule is
that if the *h-* is sounded, then *a* is the proper form. So people
who aspirate their *h*'s and follow that rule would say *a historian*
and *a historic*. This is not a new "rule." Even the venerated
language authority H. W. Fowler, in the England of 1926,
advocated *a* before *historic, historical,* and *humble. A,* in the
distributive sense (*ten hours a day*), has traditionally been
considered preferable to *per*, which originated in commercialese
and legalese. But *per* has muscled its way into idiomatic English
in phrases such as *60 miles per hour* and *one golf cart per
couple*. Although *an* could be substituted for *per* in the first of
those phrases, *a* wouldn't work well in the second.

access   Although the verb **access** is standard and common in
computing and related terminology (*only subscribers may
access the full text online*), the word is primarily a noun.
Outside computing contexts, its use as a verb in the sense of
'approach or enter a place' is often regarded as nonstandard
(*you must use a key card to access the lounge*). Even weaker is
its use in an abstract sense (*access the American dream*). It is
usually clear enough to say 'enter' or 'gain access to.'

aggravate   Though documented as existing since the 1600s,
aggravate for *annoy* or *irritate* has never gained the approval of
stylists and should be avoided in formal writing. Strictly

speaking, *aggravate* means "make worse; exacerbate": *writing a second apology might just aggravate the problem*. Even the eloquent American jurist Oliver Wendell Holmes, Jr., nodded once, using *aggravate* for *irritate* in a letter penned in 1895: "Our two countries aggravate each other from time to time." In some contexts, it's genuinely difficult to tell whether the word *aggravating* is a present participle or an adjective—e.g.: "The City of Washington is notorious for aggravating allergies, and Mr. Clinton said he expected his to be more severe there than in Arkansas." (*New York Times*; Oct. 14, 1996.) The second half of that compound sentence suggests that the writer is using *aggravating* correctly. But taken alone, the phrase in the first half of the sentence ("Washington is notorious for aggravating allergies") could refer to either (1) making allergies worse (the preferred usage), or (2) allergies that are irritating or frustrating. The confusion also occurs between the noun forms—e.g.: "Rush Limbaugh . . . has an extra tone of aggravation [read *irritation*] as he denounces the unyielding poll leads of 'the Schlickmeister' and 'noted hetero fun-seeker,' President Clinton." (*New York Times*; Sept. 25, 1996.) Perhaps *exasperate* contributes to the misuse of *aggravate* (which sounds a bit like *exasperate*) in the sense of *irritate* (which is close in meaning to *exasperate*). Also, when *aggravate* is used in this sense it often implies something more intense than merely *irritate*. It is closer in meaning to *exasperate*.

ain't Is this word used orally in most parts of the country by cultivated speakers? In 1961, *Webster's Third New International Dictionary of the English Language* (W3) said it was, provoking a firestorm of protests from journalists and academics. W3's assessment was quite a change from that of W2 (the second edition, published in 1934), which had given it a tag: "Dial. or Illit." The editor of W3, Philip Gove, explained the change by conceding that he had no large files of empirical evidence: "Knowledge of some kind of language behavior comes through contact with its observers and is not always documented because there seems to be no reason to collect additional evidence." If that's the method, then one can

confidently say that W3's treatment was flawed in its
incompleteness. In 1962, the year after W3 was published, an
apt cartoon appeared in *The New Yorker*. A man is standing in
the reception area of G. C. Merriam Co., Dictionary Division,
as the receptionist says to him, "Sorry. Dr. Gove ain't in." Yes,
ain't is used by cultivated speakers, but almost always for
either of two reasons: (1) to be tongue-in-cheek, or (2) to
flaunt their reverse snobbery. For most people, it remains a
shibboleth of poor usage.

a lot *A lot* (= many) is the standard spelling. *Alot* is a nonstandard form—e.g.: "Alot [read *A lot*] of people have noticed
that the two teams playing in the World Series have one very
important thing in common." (*Boston Globe*; Oct. 22, 2000.)
"Dalmatians are active and require alot [read *a lot*] of exercise
and attention." (*Sarasota Herald-Tribune*; Dec. 2, 2000.)

and It is rank superstition that this coordinating conjunction
cannot properly begin a sentence: "Another stumbling-block
to a certain type of academic mind is the conjunction *and*. It
is often laid down as a rigid rule that a sentence should never
begin with *and*. This was a point on which my own schoolmaster was inflexible. And quite recently a training college
student whom I asked to comment on a passage from Malory
condemned him for using 'the objectionable conjunction *and*.'
And printers have an ugly trick of emasculating my meaning
by turning my periods into commas because they happen to
be followed by *and*. Taking down my Bible and opening it at
random, I find that the eighth chapter of Exodus contains
thirty-two sentences, twenty-five of which begin with *and*."
(Philip Boswood Ballard, *Teaching and Testing English*;
1939.) "Many years ago schoolteachers insisted that it was
improper to begin a sentence with *and*, but this convention is
now outmoded. Innumerable respected writers use *and* at the
beginning of a sentence." (William Morris and Mary Morris,
Harper Dictionary of Contemporary Usage, 2d ed.; 1985.)
"And the idea that *and* must not begin a sentence, or even a
paragraph, is an empty superstition. The same goes for *but*.
Indeed either word can give unimprovably early warning of

the sort of thing that is to follow." (Kingsley Amis, *The King's English*; 1997.) Schoolteachers may have laid down a prohibition against the initial *and* to counteract elementary-school students' tendency to begin every sentence with *and*. The same superstition has plagued *but* (see note at BUT). But the very best writers find occasion to begin sentences with *and*—e.g.: "And one had better make use of whatever beauty, elegance, riches the translator's language possesses, and hope that something emotionally, intellectually, aesthetically equivalent will emerge." (John Simon, *The Sheep from the Goats*; 1989.) Oddly, *and* is frequently misused for *or* where a singular noun, or one of two nouns, is called for—e.g.: "While third-party candidates have mounted serious challenges for senator and governor in almost two dozen states this year, building an effective third-party apparatus is rare." (*New York Times*; Oct. 5, 1994.) The phrase should be "senator *or* governor"; as written, the sentence says that in each of almost 24 states, third-party candidates were running for *both* senator *and* governor—an idea belied by the context of the article. Some writers have a tendency, especially in long enumerations, to omit *and* before the final element. To do so is often infelicitous: the reader is jarred by the abrupt period ending the sentence and may even wonder whether something has been omitted. One may occasionally omit *and* before the final element in an enumeration with a particular nuance in mind. Without *and*, the implication is that the series is incomplete—rhetoricians call this construction "asyndeton." With *and*, the implication is that the series is complete. This shade in meaning is increasingly subtle in modern prose.

anxious The word *anxious* has a range of meaning. As the adjective corresponding to *anxiety*, it has long meant "uneasy, disquieted." In the most unimpeachable uses, the word stays close to that association—e.g.: "The latest holdup is the EPA's final approval of the companies' plans to test for lead at the 150 homes. . . . Some residents are getting anxious." (*Atlanta Journal Constitution*; Sept. 13, 2002.) Today the word typically encompasses both worry and anticipation—e.g.: "Creator and anchorman Brian

Lamb, the prince of un-chic, tirelessly fields the remarks of obnoxious callers, preening journalists, and anxious authors." (*National Review*; Mar. 24, 1997.) The word carries a sense of expectation, as when discussing a major life change. But when no sense of uneasiness is attached to the situation, *anxious* isn't the best word. In those instances, it displaces a word that might traditionally have been considered its opposite—namely, eager— e.g.: "Three years ago, the Latin music industry was caught up in crossover mania, anxious [read *eager*] to ride the popularity of singers such as Ricky Martin and Enrique Iglesias by selling their English-language albums to the American mainstream." (*Sun-Sentinel* [Fort Lauderdale]; Sept. 13, 2002.)

as First, it must be said that *as to* is an all-purpose preposition to be avoided whenever a more specific preposition will do. But *as to* isn't always indefensible. The phrase is most justifiable when introducing something previously mentioned only cursorily: "As to concerns the fair might lose on-track business if it offered its signal to the OTBs, [Dun said]: 'I figured we were going to lose the handle either way.' (*Portland Press Herald* [ME]; Sept. 7, 1997.) In beginning sentences this way, *as to* is equivalent to the more colloquial *as for.* In effect, the phrase is a passable shorthand form of *regarding, with regard to,* or *on the question of.* The phrase is also (minimally) defensible when used for *about,* but that word is stylistically preferable in most contexts. *As to* smells of jargon—e.g.: "The bill carries no presumptions as to [read *about*] the effect of incorporation." (*News & Observer* [Raleigh]; Mar. 17, 1997.) The main problem with *as to* is that it doesn't clearly establish syntactic or conceptual relationships, so it can hamper comprehensibility. In each of the following examples, another preposition would more directly and forcefully express the thought: "There's no rule as to [read *about*] how long you have to wait before you can enjoy your creation." (*Florida Times-Union*; Aug. 14, 1997.) "It is always possible that your neighbor is not aware of how disturbing his or her behavior is and that he or she can be more sensitive to your concerns, or you can agree as to [read *on*] certain time parameters or (if music is the culprit) what is an acceptable volume level." (*San Diego*

Union-Tribune; Aug. 24, 1997.) "The same is true as to [read *of*] other cases finding for leaders by applying the regulation." (*Bankruptcy Court Decisions*; Mar. 24, 1994.) "There is no change in the prior IRA rules with regard to an individual's participation in other qualifying retirement plans. As such, the rules remain the same as to [read *for*] the maximum amount of adjusted gross income a taxpayer can have before the IRA deduction begins to phase out." (*Gazette-Telegraph* [Colorado Springs]; Mar. 12, 1997.) "Some people are a little surprised as to [read *by* or *at*] how quickly Veniard has gotten to his present level." (*Florida Times-Union*; June 28, 199.) "During a trip to the Mars Pathfinder Mission Control Center in Pasadena this summer, House Aeronautics and Space Subcommittee member Sheila Jackson-Lee, D-Texas, inquired as to [read *into*] whether the Pathfinder Mission had taken pictures of the American flag planted by Neil Armstrong in 1969." (*San Francisco Chronicle*; Sept. 15, 1997.) (In this case, the better rewording of "inquired as to whether" would have been "asked whether.")

ass *Arse* is the spelling of the British slang term—in the anatomical sense, that is, not in the horse sense. In American English, *ass* is the spelling for both meanings. There's a story behind this. Today *ass* means both (1) "donkey" and (2) "a person's bottom." Sense 1 is the historical one; sense 2 originated in the mid-eighteenth century as the result of a phonological change, as *arse* and *ass* became homophones. By the early nineteenth century, it was possible to engage in wordplay between the words—as in an 1802 cartoon ("Neddy [a donkey] Paces at Tunbridge Wells [in Kent, England]"), in which one female rider says to another, "I'll show my Ass against any Lady's at Wells."

backward In British English, the spelling **backwards** is more common than **backward**. In American English, the adverb form is sometimes spelled **backwards** (*the ladder fell backwards*), but the adjective is almost always *backward* (*a backward glance*). Directional words using the suffix *-ward* tend to have no *s* ending in American English, although **backwards** is more common than *afterwards*, *towards*, or *forwards*. The *s* ending often (but not always) appears in the phrases *backwards and forwards* and *bending over backwards*.

black, Black   *Black* designating Americans of African heritage, became the most widely used and accepted term in the 1960s and 1970s, replacing **Negro**. It is not usually capitalized: *black Americans*. Through the 1980s, the more formal **African American** replaced **black** in much usage, but both are now generally acceptable. **Afro-American**, an earlier alternative to **black**, is heard mostly in anthropological and cultural contexts. **Colored people**, common earlier in the twentieth century, is now usually regarded as derogatory, although the phrase survives in the full name of the NAACP, the National Association for the Advancement of Colored People. An inversion, **people of color**, has gained some favor, but is also used in reference to other nonwhite ethnic groups: *a gathering spot for African Americans and other people of color interested in reading about their cultures*.

blond   The spellings **blonde** and **blond** correspond to the feminine and masculine forms in French. Although the distinction is usually retained in Britain, American usage since the 1970s has generally preferred the gender-neutral **blond**. The adjective **blonde** may still refer to a woman's (but not a man's) hair color, though use of the noun risks offense (*See that blonde over there?*): the offense arises from the fact that the color of hair is not the person. The adjective applied to inanimate objects (wood, beer) is typically spelled **blond**.

but   It is a gross canard that beginning a sentence with *but* is stylistically slipshod. In fact, doing so is highly desirable in any number of contexts, as many stylebooks have said (many correctly pointing out that *but* is more effective than *however* at the beginning of a sentence)—e.g.: "The group of Adversative conjunctions represented by BUT (called Arrestive) very often fulfil [sic] the office of relating consecutive sentences. . . . An entire paragraph is not unfrequently devoted to arresting or preventing a seeming inference from one preceding, and is therefore appropriately opened by But, Still, Nevertheless, &c." (Alexander Bain, *English Composition and*

Rhetoric, 4th ed.; 1877.) "*But* (not followed by a comma) always heads its turning sentence; *Nevertheless* usually does (followed by a comma). I am sure, however, that *however* is always better buried in the sentence between commas; *But* is for the quick turn; the inlaid *however* for the more elegant sweep." (Sheridan Baker, *The Practical Stylist*; 1962.) "Of the many myths concerning 'correct' English, one of the most persistent is the belief that it is somehow improper to begin a sentence with *and*, *but*, *for*, *or*, or *nor*. The construction is, of course, widely used today and has been widely used for generations, for the very good reason that it is an effective means of achieving coherence between sentences and between larger units of discourse, such as paragraphs." (R. W. Pence and D. W. Emery, *A Grammar of Present-Day English*, 2d ed.; 1963.) "I can't overstate how much easier it is for readers to process a sentence if you start with *but* when you're shifting direction." (William Zinsser, *On Writing Well*, 6th ed.; 1998.) "If you want to begin a sentence by contradicting the last, use *but* instead of *however*." (Christopher Lasch, *Plain Style*; 2002.) Good writers often begin sentences with *but* and have always done so. Samples from twentieth- and twenty-first-century writers follow: "But such simplicity of instinct is scarcely possible for human beings." (Bertrand Russell, *Education and the Good Life*; 1926.) "But it must not be assumed that intelligent thinking can play no part in the formation of the goal and of ethical judgments." (Albert Einstein, "Science and Religion" (1939), in *Ideas and Opinions*; 1954.) "But he had got used to that and it did not disquiet him." (Ursula K. Le Guin, *The Other Wind*; 2001.) These are not good writers on bad days. No: they were having good days. In 1963, researcher Francis Christensen found that 8.75% of the sentences in the work of first-rate writers—including H. L. Mencken, Lionel Trilling, and Edmund Wilson—began with coordinating conjunctions (i.e., *and* and *but*). In *The New York Times* (front page during the 1990s) and *U.S. News & World Report* (in 1997), the figure is about the same. To the professional rhetorician, these figures aren't at all surprising. All this enthusiasm for the construction, though, needs to be tempered to this extent: don't start consecutive sentences with *but*. Also, putting this subordinating conjunction twice in one sentence invariably makes the sentence unwieldy and less easy to read—e.g.: "But this opening misleads because the focus dissipates as the play progresses and the scattershot climax drips with sentiment but is ultimately unsatisfying." (*Pittsburgh Post-Gazette*; Oct. 10, 1997.) (A possible revision: "But this opening misleads because the focus dissipates as the play progresses. Although the scattershot climax drips with sentiment, it's ultimately unsatisfying.") The surprisingly common misuse of *but* for *and* often betrays the writer's idiosyncratic prejudice. That is, if you write that someone is "attractive but smart," you're suggesting that this combination of characteristics is atypical—e.g.: "Billy's father . . . is a man of sterling rectitude, poor but honest [read *poor and honest*], determined to pass his upcoming naturalization exams." (*Chicago Tribune*; Oct. 24, 1997.) Is the writer really suggesting that poor people are typically dishonest? The use of *but* in a negative sense after a pronoun has long caused confusion. Is it "No one but she" or "No one but her"? When *but* is a preposition (meaning "except"), the objective *her* (or *him*) follows. But when *but* is a conjunction, the nominative *she* (or *he*) is proper. The correct form depends on the structure of the sentence. If the verb precedes the *but* phrase, the objective case should be used: "None of the defendants were convicted but him." But if the *but* phrase precedes the verb, the nominative case is proper: "None of the defendants but he were convicted." That sentence is considered equivalent to "None of the defendants were convicted, but he was convicted." (Although that rewording doesn't seem to make literal sense—given that he was one of the defendants—it serves to show the grammar of the sentence excepting him from the absolute word *none*.) *But* thus acts as a conjunction when it precedes the verb in a sentence, as in this one from Thomas Jefferson: "Nobody but we of the craft can understand the diction, and find out what [the statute] means." Here the subject of *can understand* is *nobody*, and the *but* heads the understood clause: "nobody can understand, but we can understand."The logic here is based on syntax: the native English speaker instinctively rejects as alien-sounding the constructions *me know* in "No one but you and I know what is on these notice boards" and *him knew* in "No one but he knew what this had cost him."

care   *Couldn't care less* is the correct and logical phrasing, not *could care less*—e.g.: "The American people could care less [read *couldn't care less*] who's White House Chief of Staff." (George Will, on "This Week with David Brinkley"; July 3, 1994.) If you *could care less*, you're saying that you do care some. Invariably, though, writers and speakers who use the phrase mean that they don't care at all. Although some apologists argue that *could care less* is meant to be sarcastic and not to be taken literally, a more plausible explanation is that the *-n't* of *couldn't* has been garbled in sloppy speech and sloppy writing. As American linguist Atcheson L. Hench explains: "A listener has not heard the whole phrase; he has heard a slurred form. *Couldn't care* has two dental stops practically together, *dnt*. This is heard only as *d* and slurring results. The outcome is *I c'd care less*." (*American Speech*, 159; 1973.)

center   The construction **center around** (as opposed to *center on*, or *revolve around*) has been denounced as incorrect and illogical since it first appeared in the mid-nineteenth century. Although the phrase is common, it defies geometry by confusing the orbit with the fixed point: *the earth revolves around (or its revolution centers on) the sun*. A careful writer will use a precise expression, such as *centers on*, *revolves around*, *concerns*, or *involves*.

challenge   The use of **challenged** with a preceding adverb, e.g., **physically challenged**, originally intended to give a more positive tone than such terms as **disabled** or **handicapped**, arose in the U.S. in the 1980s. Despite the originally serious intention, the term rapidly became stalled by uses whose intention was to make fun of the attempts at euphemism and whose tone was usually clearly ironic: examples include cerebrally challenged, follicularly challenged, etc.

chauvinism Most traditionally, *chauvinism* (/shoh-vuh-niz-um/) refers to fanatical patriotism. The word is an eponym from Nicolas Chauvin, a French soldier who was ridiculed for being excessively devoted to Napoleon. By metaphorical extension, the word was broadened to denote excessive pride in people like oneself, especially in reference to males. Today *male chauvinism*, which (as a phrase, not a phenomenon) dates back to the late 1960s, is something of a cliché, being the word's most frequent application. Indeed, some writers have come to use *chauvinism* as if it were synonymous with *male chauvinism*—e.g.: "He betrayed his chauvinism by expressing surprise that I [Diane McFarlin] was an editor." (*Sarasota Herald-Tribune*; Nov. 8, 1998.) To the linguistic traditionalist, these uses (or misuses) are arrant nonsense. The void left by the shift in the meaning of *chauvinism* from national pride to supposed sexual superiority has been filled by *jingoism*. Essentially synonymous with *chauvinism* in its traditional sense, *jingoism* has the added layer of xenophobic and aggressive attitudes toward foreign policy— e.g.: "Gilmour goes overboard in trying to rationalize and justify Kipling's racism and jingoism. He argues, for example, that 'white' in *The White Man's Burden* does not refer to skin color but rather to 'civilization and character' and that Kipling's imperialistic beliefs were essentially humane and benevolent rather than based on greed, paternalism and self-interest." (*Houston Chronicle*; June 23, 2002.). Sometimes the word takes on an even softer sense, suggesting a provincialism or regionalism that is broader than national sovereignty—e.g.: "The prime minister's evident glee that the BA order had gone to a 'European' company is mere jingoism at bottom." (*Wall Street Journal Europe*; Aug. 27, 1998.)

chomp The original and better term for what horses do to their bits is *champ*. *Chomp* is an American variant. (Oddly, American English has transformed *champ* into *chomp*, but *stomp* into *stamp*.) The two spellings have undergone some degree of differentiation. What one *champs* is not actually eaten, but just bitten or gnawed, nervously. But to *chomp* something is to take a bite out of it and usually to consume it. In dialect, *chomp* is colloquially accompanied by the adverb *down* (*chompin' down catfish*). *Chomp* is sometimes mistakenly used in place of *champ* in the idiom—e.g.: "DreamWorks chomps [read *champs*] the bit with 'Whoa, Nelly!' a world-beat rock album by Nelly Furtado, on Sept. 26." (*Billboard*; Sept. 16, 2000.) The idiom *champing at the bit* evokes the image of an impatient horse, especially one eager for a race to start. In contemporary print sources, it is slightly more common than the variant form, *chomping at the bit*.

chronic *Chronic* is often used to mean 'habitual, inveterate,' e.g., *a chronic liar*. Some consider this use incorrect. The precise meaning of **chronic** is 'persisting for a long time,' and it is used chiefly of illnesses or other problems: *more than one million people in the United States have chronic bronchitis.*

clearly Exaggerators like this word, along with its cousins (*obviously*, *undeniably*, *undoubtedly*, and the like). Often a statement prefaced with one of these words is conclusory, and sometimes even exceedingly dubious. As a result—though some readers don't consciously realize it—*clearly* and its ilk are 'weasel words'—that is, unnecessary words that supposedly intensify the meaning of a statement, but actually weaken it. Just how much *clearly* can weaken a statement is evident in the following example, in which the author uses the word to buttress a claim about his own state of mind: "Clearly, I am not to be convinced that this is a small matter." (Stephen White, *The Written Word*; 1984.)

continual, continuous *Continual* = frequently recurring; intermittent—e.g.: "And [the police are] removing [the homeless]—by police rides to the edge of town, by continual issuing of citations for camping, by mass towing of vehicles and by routine discarding of people's belongings." (*USA Today*; Dec. 3, 1997.) *Continuous* = occurring without interruption; unceasing—e.g.: "Crow Canyon archaeologists want to study the twelfth- and thirteenth-century village to determine exactly when it was inhabited and whether it was occupied continuously or intermittently." (*Santa Fe New Mexican*; Sept. 8, 1996.) A good mnemonic device is to think of the *-ous* ending as being short for "one uninterrupted sequence." The two words are frequently confused, usually with *continuous* horning in where *continual* belongs—e.g.: "Minutes after the arrest, Wayne Forrest, a Deputy Attorney General helping prosecute the case, told the presiding judge, Charles R. DiGisi, that the sheriff's office had been engaged in a 'continuous [read *continual*] course of misconduct' in the Spath case." (*New York Times*; Jan. 18, 1992.) "Continuous [read *Continual*] interruptions are frustrating because it often means [read *they often mean*] you have to warm up all over again or don't get a complete workout." (*Montgomery Advertiser*; Jan. 1, 1996.) The two-word phrase *almost continuous* is correctly replaced by the single-word *continual*—e.g.: "The antidepressant Prozac has been in the news almost continuously [read *continually*] since it was introduced in Belgium in 1986." (*Tampa Tribune*; Nov. 24, 1996.) A related mistake is to use *continuous* for something that happens at regular (e.g., annual) intervals—e.g.: "The White House tree-lighting ceremony has been held continuously [read *annually*] since 1923." (*Herald-Sun* [Durham, NC]; Dec. 6, 1996.)

cue, queue   Though pronounced the same, these words have different meanings. *Cue* = (1) a signal to begin; a hint; or (2) a stick used in billiards, pool, or shuffleboard. *Queue* = (1) a line of people or things waiting their turn; or (2) a hanging braid of hair. Not surprisingly, the two are sometimes confused—e.g.: "Like most birds, teal don't start their migration based on air temperatures, but take their queue [read *cue*] to head south from the shortening hours of daylight." (*Times-Picayune* [New Orleans]; Sept. 25, 1994.) "People were forced to stand in long cues [read *queues*] at five emergency water stations in Amagasaki." (*Daily Yomiuri* [English language/Japan]; Jan. 19, 1995.) To *cue up* a videotape, an audiotape, or a compact disc is to have it ready for playing at a particular point—e.g.: "His brother cued up the tape, the rousing theme song from 'Rocky.' (*Hartford Courant*; Sept. 17, 1996.) To *queue up* is to line up—e.g.: "Florida State students queued up for probably the most prized ticket they would ever use." (*Sports Illustrated*; Dec. 2, 1996.) The braid of hair is spelled *queue*, not *cue*—e.g.: "Instructed by French dancing masters in the stately steps and deep curtsies of the minuet, the young men had indeed to mind their pieds (feet) and queues (pigtails) to keep from losing their balance or their huge wigs." (*Press-Enterprise* [Riverside, CA]; Nov. 15, 1995.)

cupola, copula *Copula* = (1) a linking verb, such as *be, feel*, or *seem*, that expresses a state of being rather than action; or (2) a link or connection in general—e.g.: "This is the age of parsing, a word that once referred to the grammatical analysis of sentences. Now it means playing games with words, as Bill Clinton did with the copula 'is' in worming his way out of charges of illicit copulation." (*San Francisco Chronicle*; Aug. 31, 2001.) *Cupola* = an arched or domed roof, as on an astronomical observatory. *Copula* wrongly displaces *cupola* fairly often, probably by writers not versed in architecture—e.g.: "Each has its own copula [read *cupola*], Boston Gables, as well as numerous peaks with windows galore, all topped by a metal roof." (Times-Picayune [New Orleans]; Sept. 30, 2001.)

dare It's been called "one of the subtlest and most variegated verbs in the language" (Robert W. Burchfield, *Points of View*; 1992) and also "one of the trickiest" (William Safire, "Love That Dare," *New York Times*; May 17, 1987). The subtleties arise because *dare* is both an ordinary verb (*he dares you to pick up the snake*) and a modal verb (*he dare not do it himself*). And the form it takes (*dares* vs. *dare* in those examples) changes with that grammatical function. When *dare* is used as a full verb, it behaves just like most other verbs: it takes an *-s* with a third-person singular subject (*Robert always speaks his mind bluntly and dares anyone to disagree*). The form is identifiable by the presence of an explicit infinitive (with *to*) after *dare* (here, *to disagree*). *Dare* was an Old English modal. When it is used as an auxiliary verb (like the modern modals *will, must*, and, more closely, *ought*), the infinitive either is missing its *to* (*dare he disagree with Robert?*) or is missing altogether but understood (*he dare not!*). This occurs chiefly, but not only, in interrogative or negative sentences. In those sentences, the form *dares*—although sometimes used mistakenly in striving for correctness—would be unidiomatic, because *dare* in this usage behaves like other uninflected modals (*will he disagree with Robert?* | *he must not*) As a modal verb, *dare* raises an interesting question of tense: in reference to past time, should one write (1) "Although challenged to do it, he dare not," or (2) "Although challenged to do it, he dared not"? The *Oxford English Dictionary* endorses the first and calls the second "careless," but that advice was written when that part of the great dictionary was published in 1894 (and the dandy but now archaic *durst* was still available). More recent grammarians are more lenient— e.g.: "As a modal, *dare* exhibits abnormal time reference in that it can be used, without inflection, for past as well as present time: 'The king was so hot-tempered that no one dare tell him the bad news.' The main verb form *dared (to)* might also occur here." (Randolph Quirk et al., *A Comprehensive Grammar of the English Language*; 1985.) These more modern grammarians' analyses are borne out by actual usage— e.g.: "Mayo said he dared not declare it a little blue heron without confirmation from others." (*Hartford Courant*; Dec. 23, 2001.) It is odd, however, to see the past-tense form in the set phrase *how dare you*—e.g.: " 'How dared you!' Jon shouted, waving his arms for emphasis. 'That dish was ours, the property of the entire Order! How dared you even think to appropriate it for your own uses!'" (Patricia C. Wrede, *Mairelon the Magician*; 1991.) The form *durst*, which is a past indicative and past subjunctive along with *dared*, is obsolete in American English. In British English, it still occurs rarely, always in a negative sentence or conditional clause in which there is an infinitive either understood or having no *to* (*none durst answer him*). The exclamatory construction *How dare he do that!* is an idiomatic phrasing of the interrogative *How (does/did he) dare (to) do that?* The subject/actor (*he*) appears after the verb (*dare*) and is always in the nominative case— e.g.: "How dare she tell taxpayers to take on more responsi-

bility to help neighborhood kids? How dare she be right?"
(*Cincinnati Enquirer*; Aug. 18, 2002.)

dastardly *Dastard* (= coward) is commonly muddled because of
the sound association with its harsher rhyme, *bastard*. Although
English usage authority H. W. Fowler insisted that *dastard*
should be reserved for "one who avoids all personal risk,"
modern American writers tend to use it as a printable
euphemism for the more widely objectionable epithet—e.g.:
"Samuel Ramey is the dastard of the piece, the treacherous,
lecherous, murderous Assur." (*Los Angeles Times*; May 22,
1994.) British writers, on the other hand, have remained truer
to the word's original sense—e.g.: "Last week I moved house
from London to Brighton but like a genuine spineless dastard I
flatly denied its implications on personal relationships to the
last." (*Times* [London]; Feb. 8, 1994.) Recent American
dictionaries record one meaning of *dastard* as being "dis-
honorable, despicable" or "treacherously underhanded." So the
new meaning should probably now be considered standard.
Like the noun form, the adjective *dastardly* has been subjected
to slipshod extension. Although most dictionaries define it
merely as "cowardly," it is now often used as if it meant "sneaky
and underhanded; treacherous"—e.g.: "He's b-a-a-a-c-k.
Dastardly J. R. Ewing and his oft-manipulated clan rise from
TV dustdom to air three times a day on TNN, Cable Channel
37, beginning Monday." (*Tulsa World*; Sept. 27, 1996.)

data Whether you write "data are" or "data is," you're likely to
make some readers raise their eyebrows. Technically a plural,
data has, since the 1940s, been increasingly treated as a mass
noun taking a singular verb. But in more or less formal
contexts it is preferably treated as a plural—e.g.: "The data are
derived from tests performed on expectant mothers."
(*Economist*; Mar. 24, 2001.) Many writers use it as a singular,
however, risking their credibility with some readers (admittedly
a shrinking minority)—e.g.: "No data is offered to suggest that
women are being adversely hit by the dearth of articles." (*Globe
and Mail* [Canada]; Aug. 24, 1993.) In the context of
computing and related disciplines, the singular use of *data* is

common and comfortable—e.g.: "Every time you synchronize your PDA, the data gets backed up to your PC." (PCWorld.com; Feb. 8, 2001.) In one particular use, *data* is rarely treated as a singular: when it begins a clause and is not preceded by the definite article—e.g.: "Data over the last two years suggest that the rate at which gay men get AIDS has finally begun to flatten out." (*New York Times*; Feb. 5, 1989.) *Datum*, the "true" singular, is sometimes used when a single piece of information is referred to—e.g.: "We accept the law as a necessary datum, but that is not to say that we are required to accept it in abeyance of our critical faculties." (F. R. Leavis, *The Common Pursuit*; 1952.) Still, in nonscientific contexts, *datum* is likely to sound pretentious. Because *data* can be either a plural count noun or a singular mass noun, both *many data* and *much data* are correct—e.g.: "Numerous expert and representative interests are consulted, and many data assembled, often over a long period." (Carleton K. Allen, *Law in the Making*, 7th ed.; 1964.) "But much of the data in present personnel files is highly subjective." (William O. Douglas, *Points of Rebellion*; 1970.) As Albert C. Baugh, a historian of the English language, put it in 1962, "A student with one year of Latin [knows] that *data* and *phenomena* are plural." Whatever you do, if you use *data* in a context in which its number becomes known, you'll bother some of your readers. Perhaps 50 years from now—maybe sooner, maybe later—everybody will accept it as a collective. But not yet.

deceptive   *Deceptively* belongs to a very small set of words whose meaning is genuinely ambiguous in that it can be used in similar contexts to mean both one thing and also its complete opposite. A *deceptively smooth surface* is one that appears smooth but in fact is not smooth at all, while a *deceptively spacious room* is one that does not look spacious but is in fact *more* spacious than it appears. But what is a *deceptively steep gradient*? Or a person who is described as *deceptively strong*? To avoid confusion, use with caution (or not at all) unless the context makes clear in what way the thing modified is not what it first appears to be.

deprecate, depreciate The first of these has increasingly
encroached on the figurative senses of the second, while the
second has retreated into financial contexts. *Deprecate* means
"disapprove earnestly"—e.g.: " 'Well,' he admitted, deprecat-
ingly, 'one can't suppress one's natural instincts altogether; even
if one's reason and self-interest are all the other way.' " (Dorothy
L. Sayers, *Gaudy Night*; 1936) *Depreciate*, transitively, means
"belittle, disparage"; and intransitively, "fall in value" (used in
reference to assets or investments). The familiar phrase *self-
deprecating* is, literally speaking, a virtual impossibility, except
perhaps for those suffering from extreme neuroses. Thus *self-
depreciating*, with *depreciate* in its transitive sense, has
historically been viewed as the correct phrase—e.g.: "Sadly,
Grizzard did not have the self-depreciating humor of a Jeff
Foxworthy, the self-proclaimed redneck comedian." (*St. Louis
Post-Dispatch*; July 25, 1996.) Unfortunately, though, the form
self-deprecating—despite its mistaken origins—is now 50 times
as common in print as *self-depreciating*. Speakers of American
English routinely use *self-deprecating*. However grudgingly, we
must accord to it the status of standard English—e.g.: "He's
smart, articulate, funny, alternately self-deprecating and proud
of his success." (*Los Angeles Times*; Sept. 1, 1996.)

derring-do *Derring-do* (= daring action) derives, according to
the *Oxford English Dictionary*, from a "chain of misunderstandings and errors." Originally, the term was *dorryng do*, a
verb phrase meaning "daring to do." A sixteenth-century
misprint in the poetry of John Lydgate (ca. 1370–1450) made
it *derrynge do*, which Spenser (1579) misunderstood and used
as a noun phrase meaning "manhood, chivalry." Then Sir
Walter Scott popularized the phrase in *Ivanhoe* (1820) with
the spelling *derring-do*, and this has been the settled spelling
ever since. But because of its historical and modern
associations with *daring*, writers often use the erroneous
spelling *daring-do*—e.g.: "Instead, it is also called 'Flower
Flange' and has more to do with flowers than fighting and
daring-do [read *derring-do*]." (*Knoxville News-Sentinel*; Sept.
25, 1998.)

despoliation A learned word, *spoliation* /spoh-lee-ay-shun/ means "the act of ruining, destroying, or spoiling something." In the hands and mouths of the less-than-learned, it's often misspelled and mispronounced *spoilation*. The difference between the form of the verb and of the noun arises from different paths by which the words came into English: in the fourteenth century, *spoil* was borrowed from Old French (*espoille*), whereas in the fifteenth century, *spoliation* was borrowed from Latin (*spoilātio*). *Despoliation* (= pillaging, plundering) is often misspelled *despoilation*—a blunder that surprises primarily because it occurs in otherwise highly literate writing—e.g.: "The horrors of gulag and the environmental despoilations [read *despoliations*] of the Soviet era both get their due here." (*Washington Times*; Feb. 27, 1994.) Oddly, though, the corresponding verb is *despoil*. Why the discrepancy in spelling? The answer again lies in the vagaries of linguistic history. English borrowed the verb in the thirteenth century from Old French (*despoillier*) but the noun in the seventeenth century from Latin (*despoliatio*). And those two forms—for centuries, at any rate—stuck.

dilemma *Dilemma* should be reserved for reference to a predicament in which a difficult choice must be made between undesirable alternatives: *You see his dilemma? If he moves to London, he may never see his parents again. But if he stays in Seattle, he may be giving up the best job offer of his life.* The weakened use of *dilemma* to mean simply "a difficult situation or problem" (*the dilemma of a teacher shortage*) is recorded as early as the first part of the seventeenth century, but many regard this use as unacceptable and it should be avoided in written English.

disembodied, dismembered *Disembodied* = separated from the physical body, esp. as a spirit. The word is stretched too far when used to describe a body part severed from the torso— e.g.: "Having said all that, did we really need to see the disembodied [read *severed*] heads? In a word: yuck. We got the idea with the hacksaw and the meat cleaver, thanks." (*Arizona Republic*; Nov. 21, 2002.) *Dismembered* = (1) (of bodily limbs) cut from the torso; or (2) (of a torso) character-ized by having had limbs cut off. This term does not work well with heads—e.g.: "In a flurry of recent TV appearances promoting his new book on families, the former vice president has been seen . . . floating as a dismembered [read *detached*] head in a jar on the Fox cartoon show 'Futurama,' where he's dubbed 'the inventor of the environment.'" (*Christian Science Monitor*; Nov. 19, 2002.)

due The use of **due to** as a prepositional phrase meaning 'because of,' as in *he had to retire due to an injury* first appeared in print in 1897, and traditional grammarians have opposed this prepositional usage for a century on the grounds that it is a misuse of the adjectival phrase **due to** in the sense of 'attributable to, likely or expected to' (*the train is due to arrive at 11:15*), or 'payable to' (*render unto Caesar what is due to Caesar*). Nevertheless, this prepositional usage is now widespread and common in all types of literature and must be regarded as standard English. Avoid the wordy phrase **due to the fact that** and use *because* instead, especially in writing.

edification In the phrase *for your edification* (= for your moral or intellectual instruction), the word *edification* is sometimes misused to mean "for your enjoyment" or the like—e.g.: "Dennis has come to the Tishomingo Lodge and Casino to perform daredevil dives for the edification [read *thrill*] of the casino guests." (*Rocky Mountain News* [Denver]; Feb. 15, 2002.) "Everyone says vaguely snotty things about each other and hidden cameras record, for our edification [read *titillation*], sundry couples' first kisses." (*Daily News of Los Angeles*; June 2, 2002.) "Quinn and his best friend Creedy (Gerard Butler) reenact the climactic light-saber battle between Luke Skywalker and Darth Vader for the edification [read *enjoyment*] of the local children." (*Austin American-Statesman*; July 12, 2002.)

enormity This word is imprecisely used to mean 'great size,' as in *it is difficult to comprehend the enormity of the continent,* but the original and preferred meaning is 'extreme wicked-ness,' as in *the enormity of the mass murders.* To indicate enormous size, the words *enormousness*, *immensity*, *vastness*, *hugeness*, etc., are preferable.

enthuse The verb *enthuse* is a back-formation from the noun *enthusiasm* and, like many verbs formed from nouns in this way, it is regarded by traditionalists as unacceptable. *Enthuse* has been in the language for more than 150 years, but, before using the word in formal writing, be aware that readers familiar with its Greek meaning may find casual usage misguided or irritating. *Enthusiasm* derives from a word originally meaning 'to become inspired or possessed by a god' (*en* 'in' + *theos* 'god'). From the traditionalist point of view, *inspired* or *excited* is preferable to *enthused*.

facile Always meaning "easy" in one sense or another, *facile* may connote either proficiency or shallowness. The writer must achieve clarity through context. Sometimes the word connotes the ease that comes with artistic mastery—e.g.: "Nicolai Dobrev played the jester, a noble baritone with a facile instrument." (*Boston Herald*; Mar. 30, 2002.) More often, it connotes triteness or oversimplification—e.g.: "But most mental health experts say closure is no holy grail, only rendered so by people seeking facile solutions to complex problems." (*Christian Science Monitor*; Mar. 28, 2002.)

faze, phase *Faze* = disconcert; daunt. *Phase* (verb) = carry out (a plan, program, etc.) in stages. *Phase* for *faze* is an increasingly common blunder—e.g.: "Others said they had weathered so many rumors that nothing phased [read *fazed*] them anymore." (*Boston Globe*; June 6, 1995.) The opposite error (*faze* for *phase*) also occurs, but more rarely—e.g.: "All that while shooting guard Art Mlotkowski, shadowed all over the court by Northport senior Rob Sanicola, was fazed [read *phased*] out of the offense." (*Newsday* [New York]; Feb. 26, 1995.)

fey *Fey* derives from the Old English *fæge* ("doomed to die") and carries the related sense "in an unusually excited state (like one about to die)." By an extension, the word came to mean "whimsical, otherworldly, eccentric," perhaps from confusion with *fay* (= a fairy or elf). This shift in meaning was noticed as early as 1950. Today the word's original meaning is all but forgotten—e.g.: "An upsurge of book sales in cyberspace could have dramatic effects on the fortunes of the already fey and contradictory world of book publishing." (*Washington Post*, Aug. 4, 1997.)

flaunt, flout Confusion about these terms is so distressingly common that some dictionaries have thrown in the towel and now treat *flaunt* as a synonym of *flout*. *Flout* means "contravene or disregard; treat with contempt." *Flaunt* means "show off or parade something in an ostentatious manner," but is often incorrectly used for *flout*, perhaps because it is misunderstood as a telescoped version of *flout* and *taunt*—e.g.: "In Washington, the White House issued a statement that deplored the Nigerian Government's 'flaunting [read *flouting*] of even the most basic international norms and universal standards of human rights.'" (*New York Times*; Nov. 11, 1995.) Of course, *flaunt* is more often used correctly—e.g.: "He donates millions to religious and charitable groups, yet flaunts his own wealth." (*Fortune*; Aug. 18, 1997.) *Flout*, meanwhile, almost never causes a problem. Here it's correctly used: "A record rider turnout, fueled by the mayor's earlier pledge to end the escort and crack down on cyclists flouting traffic laws, poured into the streets on an improvised route." (*San Francisco Examiner*; Aug. 3, 1997.) But the rare mistake of misusing *flout* for *flaunt* does sometimes occur—e.g.: "Mr. Talton was soon joined by almost two dozen other conservative Republicans who filed en masse into the clerk's office to flout [read *flaunt*] their disapproval for their colleague and fellow party member." (*Dallas Morning News*; May 25, 2000.) One federal appellate judge who misused *flaunt* for *flout* in a published opinion—only to be corrected by judges who later quoted him—appealed to *Webster's Third New International Dictionary of the English Language*, which accepts as standard any usage that can be documented with any frequency. The judge then attempted to justify his error and pledged to persist in it. Seeking refuge in a nonprescriptive dictionary, however, merely ignores the all-important distinction between formal contexts, in which strict standards of usage must apply, and informal contexts, in which venial faults of grammar or usage may, if we are lucky, go unnoticed (or unmentioned).

fortuitous The traditional, etymological meaning of **fortuitous** is 'happening by chance': a *fortuitous meeting* is a chance meeting, which might turn out to be either a good thing or a bad thing. In modern uses, however, *fortuitous* tends more often to be used to refer to fortunate outcomes, and the word has become more or less a synonym for 'lucky' or 'fortunate.' This use is frowned upon as being not etymologically correct and is best avoided except in informal contexts.

frog legs Some cookbook authors write *frog legs*—e.g., Irma S. Rombauer and Marion Rombauer Becker (*Joy of Cooking*; 1975), Jacqueline Killeen (*The Whole World Cookbook*; 1979), and Emeril Lagasse (*Louisiana Real & Rustic*; 1996). Others, perhaps a majority of writers on culinary matters, write *frogs' legs*—e.g., Ruth R. Tyndall (*Eat Yourself Full*; 1967), Helen Corbitt (*Helen Corbitt Cooks for Company*; 1974), and Pierre Franey (*More 60-Minute Gourmet*; 1981). This form appears to be a direct translation of the French *cuisses de grenouilles* (= legs of frogs, or frogs' legs). The other forms are less defensible. At least one writer—Jacques Pepin (*La Methode*; 1979)—uses *frog's legs*, as if they were served always in pairs (and carefully matched up). Some writers indecisively mix two or more forms—e.g., Alan Davidson, in *The Oxford Companion to Food* (1999), uses both *frog legs* and *frogs' legs*. Those citations don't quite reflect general usage in newspapers and journals. Of 1,600 examples checked in Westlaw's ALLNEWS database in January 2002, the breakdown was as follows: *frog legs*-880 (55%); *frogs' legs*-450 (28%); *frog's legs*-194 (12%); and *frogs legs*-76 (5%). Likewise, informal surveys suggest that most cultivated speakers who would order this item say *frog legs*. The cookbook writers' preference for *frogs' legs* seems a mite pedantic. In any event, the two forms to be avoided are *frog's legs* (unless you're talking about a particular frog) and *frogs legs* (unless you eat them without utensils or napkins).

fun The use of *fun* as an adjective meaning 'enjoyable,' as in *we had a fun evening*, is not fully accepted in standard English and should only be used in informal contexts. There are signs, however, that this situation is changing, given the recent appearance in American English of comparative and superlative forms *funner* and *funnest*, formed as if *fun* were a normal adjective. The adjectival forms *funner* and *funnest* have not 'arrived' in all the dictionaries, however, and if employed at all, they should be used sparingly and not in formal written English.

gay *Gay* meaning 'homosexual,' dating back to the 1930s (if not earlier), became established in the 1960s as the term preferred by homosexual men to describe themselves. It is now the standard accepted term throughout the English-speaking world. As a result, the centuries-old other senses of *gay* meaning either 'carefree' or 'bright and showy,' once common in speech and literature, are much less frequent. The word *gay* cannot be readily used unselfconsciously today in these older senses without sounding old-fashioned or arousing a sense of double entendre, despite concerted attempts by some to keep them alive. *Gay* in its modern sense typically refers to men (**lesbian** being the standard term for homosexual women), but in some contexts it can be used of both men and women.

gender The word *gender* has been used since the fourteenth century primarily as a grammatical term, referring to the classes of noun in Latin, Greek, German, and other languages designated as *masculine, feminine,* or *neuter*. It has also been used since the fourteenth century in the sense 'the state of being male or female,' but this did not become a common standard use until the mid twentieth century. Although the words *gender* and *sex* both have the sense 'the state of being male or female,' they are typically used in slightly different ways: *sex* tends to refer to biological differences, while *gender* tends to refer to cultural or social ones.

golf One may either *play golf* (the phrase dates from ca. 1575) or simply *golf* (ca. 1800)—that is, *golf* can be a verb as well as a noun. Most golfers use the older phrasing and say that they *play golf* (*I'll be playing golf on Saturday*), whereas nowadays nongolfers tend to be the ones who use *golf* as a verb (*she'll be golfing on Saturday*). In modern print sources, *played golf* is 20 times as common as *golfed*. Writers on golf often disparage the verb *golf* as symptomatic of linguistic dufferdom—e.g.: One writer states: "If you call yourself a golfer, you never use *golf* as a verb. You never say 'We went golfing.' *Golf* to a golfer is a noun. A guy tells you he 'golfs,' and you know he's clueless." (*San Francisco Examiner*; June 14, 1998.) If you're serious about golf and writing, stick to the noun uses of *golf*. That will never get anyone teed off.

handicapped *Handicapped* in the sense referring to a person's mental or physical disabilities is first recorded in the early twentieth century. For a brief period in the second half of the twentieth century, it looked as if *handicapped* would be replaced by *disabled*, but both words are now acceptable and interchangeable in standard American English, and neither word has been overtaken by newer coinages such as *differently abled* or *physically challenged*.

historic, historical *Historical*, meaning "of or relating to or occurring in history," is called upon for use far more frequently than historic. *Historic* means "historically significant" *the Alamo is a historic building*. An event that makes history is historic; momentous happenings or developments are historic—e.g.: "The Supreme Court's historic decision about whether mentally competent, dying patients and their doctors have the right to hasten death won't be known for months." (*USA Today,* Jan. 10, 1997). A documented fact, event, or development—perhaps having no great importance—is *historical*. E.g.: "Despite the historical data, some people just don't feel comfortable knowing their loan's rate can drift up 5 or 6 points." (Chicago Sun-Times, Jan. 24, 1997). Examples of *historic* used incorrectly for *historical* could easily run for several pages—e.g.: "The

Sunday Trading Act, which formally became law yesterday, removes historic [read *historical*] anomalies of the kind that allowed shopkeepers to sell pornographic magazines but not Bibles on the Sabbath, and instant but not ground coffee." (*Times* (London), Aug. 27, 1994). "The odds are now on a further easing of monetary policy and there is a good historic [read *historical*] correlation between falling interest rates and a rising stock market." (*Financial Times*, June 13, 1996). "Rape is also an historic [read a *historical*] soldiers' sport." (*Harper's Magazine*, Jan. 2003). The far less common mistake is misusing *historical* for *historic*—e.g.: "Gary Pinkel didn't know what to expect after Toledo and Nevada found themselves going into a historical [read *historic*] overtime in the Las Vegas Bowl." (*Austin Am.-Statesman*, Dec. 16, 1995).

hopefully Four points about this word: First, it was widely condemned from the 1960s to the 1980s. Briefly, the objections are that (1) *hopefully* properly means "in a hopeful manner" and shouldn't be used in the radically different sense "I hope" or "it is to be hoped"; (2) if the extended sense is accepted, the original sense will be forever lost; and (3) in constructions such as "Hopefully, it won't rain this afternoon," the writer illogically ascribes an emotion (*hopefulness*) to a nonperson. *Hopefully* isn't analogous to *curiously* (= it is a curious fact that), *fortunately* (= it is a fortunate thing that), and *sadly* (= it is a sad fact that). How so? Unlike all those other sentence adverbs, *hopefully* can't be resolved into any longer expression involving the word *hopeful*— but only *hope* (e.g., *it is to be hoped that* or *I hope that*). Second, whatever the merits of those arguments, the battle is now over. *Hopefully* is now a part of American English, and it has all but lost its traditional meaning—e.g.: "Hopefully, one day we will all grow older." (*San Diego Union-Tribune*; Nov. 26, 1997.) Sometimes, the word is genuinely ambiguous (if the original meaning is considered still alive)—e.g.: "Dave Krieg will take the snaps and, hopefully, hand off to RB Garrison Hearst." (*USA Today*; Sept. 1, 1995.) (Is Krieg hoping for the best when Hearst runs? Or is the writer hoping that Krieg won't pass the football or hand off to another running back?) Indeed, the original meaning of *hopefully* is alive, even if moribund—e.g.: "Officials recently have pointed hopefully to signs of increased usage of the garage." (*Boston Globe*; Oct. 9, 1994.) Third, some stalwarts continue to condemn the word, so that anyone using it in the new sense is likely to have a credibility problem with some readers—e.g. "Professor Michael Dummett, an Oxford logician, condemns the new usage of *hopefully* because only a person can be hopeful, and in many such cases there is nobody around in the sentence to be hopeful." (*Daily Telegraph* [UK]; Dec. 11, 1996.) "Although various adverbs may be used to modify entire clauses, *hopefully* isn't among them—yet. I only hope I won't have to concede that it is until I'm an old, old woman." (Barbara Wallraff, *Word Court*; 2000.) Fourth, though the controversy swirling around this word has subsided, any use of it is likely to distract some readers. Avoid it in all senses if you're concerned with your credibility: if you use it in the traditional way, many readers will think it odd; if you use it in the newish way, a few readers will tacitly tut-tut you. Throughout the late twentieth century, the common wisdom was that the use of *hopefully* as a sentence adverb had begun sometime around the early 1930s. Then, in 1999, a lexicographic scholar named Fred Shapiro, using computer-assisted research, traced it back to Cotton Mather's 1702 book, *Magnalia Christi Americana*, in this sentence: "Chronical diseases, which evidently threaten his Life, might hopefully be relieved by his removal." The evidence then skips to 1851, then to the 1930s.

ignoramus Until 1934 in England, if a grand jury considered the evidence of an alleged crime insufficient to prosecute, it would endorse the bill *ignoramus*, meaning literally "we do not know" or "we know nothing of this." Long before, though, the word *ignoramus* had come to mean, by extension, "an ignorant person." In 1615, George Ruggle wrote a play called *Ignoramus*, about a lawyer who knew nothing about the law; this fictional lawyer soon gave his name to all manner of know-nothings, whether lawyers or nonlawyers. The modern nonlegal meaning appears most frequently—e.g.: "There's no surprise—or challenge—in watching a sycophantic, misogynistic ignoramus like Burdette win out over the self-effacing, truth-loving Hutchinson." (*Chicago Tribune*; Aug. 5, 1997.) The plural is *ignoramuses*. The form *ignorami* is a pseudo-learned blunder, since in Latin *ignoramus* is a verb and not one of the Latin nouns ending in *-us*.

impact *Impact* has traditionally been only a noun. In recent years, however, it has undergone a semantic shift that has allowed it to act as a verb. Such use has become widespread (and also widely condemned by stylists)—e.g.: "The researchers concluded that this low level of intensity may have impacted [read *affected*] the results." (*Tampa Tribune*; July 17, 1997.) This use of the word would be perfectly acceptable if *impact* were performing any function not as ably performed by *affect* or *influence*. If *affect* as a verb is not sufficiently straightforward in context, then the careful writer might use *have an impact on*, which, though longer, is probably better than the jarring impact of *impacted*. Reserve *impact* for noun uses and *impacted* for wisdom teeth. Interestingly, *impact* as a verb might have arisen partly in response to widespread diffidence about the spelling of *affect* (often confused with *effect*).

infer Properly used, *infer* means "deduce; reason from premises to a conclusion"—e.g.: "We get no sense of the man himself from this book except what we can infer from the biographical facts that Mr. Magida presents." (*New York Times*; Aug. 18, 1996.) Writers frequently misuse *infer* when *imply* (= hint at; suggest) would be the correct word—e.g.: "And no team is, of course, inferring [read *implying*] that Dallas isn't talented." (*New York Times*; Jan. 12, 1996.) Remember: a speaker or writer *implies* something without putting it expressly. A listener or reader *infers* beyond what has been literally expressed. Or, as Theodore Bernstein put it, "The *implier* is the pitcher; the *inferrer* is the catcher." (*The Careful Writer*; 1965.) Stylists agree that the important distinction between these words deserves to be maintained.

in like Flynn This phrase, meaning "assured of success," first became widespread during World War II as an allusion to the actor Errol Flynn's legendary prowess in seducing women. (In

1942, Flynn was prosecuted for the statutory rape of two teenage girls—and was acquitted.) Today the phrase has generally lost any sexual connotation—e.g.: "By these standards, Gore should be in like Flynn." (*Commercial Appeal* [Memphis]; Feb. 13, 2000.) "Based on the results of our Triangle Census, you'll be in like Flynn." (*News & Observer* [Raleigh]; Mar. 27, 2000.) "Follow the formula, and you're in like Flynn." (*BusinessWeek,* Aug. 7, 2000.) The phrase has been the subject of wordplay and consequent confusion. In 1966 appeared *Our Man Flint,* a film starring James Coburn and spoofing the James Bond series; the following year, its sequel, *In Like Flint,* was released. The popularity of these films—especially the latter with its pun on *in like Flynn*—sparked lingering confusion about what the proper phrase should be. Thus, during coverage of the 2000 Republican Convention, Mark Shields, a PBS commentator, said that George W. Bush might be "in like Flynn, or in like Flint—whatever we say" (PBS Convention Coverage, Aug. 3, 2000). This confusion had already surfaced in print—e.g.: "Yep, with my peacoat, I was in like Flint [read *Flynn*], I thought, able to hubbub with the highbrows or hang with the homeboys." (*News & Observer* [Raleigh]; Jan. 11, 1998) (in this example, *hubbub* should probably be *hobnob*). "If you want to be 'in like Flint [read *Flynn*],' there has to be a measure of exclusivity." Larry Lipson, (*Daily News* [L.A.]; Aug. 27, 1999.) "Finder praises Gawande as a quick learner. If he failed to incorporate advice initially, says Finder, 'the second time he was in like Flint [read *Flynn*].' (*Boston Globe,* Nov. 10, 1999.) Although this usage occasionally appears in tongue-in-cheek references to Flint, Michigan, and to flint as stone, it shouldn't appear in sentences such as those just quoted. Errol Flynn is reported to have resented the phrase, but it will always be linked etymologically to him.

innocent *Innocent* properly means 'harmless,' but it has long been extended in general language to mean 'not guilty.' The jury (or judge) in a criminal trial does not, strictly speaking, find a defendant 'innocent.' Rather, a defendant may be *guilty* or *not guilty* of the charges brought. In common use, however, owing perhaps to the concept of the *presumption of innocence*, which instructs a jury to consider a defendant free of wrong-doing until proven guilty on the basis of evidence, *not guilty* and *innocent* have come to be thought of as synonymous.

interment, internment *Interment* = burial (*interment will take place just after the funeral service*). *Internment* = detention, esp. of aliens in wartime (*the internment of Japanese Americans during World War II*). *Interment* is sometimes, especially in obituaries, confounded with *internment*—e.g.: "Graveside ceremony and internment [read *interment*] will be at Hillside Cemetery in Peekskill immediately following." (*Times Union* [Albany]; Aug. 22, 2000.)

it The possessive form of *it* is *its*; the contraction for *it is* is *it's*. But the two words are often confounded—e.g.: "Potter County was ordered by the state to do something about overcrowding in in it's [read *its*] system." (*Canyon News* [TX]; Jan. 13, 1994.) Confusion is just as much a problem in British English as it is in American English—e.g.: "But fear not because fashion does award it's [read *its*] very own New Year's Honour's list of modern classics." (*Independent* [UK]; Jan. 16, 2000.) Also, the possessive *its* should never be used—as it sometimes is—as a personal pronoun in place of *his*, *her*, or *his or her*.

jodhpur *Jodhpur* /jod-per/ derives from the city of Jodhpur, India. The word (almost invariably used in the plural) refers to a type of flared-at-the-thigh pants used in English horse-riding. Through a kind of visual metathesis, the word is often mispronounced /jod-fer/. And believe it or not, this error pervades the horse-riding industry. The mispronunciation sometimes results in the obvious misspelling—e.g.: "Wealthy suburbanites clad in fancy jodphurs [read jodhpurs] and riding boots will replace overall-clad cowboys like Mizer." (*Palm Beach Post*, 14 July 2002.) By inevitable extension, the misspelling also goes back to the source of the word—e.g.: "His name is Ali Akbar Khan, above, whose family traces its musical roots to the sixteenth century, when an ancestor was court musician to the Emperor Akbar, as Ali Akbar Khan was

to the Maharajah of Jodphur [read Jodhpur] in his 20's."
(*N.Y. Times*, 7 Nov. 2002.) How did Jodhpur, a town in
northwestern India, come to be famously associated with
riding pants? It seems that Rao Raja Hanut Singh, who
represented Jodhpur at Queen Victoria's 60th jubilee in 1897,
had designed some comfortable riding trousers that ballooned
at the thigh and narrowed at the knee so that they could be
tucked into boots. While in London, he had the pants copied
by a London tailor, who then began making and selling them.
By 1899, the pants were well on their way to international
popularity.

lay, lie The verb lay means, broadly, 'put something down': *they
are going to lay the carpet*. The past tense and the past
participle of lay is laid: *they laid the groundwork; she had laid
careful plans*. The verb lie, on the other hand, means 'assume
a horizontal or resting position': *why don't you lie on the floor?*
In practice, many speakers inadvertently get the **lay** forms and
the **lie** forms into a tangle of right and wrong usage. Here are
some examples of typical incorrect usage: *have you been laying
on the sofa all day?* (should be **lying**); *he lay the books on the
table* (should be **laid**); *I had laid in this position so long, my
arm was stiff* (should be **lain**).

less, fewer Strictly, *less* applies to singular nouns (*less tonic
water, please*) or units of measure (*less than six ounces of
epoxy*). *Fewer* applies to plural nouns (*fewer guests arrived
than expected*) or numbers of things (*we have three fewer
members this year*). The exception in using *fewer* occurs when
count nouns essentially function as mass nouns because the
units are so very numerous or they aren't considered discrete
items (the idea of individual units becomes meaningless).
Hence *less* is used correctly with time and money: one isn't,
ordinarily, talking about the number of years or the number of
dollars but rather the amount of time or the amount of
money—e.g.: "On that mantra, Larry Clark has built a $45
million-a-year company in less than five years." (*Arizona
Business Gazette*; Nov. 30, 1995.) "Okay, how about $50 a
month for such an apartment—less than two dollars a day?"

(*Village Voice*; Apr. 29, 1997.) *Fewer*, in fact, is incorrect when intended to refer to a period of time—e.g.: "You can run from sea level to the sky and back to earth in as fast as 45 minutes (so far), but even today, going round-trip in fewer [read *less*] than 60 minutes carries a special cachet." (*Anchorage Daily News*; June 29, 1997.) But if the units of time are thought of as wholes, and not by fractions, then *fewer* is called for (*fewer days abroad | fewer weeks spent apart*). Hence we say *less documentation* but *fewer documents*; *less whispering* but *fewer remarks*; *less of a burden* but *fewer burdens*; *less fattening* but *fewer calories*. Fastidious writers and editors preserve the old distinction. But the loose usage crops up often—e.g.: "You will have less [read *fewer*] people to call and haunt about paying for their outfits and buying their accessories." (*Boston Herald* [magazine]; Oct. 19, 1997.) The linguistic hegemony by which *less* has encroached on *fewer*'s territory is probably now irreversible. What has clinched this development is something as mundane as the express checkout lines in supermarkets. They're typically bedecked with signs cautioning, "15 items or less." These signs are all but ubiquitous in the United States. But the occasional more literate supermarket owner uses a different sign: "15 or fewer items." Finally, even with the strict usage, it's sometimes a close call whether a thing is a mass noun or a count noun, and hence whether *less* or *fewer* is proper. Take, for example, a percentage: should it be "less than 10% of the homeowners were there" or "fewer than 10% of the homeowners were there"? One could argue that a percentage is something counted (i.e., 10 out of 100), and thus requires *fewer*. One could also argue that a percentage is a collective mass noun (akin, e.g., to money), and thus requires *less*. The latter is the better argument because most percentages aren't whole numbers anyway. And even if it were a toss-up between the two theories, it's sound to choose *less*, which is less formal in tone than *fewer*. If, in strict usage, *less* applies to singular nouns and *fewer* to plural nouns, the choice is clear: "one less golfer on the course," not "one fewer golfer." This is tricky only because *less* is being applied to a singular count noun, whereas it usually applies to a mass noun. Lyricist Hal David got it right in "One Less Bell to Answer" (1970). Nearly a quarter of the time, however, writers use *one fewer*, an awkward and unidiomatic phrase. One can't help thinking that this is a kind of hypercorrection induced by underanalysis of the *less*-vs.-*fewer* question. *Lesser*, like *less*, refers to quantity, but is confined to use as an adjective before a singular noun and following an article (*the lesser crime*) or alone before a plural noun (*lesser athletes*), thus performing a function no longer idiomatically possible with less. Dating from the thirteenth century, this formal usage allows *lesser* to act as an antonym of *greater*.

lie In the sense of telling an untruth, the verb is inflected *lie, lied, lied*. The more troublesome inflections belong to the senses of reclining, being placed, and being situated: *lie, lay, lain*. A murderer may *lie in wait*. Yesterday he *lay in wait*. And for several days he *has lain in wait*—e.g.: "The Ramseys say an intruder may have lay [read *lain*] in wait for hours before killing the 6-year-old beauty queen." (*Austin American-Statesman*; Mar. 18, 2000.)

majority Strictly speaking, **majority** should be used with countable nouns to mean 'the greater number': *the majority of cases*. The use of **majority** with uncountable nouns to mean 'the greatest part' (*I spent the majority of the day reading*), although common in informal contexts, is not considered good standard English.

man Traditionally, the word **man** has been used to refer not only to adult males but also to human beings in general, regardless of sex. There is a historical explanation for this: in Old English, the principal sense of **man** was 'a human being,' and the words *wer* and *wif* were used to refer specifically to 'a male person' and 'a female person,' respectively. Subsequently, **man** replaced *wer* as the normal term for 'a male person,' but the older sense 'a human being' remained in use. In the second half of the twentieth century, the generic use of **man** to refer to 'human beings in general' (*reptiles were here long before man appeared on the earth*) became problematic; the use is now often regarded as sexist or old-fashioned. In some contexts, terms such as **the human race** or **humankind** may be used instead of **man** or **mankind**.

media, medium Strictly speaking, the first is the plural of the second (*the media were overreacting*). But *media*—as a shortened form of communications *media*—is increasingly used as a mass noun (*the media was overreacting*). While that usage still makes some squeamish, it must be accepted as standard. But it's still possible (and preferable) to draw the line at *medias*, which has recently raised its ugly head—e.g.: "The staff will use several medias [read *media*] and visuals to help get their points across." (*Virginian-Pilot & Ledger Star* [Norfolk]; Jan. 17, 1996.) *Mediums* is the correct plural when the sense of *medium* is "a clairvoyant or spiritualist"—e.g.: "Contact is initiated by the deceased, and no psychics, mediums or devices are involved." (*St. Petersburg Times*; Oct. 14, 1996.) Otherwise, the form should be avoided—e.g.: "Reporters for printed mediums [read *media*] also focus criticism on television for using all-purpose experts to express an opinion on a wide variety of subjects." (*New York Times*; May 4, 1990.)

Meritage "Some people find the word 'Meritage' meritorious. Others find it meretricious. But most people have no idea what it means." (*Denver Post*; June 8, 1994.) And the dictionaries provide no help: as of early 2003, no major dictionary had an entry on the term—which has an interesting history. In 1988, California winemakers sponsored an international contest to create an upscale term for a table wine blended from two or more Bordeaux varietals grown in the United States. A California grocery-store wine buyer won the contest with "Meritage," a portmanteau word formed by combining *merit* with *heritage*. The word rhymes with *heritage*; it's pronounced /mer-it-ij/. Yet many wine enthusiasts mistakenly give it a Frenchified pronunciation (/mar-i-tahzh/), which has become lamentably widespread. To help keep prices reasonable, insist on the unpretentious pronunciation rhyming with *heritage*. With the faux-French affectation, prices will surely get out of hand.

misnomer Speakers and writers frequently misuse this word, meaning "an inappropriate name," to mean "a popular misconception"—e.g.: " 'The last I remember, only 7 percent of Division I programs operate in the black. The common misnomer [read *misconception*] is that people see this as a multi-million-dollar business.' " (*Times Union* [Albany]; Dec. 24, 2000.) Oddly enough, this mistake is itself a kind of misnomer based on a misconception. Although the error is less common in edited text, it does surface—e.g.: "The old theory that was heard at UW for years is that the school needs a big-name coach. That's really a misnomer [read *misconception*] because UW usually has succeeded in developing its own big-name coach." (*Wyoming Tribune-Eagle*; Nov. 21, 2002.) Typically, when the term is used correctly it will accompany a misleading word or title, often in quotation marks—e.g.: "Old countries are sometimes world-weary and cynical, urging a 'realism' that is sometimes a misnomer for the moral corruption they know so very well." (*Washington Post*; Oct. 15, 2002.)

mutual Traditionalists consider using **mutual** to mean 'common to two or more people' (*a mutual friend*; *a mutual interest*) to be incorrect, holding that the sense of reciprocity is necessary (*mutual respect*; *mutual need*). However, both senses are well established and acceptable in standard English.

myself *Myself* is best used either reflexively (*I have decided to exclude myself from consideration*) or intensively (*I myself have seen that* | *I've done that myself*). The word shouldn't appear as a substitute for *I* or *me* (*my wife and myself were delighted to see you*). Using it that way, as an "untriggered reflexive," is thought somehow to be modest, as if the reference were less direct. Yet it's no less direct, and the user may unconsciously cause the reader or listener to assume an intended jocularity, or that the user is somewhat doltish—e.g.: "Those ins and outs are largely a self-learning process, though knowing the experience of someone like myself [read *me*] might make the learning shorter, easier, and a lot less painful." (Mark H. McCormack, *What They Don't Teach You at Harvard Business School*; 1984.) "The exclusion of women and women's concerns is self-defeating. For instance, myself and other women in Hollywood [read *many women in Hollywood, including me,*] would deliver millions of dollars of profit to the film industry if we could make films and television shows about the lives of real women." (*Los Angeles Times*; Oct. 22, 1989.) "My wife and myself [read *I*] were in a religious cult for over 15 years before the leader fell over dead." (*Pantagraph* [Bloomington, IL]; Apr. 6, 1997.)

Native American The term *Native American* proliferated in the 1970s to denote groups served by the federal Bureau of Indian Affairs: American Indians as well as the Eskimos and Aleuts of Alaska. Later, the term was interpreted as including Native Hawaiians and Pacific Islanders, and it fell into disfavor among some Indian and Alaskan groups, who came to prefer *American Indian* and *Alaska Native*. Yet views are unpredictable: some consider *Native American* more respectful than *American Indian*. As an equivalent to *American Indian*, the phrase *Native American* was long thought to be a twentieth-century innovation. In fact, the phrase *Native American*—though it came into vogue in the early and mid-1970s—dates back to at least 1737 in this sense. And it made literal sense (for the most part) in 1737, since at that time most people who had been born in the New World were indigenous—not of European descent. By the nineteenth century, when the phrase *native American* (lowercase *n-*) was fairly common, it had become ambiguous, since it often referred to any person born in the United States, whether of indigenous or of European descent. Here, in a mid-twentieth-century passage, it refers to place of birth: "Dr. Flesch . . . was born in Vienna, but writes more like a native American than do most native Americans; in fact, he teaches the natives how to write like natives; it is always amazing to recall that he came to America as lately as the 1930's." (Gorham Munson, *The Written Word*, rev. ed.; 1949.) The phrase *indigenous American*, which is a more logical and etymologically correct way of referring to an American Indian, does have some support—e.g.: "Hundreds of high schools and colleges have dropped their Indian symbols over the past 30 years as many indigenous American groups and their members have called for sports teams to drop the names." (*J. News* [Westchester Co., NY]; June 3, 2002.) Meanwhile, the synonymous phrase *autochthonous American* hasn't ever caught on. No surprise there.

nice Nice originally had a number of meanings, including 'fine, subtle, discriminating' (*they are not very nice in regard to the company they keep*); 'refined in taste, hard to please, fastidious' (*for company so nice, the finest caterers would be engaged*); and 'precise, strict' (*she has a nice sense of decorum*). The popular overuse of nice to mean 'pleasant, agreeable, satisfactory' has rendered the word trite: *we had a very nice time*; *this is a nice room*; *he's a nice boy*.

nimrod According to all the standard dictionaries, this word means "a skillful hunter." The term derives from the name of a king of Shinar (Southern Babylonia)—that is, King Nimrod, who is described in Genesis as a mighty hunter. And the word is often used in this traditional sense—e.g.: "Some sportsmen, of course, would say Mealey has a fatal flaw. . . . Nimrods and anglers believe he's too cozy with groups as varied as ranchers, miners, loggers and even environmentalists." (*Spokesman-Review* [Spokane]; Aug. 5, 1997.) In late-twentieth-century slang, though, the word has come to mean "a simpleton; dunderhead; blockhead"—e.g.: "Hey all you mack daddies (cool guys) out there: if you don't want to sound like a nimrod (geek) on your next trip to kili cali (Southern California), don't get all petro (worried)." (*Washington Post*; July 20, 1997.) "V.P. Marketing: 'You'd call Messier that to his face?' Quinn: 'No, I'm calling it to yours, ya nimrod.' " (*Financial Post* [Canada]; July 31, 1997.) Though this sense isn't recorded in most standard dictionaries, it certainly exists and is well known among the younger generations. For now, it remains slang. But it surely threatens to kill off the hunter sense.

nonplussed In standard use, **nonplussed** means 'surprised and confused': *the hostility of the new neighbor's refusal left Mrs. Walker nonplussed*. In American English, a new use has

developed in recent years, meaning 'unperturbed'—more or less
the opposite of its traditional meaning: *hoping to disguise his
confusion, he tried to appear nonplussed.* This new use probably
arose on the assumption that **non-** was the normal negative
prefix and must therefore have a negative meaning. Although
the use is common, it is not yet considered standard. Note that
the correct spelling is *nonplussed*, not *nonplused*.

octopus Because this word is actually of Greek origin—not
Latin—the classical plural is *octopodes* (ok-top-uh-deez), not
octopi. But the standard plural is *octopuses*. Still, some writers
mistakenly use the supposed Latin plural—e.g.: "The nearby
mangrove swamps have become nurseries and breeding
grounds for a whole new ecosystem, including sponges, octopi
[read *octopuses*], shrimp, oysters, sharks, fiddler crabs, and
man." (*Christian Science Monitor*; Mar. 14, 1984.)
Occasionally the pedantic *octopodes* appears, but it is relatively
rare—e.g.: "The baby octopus salad, made with finger-sized
octopodes, whole and purplish, were marinated in a tasty,
sesame oil dressing and lightly sprinkled with sesame seeds."
(*Newsday* [New York]; Oct. 19, 2001.)

odorous In practice, *odorous* (= having a pronounced odor) is
neutral in connotation (*an odorous bouquet* | (*an odorous locker
room*). Although, in *A Dictionary of Contemporary American
Usage* (1957), the Evanses insisted that *odorous* be "strictly
confined to pleasant fragrances", today it is used with a
negative sense about twice as often as a positive one. *Malodorous* carries even stronger negative connotations (*a malodorous
bathroom*). *Odoriferous*, a frequently misused term, has
historically had positive connotations in the sense "fragrant"
(*odoriferous rose gardens*). It shouldn't be used in reference to
foul odors—e.g.: "The only thing that gave him trouble was
finding a toad; the rest of the stuff, though mostly nasty and
odoriferous [read *odorous* or *malodorous*], was obtained with
little difficulty." (Theodore R. Cogswell, "The Wall Around the
World" (1953), in *The Mammoth Book of Fantasy*, Mike Ashley
ed.; 2001.) *Odiferous* is an erroneous shortening of *odoriferous*,
and it's often misused for *odorous* or *malodorous*. Only

someone familiar with garlic plants knows whether the odor in the following example is nice or foul (probably the latter): "They are underplanted with useful plants ranging from fragrant peppermint to odiferous [read *malodorous, odorous,* or, if pleasant-smelling, *odoriferous*] garlic chives." (*Boston Herald*; Aug. 3, 1997.) Just as *odious* (= offensive) is sometimes misused to describe a foul smell, so *odoriferous* is sometimes misused to mean "corrupt" or at least "suspicious" —e.g.: "There does seem to be something odoriferous underfoot." (*Orlando Sentinel Tribune*; Dec. 29, 2002.) Unfortunately, the use is common enough that at least one dictionary (*Merriam-Webster's Collegiate Dictionary*, 11th ed.; 2003) lists "morally offensive" as an alternative definition of *odoriferous*. In one sense that's understandable, because corruption and bad smells have always been associated (the usage passes the sniff test). But in a larger sense it's unfortunate, since we can't clearly distinguish all the odor words we already have—and it just continues the degeneration of the word's connotations.

one   One is used as a pronoun to mean 'anyone' or 'I (or me) and people in general,' as in *one must try one's best*. In modern English, it is generally used only in formal and written contexts. In informal and spoken contexts, the normal alternative is **you**, as in *you must try your best*. Until quite recently, sentences in which **one** is followed by **his** or **him** were considered perfectly correct: *one must try his best*. These uses are now held to be less than perfectly grammatical (and possibly sexist as well).

only   In normal, everyday English, the tendency is to place the word **only** as early as possible in the sentence, generally just before the verb, and the result is rarely ambiguous. Misunderstandings are possible, however, and grammarians have debated the matter for more than two hundred years. Advice varies, but in general, ambiguity is less likely if *only* is placed as close as is naturally possible to the word(s) to be modified or emphasized: The wording *Bill ate only the salad* explains that the salad was the sole item that Bill ate. There is no doubt what the statement means. The clear implication is that Bill did not eat the ham, the dessert, or anything else that may have been available. The wording *Bill only ate* the salad almost certainly means the same thing, but in a literal sense, there is indeed some doubt. The linking of *only* with *ate* could imply that what Bill did to the salad was simply eat it; he did not prepare it, or spill it, or throw it across the room, or anything else that one could imagine doing to a salad. In normal conversation, the second statement would probably not be so misunderstood, but, especially when writing, it's never a mistake to favor the less ambiguous wording.

palpable   *Palpable* (literally, "touchable") = tangible; apparent. There is nothing wrong with using this word in figurative senses (*palpable weaknesses in the argument*), as it has been used since at least the fifteenth century. What is nonsensical, however, is to say that the *level* of frustration, tension, etc., is *palpable*—e.g.: "When they share a scene, the energy level is palpable [read *the energy is palpable*]." (*Daily News* [New York]; Sept. 24, 2002.)

Paparazzi   *Paparazzi* (= photographers who follow celebrities, often aggressively, in hopes of snapping candid photos) is a plural; *paparazzo* is the singular. Originally Italian—invented for Federico Fellini's film *La Dolce Vita* (1960)—the term first surfaced in English in the mid-1960s. Unfortunately, because the singular form is so rare, some writers have begun using the misbegotten double plural *paparazzis*—e.g.: "The paparazzis [read *paparazzi*] even left the Clintons to find her [Princess Diana] on the Vineyard." (*Boston Herald*; Dec. 25, 1994.) On August 31, 1997, the day Diana died after a car crash while being chased by paparazzi, many television commentators used the incorrect form—no doubt spreading the mistake among millions of viewers.

penultimate   *Penultimate* (= next-to-last) is sometimes misused for *ultimate* or *quintessential*—e.g.: "As our cover story points out, data warehouses have been sold by many vendors as the penultimate [read *quintessential*] business solution." (*ComputerWorld*; Apr. 1, 1996.) Sometimes, too, the word is misspelled *pentultimate* (perhaps through sound association with *pent-up*)—e.g.: "When Poole secured a 4–2 in the pentultimate [read *penultimate*] race the scores were level at 42–42." (*Birmingham Evening Mail* [UK]; Apr. 8, 2003.)

plethora According to the *Oxford English Dictionary* (OED) and most other dictionaries, this word refers (and has always referred) to an overabundance, an overfullness, or an excess. The phrase *a plethora of* is essentially a highfalutin equivalent of *too many*—e.g.: "Our electoral politics now is beset with a plethora of [read *too many*] players and a confusing clutter of messages." (*Brookings Review*; Jan. 1, 2002.) But sometimes, when not preceded by the indefinite article, the word is genuinely useful—e.g.: "Critics say the plethora of scrip circulating in Argentina risks running out of control." (*Wall Street Journal*; Dec. 26, 2001.) Unfortunately, through misunderstanding of the word's true sense, many writers use it as if it were equivalent to *plenty* or *many*. This meaning is unrecorded in the OED and in most other dictionaries. And it represents an unfortunate degeneration of sense—e.g.: "Buffalo may seem like a boring city, but we've managed to produce a plethora [read *plenty*] of famous people, the Goo Goo Dolls, Ani Difranco, David Boreanaz and now, Chad Murray." (*Buffalo News*; Jan. 8, 2002.) "The old policies did not anticipate a plethora [read *series* or *group* or *lot*] of suicide bombers." (*Orlando Sentinel*; Jan. 10, 2002.) (One suicide bomber is too many—so plethora doesn't work.) Phrases such as *a whole plethora of* are likewise ill-considered—e.g.: "Then, once you get to the airport ticket counter, there's a whole plethora [read *a whole range* or *a wide variety*] of biometric identifiers you could use to tie the background checks you've done to the individuals who present themselves at the ticket counter." (*Boston Globe*; Jan. 6, 2002.) The word is pronounced /pleth-er-uh/, not /pluh-thor-uh/.

principal, principle These two words, though often confused and used incorrectly and interchangeably, share no common definitions. Generally, it's enough to remember that *principal* (= chief, primary, most important) is usually an adjective and that *principle* (= a truth, rule, doctrine, or course of action) is virtually always a noun. Although *principle* is not a verb, we have principled as an adjective. But *principal* is sometimes a noun—an elliptical form of *principal official* (*Morgan is principal of the elementary school*) or *principal investment* (*principal and interest*). Substituting *principal* for *principle* is a fairly common blunder—e.g.: "The Ways and Means bill approved today, after more than a month of deliberation and voting, preserves two of the central principals [read *principles*] put forth by the President: universal coverage and the requirement that employers assume 80 percent of its cost for their workers." (*New York Times*; July 1, 1994.) Substituting *principle* for *principal* is perhaps even more common—e.g.: "Audio CDs are a principle [read *principal*] source of material for making music with samples." (*Electronic Musician*; June 1994.)

queer The word queer was first used to mean 'homosexual' in the early 20th century: it was originally, and often still is, a deliberately offensive and aggressive term when used by heterosexual people. In recent years, however, many gay people have taken the word queer and deliberately used it in place of *gay* or *homosexual*, in an attempt, by using the word positively, to deprive it of its negative power. This use of queer is now well established and widely used among gay people (esp. as an adjective or noun modifier, as in *queer rights*; *queer theory*) and at present exists alongside the other, deliberately offensive, use. (This use is similar to the way in which a racial epithet may be used *within* a racial group, but not by outsiders.)

reason is because This construction is loose because *reason* implies *because* and vice versa. As Robert W. Burchfield, the distinguished *Oxford English Dictionary* lexicographer, put it: "Though often defended by modern grammarians, the type 'the reason . . . is because' (instead of 'the reason . . . is that') aches with redundancy, and is still as inadmissible in Standard English as it was when H. W. Fowler objected to it in 1926." Points of View 116 (1992). After *reason is*, you'll need a noun phrase, a predicate adjective, or a clause introduced by *that*. The best cure for *reason is because* is to replace *because* with *that*—e.g.: "Marcello (Jean Reno) has one frantic mission in life: to keep anyone from dying in the small Italian village where he lives. The reason is because [read *reason is that*] there are only three plots left in the local cemetery and his terminally ill wife, Roseanna (Mercedes Ruehl), wishes only that she be buried next to their daughter." (*Star-Ledger* [Newark]; June 27, 1997.) Variations such as *reason is due to* are no better—e.g.: "It's a challenge for any athlete to come back after four years of inactivity. The challenge is even greater when the reason is due to injury [read *the layoff is due to injury* or *injury is the cause*]." (*Tulsa Tribune & Tulsa World*; May 4, 1997.)

rebut *Rebut* means "attempt to refute." *Refute* means "defeat (countervailing arguments)." Thus one who *rebuts* certainly hopes to *refute*; it is immodest to assume, however, that one has *refuted* another's arguments. See also note at refute. *Rebut* is sometimes wrongly written *rebutt*.

recant, recount *Recant* = publicly repudiate a previous statement, belief, or accusation. *Recount* = narrate a past event, esp. from personal experience. *Recant* sometimes erroneously displaces the similar-sounding *recount*—e.g.: "Dressed in a top hat and tails, Garrett chats with his riders and recants [read *recounts*] tales of Weston's glory days." (*Des Moines Register*; May 19, 2002.) The *Oxford English Dictionary* does give "recount" as one sense of *recant* but labels it obsolete and rare. The most recent example is from 1611. *Recant* is best reserved for use with personal statements and public positions (think *cant* = sing). Other words are better suited when the thing taken back is something other than words—e.g.: "The state's consumer counsel has asked state regulators to recant [read *reverse*] a recent decision under which she said Yankee Gas ratepayers would bear all of the costs of the company's proposed multimillion-dollar system expansion." (*Hartford Courant*; Feb. 14, 2002.) "Why do I feel like I'm listening to a deathbed confession by someone who's been a bastard all his life and suddenly, at the 11th hour, is terrified and wants to recant [read *make up for* or *renounce*?] his evil ways?" (*Daily News Leader* [Staunton, VA]; Mar. 5, 2002.) *Recant* may be transitive (as in the first use in the following example) or intransitive (as in the second): "Police have a follow-up interview scheduled with Olowokandi's former girlfriend, Suzanne Ketcham, who says she plans to recant her original statements to them and a representative of the district attorney's special victims unit. 'It's not unusual for victims of domestic abuse to recant,' Nilsson said." (*Los Angeles Times*; Dec. 7, 2001.)

recoup, recuperate *Recoup*, dating from the fifteenth century as an English word, is a transitive verb with two senses: (1) "get back (lost money, etc.)"; or (2) "pay back (money owed, etc.)." Although sense 2 is older, sense 1 is now predominant. *Recuperate*, dating from the mid-sixteenth century, is almost always an intransitive verb with the sense "get well; regain one's strength after a medical procedure or an illness." The misuse of *recoup* for *recuperate* is not uncommon—e.g.: "Still recouping [read *recuperating*] from foot surgery and planning to strike a long-term performance deal in Las Vegas for early next year, Cassidy kicked back and watched hours of rare footage of the Rats in action." (*Las Vegas Review-Journal*; July 23, 1999.) A related mistake is the misspelling *recouperate*— e.g.: "Lance Diamond, the godfather of Buffalo soul, is in Mercy Hospital recouperating [read *recuperating*] from a flu-like illness." (*Buffalo News*; Nov. 30, 2000.) Another error is the misuse of *recuperate* for *recoup*—e.g.: "The funeral provider would have to file a civil lawsuit to recuperate [read *recoup*] its money, Yabuno said." (*Press-Enterprise* [Riverside, CA]; July 19, 2000.) "They have demanded a jury trial in the hopes of recuperating [read *recouping*] losses they claim are a result of 'incompetence' by the attorneys they are suing." (*South Bend Tribune*; Aug. 4, 2000.)

refute *Refute* is not synonymous with *rebut* or *deny*. That is, it doesn't mean merely "counter an argument" but "disprove beyond doubt; prove a statement false." Yet the word is commonly misused for *rebut*—e.g.: "Ontario Hydro strongly refuted [read *rebutted* or *denied*] the charges, saying none of its actions violate the Power Corporations Act." (*Ottawa Citizen*; Apr. 25, 1997.) See also note at *rebut*. Sometimes *refute* is misused for *reject*—e.g.: "Two-thirds of people refuted [read *rejected*] [Nicholas Ridley's] belief that European Monetary Union is a 'German racket to take over the whole of Europe.' " (*Sunday Telegraph* [UK]; July 15, 1990.) *Confute* is essentially synonymous with *refute* in the sense "prove to be false or wrong." It's probably the stronger term, but it's much rarer.

regard As a noun in *with regard to* and *in regard to*, the singular noun is correct. The plural form (as in *with regards to* and *in regards to*) is, to put it charitably, poor usage—e.g.: "Single men and women are overwhelmed and confused by a barrage of information and advice on what to do and what not to do in regards to [read *in regard to*] finding Mr. Right and Ms. Girl-of-My-Dreams." (*Ebony*; Dec. 1997.) The acceptable forms are best used as introductory phrases. But even these may be advantageously replaced by a single word such as *concerning*, *regarding*, or *considering*, or even *in*, *about*, or *for*. The plural *regards* is acceptable in this sense only in the phrase *as regards*, a traditional literary idiom (though now a little old-fashioned). But some writers mistakenly use with *regards to*—e.g.: "He became furious at the mere mention of . . . the columnist who accused him recently of 'judicial exhibition-ism' with regards to [read *with regard to*] his trade-agreement ruling." (*New York Times*; Sept. 17, 1993.) The verb *regard* commonly appears in two combinations. The one phrase, *highly regarded*, is a vague expression of praise; the other, *widely regarded as*, usually leads to words of praise—though it would certainly be possible to say that someone is "widely regarded as beneath contempt." It's a mistake, however, to truncate the latter phrase—to say *widely regarded* in place of *highly regarded*: "Crotty has published four novels since leaving the newspaper, and he's widely regarded [read *highly regarded*] by both fiction writers and journalists."

rein, reign Like many homophones, these words are frequently mistaken for each other in print—but perhaps no other pair is confused in so many different ways. *Rein in*, not *reign in*, is the correct phrase for "check, restrain." The metaphorical image is of the rider pulling on the reins of the horse to slow down (i.e., "hold your horses")—e.g.: "With every disclosure it becomes clearer that Yeltsin is unwilling or unable to reign in [read *rein in*] his protégé." (*Times Magazine* [London]; Mar. 11, 1995.) The error also occurs with the noun forms: one holds the *reins*, not the *reigns*—e.g.: "Ron Low has a hold of the Oilers' reigns [read *reins*] for now, but should he not work out, look for former Canucks and Flyers coach Bob McCammon to take over as coach next season." (*Tampa Tribune*; Apr. 16, 1995.) "In other cases, the computer recommended keeping tighter reign [read *rein*] on inventory, pressing the vendor for more discounts, or raising prices." (*New York Times*; May, 20, 2001.) The opposite error (*rein* for *reign*) occurs as well—e.g.: "His rein [read *reign*] as Fort Meade's tobacco-chewing, play-calling leader ended abruptly in September 1993." (*Tampa Tribune*; Sept. 1, 1995.) "Confusion reined [read *reigned*] when everyone within a five-mile radius was asked to evacuate." (*Houston Chronicle*; Jan. 4, 2003.)

rhetoric *Rhetoric* = (1) the art of using language persuasively; the rules that help one achieve eloquence; (2) the persuasive use of language; (3) a treatise on persuasive language; (4) prose composition as a school subject. These are the main senses outlined in the *Oxford English Dictionary*. There should probably be added a new sense, related to but distinct from the first sense: (5) the bombastic or disingenuous use of language to manipulate people. Older books defined *rhetoric* in line with sense 1: "Rhetoric is the Art of speaking suitably upon any Subject." (John Kirkby, *A New English Grammar*; 1746.) "Rhetoric is the art of adapting discourse, in harmony with its subject and occasion, to the requirements of a reader or hearer." (John F. Genung, *The Working Principles of Rhetoric*; 1902.) But the slippage toward the pejorative sense 5 began early. In "Some Fruits of Solitude" (1693), William Penn suggested its iniquitous uses: "There is a Truth and Beauty in Rhetorick; but it oftener serves ill Turns than good ones." (Charles W. Eliot, ed., *Harvard Classics*; 1909.) By the twentieth century, some writers with a classical bent were trying hard to reclaim the word—e.g.: "No one who reads [ancient authors] can hold the puerile notions of rhetoric that prevail in our generation. The ancients would have made short work of the cult of the anti-social that lies behind the cult of mystification and the modern hatred of rhetoric. All the great literary ages have exalted the study of rhetoric." (Van Wyck Brooks, *Opinions of Oliver Allston*; 1941.) But T. S. Eliot probably had it right when he acknowledged that the word is essentially ambiguous today—generally pejorative but with flashes of a favorable sense: "The word [*rhetoric*] simply cannot be used as synonymous with bad writing. The meanings which it has been obliged to shoulder have been mostly opprobrious; but if a precise meaning can be found for it this meaning may occasionally represent a virtue." ("'Rhetoric' and Poetic Drama," in *The Sacred Wood*, 7th ed.; 1950.)

rift, riff These two are sometimes confused. *Riff* is now largely confined to jazz and pop-music contexts. It refers to a melodic phrase, usually repeated and often played in unison by several instruments; sometimes it's a variation on a tune, and it may be either an accompaniment to a solo or the only melodic element—e.g.: "With guitar riffs so rudimentary they seem to have been made up on the spot, . . . the U.K. sextet played with rude ebullience." (*Chicago Tribune*; Sept. 29, 2000.) The term dates only from the mid-twentieth century—and has little discernible relation to the older, mostly obsolete senses of *riff* (= [1] a string of onions, [2] the diaphragm, or [3] the mange; an itchy rash). That's probably because this particular *riff* seems to have originated as a truncated form of the musical term *refrain*. *Rift* arose in Middle English in the sense "a fissure or divide; a split or crack"—the meaning it still carries—e.g.: "Word out of Washington is that Bondra wants to change teams because of a rift with coach Ron Wilson." (*Boston Globe*; Oct. 1, 2000.) Occasionally the term also refers to the rapids formed by rocks protruding from the bed of a stream. It formerly also meant "a burp"—a sense long obsolete. Although the *Oxford English Dictionary* records two

early-seventeenth-century uses of *riff* in the obsolete sense
"rift, chink," the modern use of the word in that sense appears
to be nothing more than rank word-swapping resulting from
sound association—e.g.: "The way he sees it, things aren't bad
at all. No riffs [read *rifts*] between him and crew chief Todd
Parrott." (*USA Today*; May 26, 2000.)

sailor, sailer   A *sailor* is one who sails—always in reference to a
person. A *sailer* is a vessel or vehicle that sails, or that moves
by the use of a sail—e.g.: "The second part of the project is to
launch an operational solar sailer with eight sails to be tested
in an 850-km (528-mi.) circular orbit, also using a Volna
rocket." (*Aviation Week & Space Technology*; July 16, 2001.) It
isn't unusual to see *sailer* misused for *sailor*—e.g.: "The
current exercises involve about 15,000 sailers [read *sailors*]
and Marines, and include cruisers and destroyers, with
nonexplosive bombs dropped from the air, according to the
Associated Press." (*Chicago Sun-Times*; Apr. 30, 2001.)

scarify, scorify   *Scarify* (from *scar*, but pronounced as if from
scare) means (1) "make superficial marks or incisions in; cut off
skin from"; (2) "break up the surface of (the ground) with a
spiked machine [a scarifier] for loosening soil or building
roads"; or (3) "pain by severe criticism." Sense 1 is most
common—e.g.: "Rub the seed across some sandpaper to weaken
the hard seed coat or scarify it with a knife for better germina-
tion." (*Virginian-Pilot* [Norfolk]; Apr. 20, 1997.) This sense
applies also to body adornment by cutting and scraping—e.g.:
"Worse, once piercing becomes commonplace among people
like, well, Leslie, the trendsetters up the ante with other forms of
body alteration: cutting (scarification as adornment), branding
(searing flesh with high heat in artistic patterns) and—please
don't eat during this next sentence—tongue splitting, in which
the tongue is cleaved nearly in half so as to cause it to fork like a
lizard's." (*Washington Post*; Feb. 11, 2003.) Sense 3 is also fairly
common—e.g.: "With a combination of dazzling philosophical
acumen and scarifying wit, Stove does for irrationalism in Karl
Popper's philosophy . . . what the Romans did for Carthage in
the Third Punic War." (*New Criterion*; Mar. 1997.) An

identically pronounced, but separate, *scarify*, based on the root word *scare*, dates from the late 18th century but remains mostly dialectal. It often carries a lighthearted connotation—e.g.: "The cost-of-living index had taken a scarifying new jump of 1.2 percent in February, to an annual rate of 15 percent." (*Newsweek*; Apr. 2, 1979.) *Scorify* = reduce to dross or slag. The term surfaces most commonly in cognate forms, such as *scorifier*—e.g.: "Hanging adjacent to the furnace are the specialized tongs for handling crucibles, cupels and the dishlike ceramic containers called scorifiers." (*Bulletin* [Bend, OR]; Apr. 2, 1997.)

stratagem The mistaken spelling *strategem* (on the analogy of *strategy*) appears about 20% as often as the correct spelling *stratagem*. Though the words *stratagem* and *strategy* are etymologically related, they came into English by different routes, and their spellings diverged merely as a matter of long-standing convention. What happened is that the Latin *strategema* became *stratagema* in Romance languages such as French. (The *Century Dictionary* calls the Romance spelling "erroneous.") *Stratagem* came into English in the fifteenth century, through French. But it wasn't until the early nineteenth century that English and American writers borrowed *strategy* (originally a Greek term) from Latin. Hence our incongruous spellings today.

there is, there are These phrases, though sometimes useful, can also be the enemies of a lean writing style, as several commentators have observed—e.g.: "The habit of beginning statements with the impersonal and usually vague *there is* or *there are* shoves the really significant verb into subordinate place instead of letting it stand vigorously on its own feet." (David Lambuth et al., *The Golden Book on Writing*; 1964.) "The *there* construction is not to be condemned out of hand; it is both idiomatic and common in the best literature; it is clumsy and to be avoided with a passive verb; and in view of the prejudice against it [for promoting wordiness], the writer who uses it discriminatingly should take heart and be prepared to defend himself, for defense is indeed possible." (Roy

H. Copperud, *American Usage and Style: The Consensus*;
1980.) When is the phrase *there is* defensible? When the
writer is addressing the existence of something. That is, if the
only real recourse is to use the verb *exist*, then *there is* is
perfectly fine—e.g.: "There is unlimited competition for our
entertainment dollars." (*Kansas City Star*; Sept. 21, 1997.)
Otherwise, though, the phrase should typically be cut—e.g.:
"There is wide support among congressional Republicans for
a flat tax." (*Dallas Morning News*; Sept. 20, 1997.) (A possible
revision: "Congressional Republicans tend to support a flat
tax." Or: "Many congressional Republicans support a flat
tax.") The phrase *there is wide support* has become a cliché
among political commentators. And it robs the sentence of a
good strong verb. The number of the verb is controlled by
whether the subject that follows the inverted verb is singular
or plural. Mistakes are common—e.g.: "He said there is [read
there are] several truckloads of nuclear waste." (*Knoxville
News-Sentinel*; Apr. 18, 1996.) "There seems [read *there
seem*] to be two key reasons for Capriati's renaissance."
(*USA Today*; Jan. 26, 2000.) Especially when followed by a
negative, *there* has in many minds come to represent a single
situation. It therefore often appears, though wrongly, with a
singular verb—e.g.: " There wasn't [read *there weren't*] any
other witnesses. " (*Austin American-Statesman*; Dec. 9, 1994.)

they The word *they* (with its counterparts *them*, *their*, and
themselves) as a singular pronoun to refer to a person of
unspecified sex has been used since at least the sixteenth
century. In the late twentieth century, as the traditional use of *he*
to refer to a person of either sex came under scrutiny on the
grounds of sexism, this use of *they* has become more common. It
is now generally accepted in contexts where it follows an
indefinite pronoun such as *anyone*, *no one*, *someone*, or a *person*:
anyone can join if they are a resident; *each to their own*. In other
contexts, coming after singular nouns, the use of *they* is now
common, although less widely accepted, esp. in formal contexts.
Sentences such as *ask a friend if they could help* are still
criticized for being ungrammatical.

thus There is never a need to expand the adverb **thus** to "thusly."

till *Till* is, like *until,* a bona fide preposition and conjunction. Though less formal than *until, till* is neither colloquial nor substandard. As Anthony Burgess put it, "In nonpoetic English we use 'till' and 'until' indifferently." (*A Mouthful of Air*; 1992.) It's especially common in British English—e.g.: "After the First World War, Hatay, named by Attaturk after the Hittites, fell into the hands of the French, who did not return it till 1939." (*Independent* [UK]; Apr. 1, 1995.) "He works from dawn till dusk, six days a week." (*Daily Telegraph* [UK]; Mar. 31, 1997.) And it still occurs in American English—e.g.: "In medium skillet, sauté the garlic till golden. Add onion, wait till brown." (*Palm Beach Post*; Mar. 23, 1995.) But the myth of the word's low standing persists. Some writers and editors mistakenly think that *till* deserves a bracketed *sic*— e.g.: " 'Trading in cotton futures was not practiced till [sic] after the close of the Civil War, spot cotton being quoted like other stocks in cents, halves, quarters, etc.' " (*School Science and Mathematics*; Apr. 1, 1997 [in which the *sic* appeared in the original source being quoted].) If a form deserves a *sic*, it's the incorrect *'til*. Worse yet is *'till*, which is abominable—e.g.: "A month or two remain 'till [read *till*] you grab your dancing shoes, plus a crew of pals or that special date." (*Denver Post*; Mar. 21, 1997.)

titmouse *Titmouse* (= a small songbird) is also known as a *tit*, but only serious birdwatchers use the shortened form (because of the vulgar homonym). The vastly predominant plural (and the one recognized by dictionaries) is *titmice*, not *titmouses*— e.g.: "In recent days chickadees, titmice, robins, cardinals, and white-breasted nuthatches seemed to celebrate the return of blue skies and sunshine." (*Pittsburgh Post-Gazette*; Mar. 16, 2003.) The form *titmouses*, though perhaps logical (since it's not a mouse at all), occurs so infrequently as to be ill-advised—e.g.: "Other visitors to the Gibbs' yard Monday were cardinals, white-throated sparrows, . . . titmouses [read *titmice*], chickadees, juncos, Carolina wrens, bluebirds and goldfinches." (*Augusta Chronicle* [GA]; Jan. 24, 2003.)

transpire The common use of **transpire** to mean 'occur, happen' (*I'm going to find out exactly what transpired*) is a loose extension of an earlier meaning, 'come to be known' (*it transpired that Mark had been baptized a Catholic*). This loose sense of 'happen,' which is now more common in American usage than the sense of 'come to be known,' was first recorded in American English toward the end of the eighteenth century and has been listed in American dictionaries from the nineteenth century. Careful writers should note, however, that in cases where *occur* or *happen* would do just as well, the use of **transpire** may strike readers as an affectation or as jargon.

unique Strictly speaking, *unique* means "being one of a kind," not "unusual." Hence the phrases *very unique, quite unique, how unique,* and the like are slovenly. *The Oxford English Dictionary* notes that this tendency to hyperbole—to use *unique* when all that is meant is "uncommon, unusual, remarkable"— began in the nineteenth century. However old it is, the tendency is worth resisting. Unless the thing is the only one of its kind, rarity does not make it unique. For instance, if a thing is one in a million, logically there would be two things in two million. Rare indeed but not unique. Who can demand responsible use of the language from an ad writer who is reckless enough to say, in a national advertisement, that a certain luxury sedan is "so unique, it's capable of thought"? And what are we to make of the following examples? "This year the consensus among the development executives seems to be that there are some fantastically funny, very exciting, very, very unique talents here." (*Time*; Aug. 16, 1993.) "Residents of college basketball's most unique unincorporated village were in place yesterday afternoon, the day before their Blue Devils will face North Carolina." (*New York Times*; Feb. 2, 1995.) Arguably, our modern culture lacks and does not want absolutes, in intellectual life or in language. But stick with the incomparable *unique*, and you may stand out as almost unique.

up to—or more This bit of illogic crops up fairly often in print ads and store signs. At a sale touted as offering "up to 50% off and more," for example, all we know is that the sale price is (1) less than 50% off, (2) 50% off, or (3) more than 50% off. The number itself, then, is meaningless and serves only as bait in big, bold type. The small type, as usual, taketh away. Versions of the phrase appear in places other than signs announcing sales—e.g.: "Some lakes and forests devastated by acid rain will likely take up to 70 years or more to recover." (*Post-Standard* [Syracuse]; Mar. 26, 2001.) (A possible revision: "Some lakes and forests devastated by acid rain could take 70 years or more to recover.") "Use live bait or cut bait for yellow perch up to 1½ pounds or more." (*Richmond Times-Dispatch*; Mar. 30, 2001.)

who, whom Edward Sapir, the philosopher of language, prophesied that "within a couple of hundred years from to-day not even the most learned jurist will be saying 'Whom did you see?' By that time the *whom* will be as delightfully archaic as the Elizabethan *his* for *its*. No logical or historical argument will avail to save this hapless *whom*." (*Language*; 1921.) A safer bet might be that no one will be spelling *to-day* with a hyphen. In any event, writers in the twenty-first century ought to understand how the words *who* and *whom* are correctly used. *Who*, the nominative pronoun, is used (1) as the subject of a verb (*it was Kate who rescued the dog*); and (2) as the complement of a linking verb, i.e., as a predicate nominative (*they know who you are*). *Whom*, the objective pronoun, is used (1) as the object of a verb (*whom did you see?*); and (2) as the object of a preposition (*the person to whom we're indebted*). It's true that in certain contexts, *whom* is stilted. That has long been so: "Every sensible English speaker on both sides of the Atlantic says *Who were you talking to?* [—not *Whom*—] and the sooner we begin to write it the better." (J. Y. T. Greig, *Breaking Priscian's Head*; ca. 1930.) But there are other constructions in which *whom* remains strong—and more so in American English than in British English. Although writers have announced the demise of *whom*, it persists in American English—e.g.: "Susan McDonough's classroom is filled with primary-school children of different ages, all of whom are lagging behind in reading skills." (*Washington Post*; Sept. 28, 1997.) "He was implicated in the murder of a man whom his workers caught tampering with some stone blocks." (*SmartMoney*; Oct. 1, 1997.) (In this sentence, *that* might work more naturally than *whom*.) The correct uses of *who* are sometimes tricky. But if the pronoun acts as the subject of a clause, it must be *who*, never *whom*— e.g.: "Alan Alda, who you quickly realize is sorely missed on TV, stars as Dan Cutler, a type-A personality advertising executive." (*Sun-Sentinel* [Fort Lauderdale]; May 20, 1994.) (*Who* is the subject of *is*.)While the subject of a finite verb is nominative (*I know she is good*), the subject of an infinitive is in the objective case (*I know her to be good*). The same is true of *who* and *whom*. Strictly, *whom* is always either the object of a verb or preposition, or else the subject of an infinitive—e.g.: "Do all you can to develop your intuition—this will help you to know when to act and when to wait, whom to be cautious about and whom to trust." (*Washington Times*; July 9, 1997.) But often journalists don't get it right, perhaps because they consider the word stuffy—e.g.: "And he [nominee Stephen G. Breyer] promised, following the admonition of the late Justice Arthur Goldberg, who [read *whom*] he served as a law clerk 30 years ago, to do his best to avoid footnotes." (*Washington Post*; May 17, 1994.) "A polite, helpful 11-year-old who [read *whom*] everybody called Jake was fatally shot in his bedroom in this small rural town on Thursday, and a 13-year-old friend was charged hours later with killing him." (*New York Times*; Sept. 3, 1994.) (Replacing *who* with *that* would also work naturally here.) "Those friends include Myra Guarino, 62, of Valdosta, who [read *whom*] Mrs. Helms represents in a suit against the manufacturer of silicone breast implants." (*New York Times*; July 7, 1995.) In the citations just listed, *who* is defensible in informal contexts. But the objective *who* is not idiomatically normal after a preposition. For example, *one of whom* is something of a set phrase—e.g.: "Parents proudly whooped it up for the players, not one of who [read *one of whom*] wore shoulder pads." (*USA Today*; Jan. 27, 2003.) Among the toughest contexts in which to get the pronouns right are those involving linking verbs. We say, for example, *who it is* for the same reason we say *this is he*, but some very good writers have nodded. In any event, *whom* shouldn't be used as the subject of any finite verb—e.g.: "The distinguished political and social philosopher Russell Kirk used the word 'energumen' to describe . . . whom [read *who*] it is I agitate against." (William F. Buckley, *The Jeweler's Eye*; 1969.) (*Who* is needed as the inverted subject of *is*: *it is who*, as in *it is he*.) "Police went to several addresses looking for a 17-year-old whom [read *who*] they thought was staying with his aunt." (*San Francisco Chronicle*; Apr. 20, 1994.) (*Who* is needed as the subject of *was*.) "In the other corner are the anti-Stratfordians, the heretics and conspiracy theorists of literature, most of them devoted amateurs whose dogged sleuthing and amassing of evidence (albeit mostly circumstantial) continues to enlarge the body of contention that Shakespeare wasn't himself. But if not he, then whom [read *who*]?" (*Washington Post*; May 17, 1994.) (*Who* is needed in a parallel phrasing with *he*.) "But Beck ought to serve as an inspiration for a host of other superb golfers whom [read *who*] naysayers claim 'can't win the big ones.' " (*Sky*; Sept. 1995.) (*Who* is needed as the subject of *can't win*.) "Sam divorced in 1969, and is survived by his son, Sam III, his wife, Angela, and their daughter, Samantha, of Clarksville, Tennessee; his daughter, Marguerite; the mother of Matthew and Grace, whom [read *who*] all lived with Sam in Austin." (*Austin American-Statesman*; Feb. 10, 1996.) (*Who* is needed as the subject of *lived*.) William Safire takes an interesting approach for those who fear seeming pedantic (by using *whom*) or being incorrect (by using *who* for *whom*): "When *whom* is correct, recast the sentence." (*New York Times*; Oct. 4, 1992.) Thus "Whom do you trust?" becomes, in a political campaign, "Which candidate do you trust?" The relative pronoun *that* can also substitute in many situations. But one commentator, Steven Pinker, calls Safire's suggestion an "unacceptable pseudo-compromise." And Pinker has a point: "Telling people to avoid a problematic construction sounds like common sense, but in the case of object questions with *who*, it demands an intolerable sacrifice. People ask questions about the objects of verbs and prepositions a lot." (*The Language Instinct*; 1994.) Moreover, a phrase such as *which person* is wordier and slightly narrower than *who* or *whom*. Perhaps the most sensible approach was the one taken by Robert C. Pooley in 1974: "Considering the importance some people place on mastery of [the textbook rules for *whom*], the schoolbooks may be justified in distinguishing the case forms for the relative pronouns for literary usage. But to insist that these literary and formal distinctions be made in informal writing and speech as necessary to achieve 'correctness' is to do violence to the readily observed facts of current usage." (*The Teaching of English Usage*, 2d ed.; 1974.) *Who* is the relative pronoun for human beings (though *that* is also acceptable); *that* and *which* are the relative pronouns for anything other than humans, including entities created by humans. But writers too often forget this elementary point— e.g.: "The best borrowers are grabbed by the banks and financial institutions who [read *that*] are in a position now to offer finer rates." (*Business Standard*; Oct. 25, 1997.) Some inattentive writers use *which* in referring to human beings—e.g.: "The bakery employs 11 people, two of which [read *whom*] are English (non-Amish) women, and one who is a salesman." (*Plain Dealer* [Cleveland]; June 13, 1995.) *That*, of course, is permissible when referring to humans: "the people that were present" or "the people who were present." Editors tend, however, to prefer the latter phrasing.

wrought In the phrase **wrought havoc**, as in *they wrought havoc on the countryside*, **wrought** is an archaic past tense of **work**. It is not, as is sometimes assumed, a past tense of **wreak**.

y'all This sturdy Southernism is most logically *y'all*, not *ya'll*. Only the *you* of *you all* is contracted. And in modern print sources, *y'all* is ten times as common. So *ya'll* (which misleadingly resembles *he'll*, *she'll*, and *we'll*) deserves an edit— e.g.: " 'Ya'll [read *Y'all*] have got to help me a lot,' Bentley, a registered nurse at Chalmette Medical Centers, told the students about class planning." (*Times-Picayune* [New Orleans]; Feb. 25, 1997.) In the late twentieth century, some writers began spelling the term without an apostrophe: *yall*. This spelling is not yet widespread (and not recommended).

Why has the spelling been so much trouble? *Y'all* is the only contraction in English in which a stressed form is contracted to an unstressed one. Although the traditional use of *y'all* is plural, and although many Southerners have stoutly rejected the idea that it's ever used as a singular, there does seem to be strong evidence that it can refer to a single person—for example, "See y'all later" spoken to someone without a companion. One possibility is that the speaker means "you and anyone else who may be with you" or "you and anyone else who comes along." Another possibility is that *y'all* may in fact refer to one person. Getting at the truth depends on understanding the speaker's state of mind. Many speakers in the South and Southwest, even highly educated ones, use the uncontracted *you all* as the plural form of *you*. This is a convenient usage, since *you* alone can be either singular or plural—and therefore is sometimes ambiguous. True, *you all* is unlikely to spread beyond regional usage. But speakers who grew up with the phrase won't be easily dispossessed of it. It's handy, and it's less susceptible to raised eyebrows than *y'all*. There is, however, a noticeable tendency in urban areas to replace this phrase with *you guys*. This may have resulted from the great influx of a geographically diverse population in major cities such as Dallas throughout the 1980s and 1990s, coupled with a growing sense among natives that *you all* and *y'all* signal provincialism.

CHAPTER 4

100 Rare Fifty-Cent Words and Their Meanings

INTRODUCTION

Hemingway used to call them "ten-dollar words." He claimed he knew them, but just didn't want to use them. Faulkner, who was not shy about using big, unusual, arcane words, said that Hemingway "has never used a word where the reader might check his usage in a dictionary." Well, *chacun à son goût* (see Chapter 2). However, the point is that not everyone writes as simply as Hemingway. You will have a hard time avoiding those fifty-cent words in a career of reading. William F. Buckley Jr. alone is enough to warrant this chapter.

And if WFB Jr. isn't a good enough reason, well, there's always Henry James.

abligurition [ab-lig-yoo-rish-un] the spending of an unconscionable amount on food. This comes from a Latin word meaning 'to spend freely and indulgently on luxuries', which was itself derived from another Latin word meaning 'to lick'.

absterge [ab-sturdj] to clean by wiping, to purge. From a Latin word meaning 'to wipe'.

ageustia [ug-yoo-stee-uh] the loss of the sense of taste.

anopisthograph [an-oh-pis-thoh-graf] something that has writing on only one side. From Greek words that mean 'written on the back or cover'.

balbutiate [bal-byoo-shee-ate] to stutter or stammer. From a Latin word meaning 'to stammer'. Someone who is *balbutient* is stammering.

banausic [buh-naw-sick] an adjective meaning 'merely mechanical, without art, requiring no initiative'. From a Greek word meaning 'mechanical'.

battologist [bat-tah-luh-djist] someone who repeats the same thing needlessly. From a Greek word meaning 'stammerer'.

bombilation [bahm-buh-lay-shun] a buzzing, droning, or humming sound.

capilotade [kap-i-loh-tahd] any hashed-together story. From the name of a dish made of minced veal, chicken, capon, or partridge, separated by beds of cheese.

chiliad [kill-ee-ad] a group of a thousand things, especially a period of a thousand years.

consuetudinary [kahns-wi-t(y)oo-duh-ner-ee] a guide to customs, rituals, or practices, especially those of a religious order.

crumenically [kroo-mee-nick-lee] an adverb meaning 'relating to the purse'.

cryptaesthesia [krip-tiss-thee-zhuh] any kind of supernormal perception, including clairvoyance and telepathy. From *crypto-* and a Greek word meaning 'perception'.

cymbocephalic [sim-boh-suh-fal-ick] having a skull shaped like a boat, especially when seen from above; having a long and narrow skull. From Greek words meaning 'boat' and 'head'.

delassation [dee-lass-say-shun] fatigue, tiredness. From a Latin word meaning 'to tire out'.

delitescent [dell-i-tess-unt] an adjective meaning 'hidden, concealed'.

deuterogamist [d(y)oo-ter-rah-guh-mist] someone who marries a second time.

dyslogistic [dis-luh-djiss-tick] expressing disapproval or opprobrium. The antonym of *eulogistic*.

dysteleology [dis-tell-ee-ah-luh-djee] the study of the organs of plants and animals without admitting that there is any purpose to their design. The antonym is *teleology*, studying things with the idea that there is a purpose for everything in nature.

eboulement [ay-**bool**-munt] the crumbling or falling of a wall, especially a fortification.

emmetropia [em-uh-**troh**-pee-uh] the condition of the eye in which no correction of vision is needed—in other words, 20/20 vision or better. From Greek words meaning '(well) proportioned' and 'eye'. If both eyes have the same vision, they are *isometropic*.

epagomenic [ep-uh-**gah**-muh-nick] days left off the calendar (before calendar reform). Also, gods worshipped on those days.

equivoque [**eck**-wuh-voke] something that has the same name as something else.

finnimbrun [fin-**nim**-brun] a knickknack, a trinket.

flambuginous [flam-**byoo**-djuh-nus] a rare adjective meaning 'deceptive, fictitious, sham'. Related to the *flam* of *flimflam* and *flamfew,* 'a gewgaw'. *Flamfew* is related to a Latin word meaning 'a bubble, a lie'.

fleechment [**fleech**-munt] flattery, cajolery, persuasive but untruthful talk. Its origin is obscure.

flosculous [**flahs**-kyuh-lus] an adjective meaning 'like a flower' or 'flowery'. Also written *flosculose*. From a Latin word meaning 'little flower', which also gives us *floscule*, 'something shaped like a little flower' or 'a flowery speech' and *flosculation*, 'speaking in a flowery way'.

furciferous [fur-**sif**-er-us] an adjective meaning 'like a rascal'. From a Latin word meaning 'fork-bearer', which, by analogy with the forked yoke put on the necks of criminals, also came to mean 'jailbird'.

geoponic [djee-uh-**pah**-nick] an adjective meaning 'relating to farming or agriculture', and, like most farming words, it has an extended humorous meaning of 'rustic, countrified'. As a noun, *geoponic* means 'a book about agriculture' or 'a writer on agricultural topics'. A *geoponist* is a student of agriculture.

gleimous [**glay**-mus] a rare word meaning 'full of phlegm or mucus'. *Gleimousness* is stickiness, but if something is *engleimous*, it is both slimy and venomous.

gnast [nast] an obsolete word meaning 'a spark; the snuff of a candle'.

halieutic [hal-i-yoo-tik] an adjective meaning 'of or about fishing'. Ultimately from a Greek word meaning 'the sea'.

harbergery [har-ber-djuh-ree] a place of entertainment, an inn. From an Old French word meaning 'to lodge'. Grab it as the name for your restaurant now.

heptamerous [hep-tam-er-us] an adjective meaning 'having seven parts or members'.

heterarchy [het-er-ahr-kee] government by strangers or foreigners. Literally, 'rule of an alien'.

iatraliptic [eye-at-ruh-lip-tick] a doctor who cures diseases with lotions or creams. As an adjective, it means 'of or about the curing of diseases with lotions or creams'.

ichnography [ick-nog-ruh-fee] a floor plan for a building. From Greek words meaning 'track' and 'writing'.

ideokinetic [eye-dee-oh-ki-net-ik] a kind of apraxia in which the sufferer still has the physical ability to perform an action or movement and understands a request to perform it, but is unable to do so when asked.

imbriferous [im-brif-er-us] bringing rain; rainy. From a Latin word meaning 'a shower'.

imparidigitate [im-par-i-didj-i-tate] having an odd number of digits (toes or fingers) on each limb. The specific word for having an odd number of toes is *perissodactyl*. *Imparidigitate* comes from Latin for 'unequal' plus 'digit'; *perissodactyl* comes from the Greek for 'uneven' plus 'digit'.

impluvious [im-ploo-vee-us] a rare adjective meaning 'wet with rain'.

infelicific [in-fee-luh-sif-ik] an adjective meaning 'making unhappy'.

infrendiate [in-fren-dee-ate] to gnash the teeth.

isocephaly [eye-soh-sef-uh-lee] the principle observed in some ancient Greek reliefs, esp. in friezes, of representing the heads of all the figures at nearly the same level.

jaculiferous [jack-yuh-lif-er-us] an adjective meaning 'having prickles'.

jectigation [jeck-ti-gay-shun] a wagging or trembling movement. From a Latin word meaning 'to throw'.

jocoserious [joh-koh-sear-ee-us] half jocular, half serious; partly silly and partly somber; blending jokes and serious matters. The noun is *jocoseriosity*.

kakistocracy [kack-i-stah-kruh-see] the government of a state by its worst citizens.

kalokagathia [kal-oh-kuh-gath-ee-uh] nobility and goodness of character. From Greek words meaning 'beautiful' and 'good', describing the perfect character.

katavothron [kat-uh-vah-thrun] a subterranean channel or deep chasm formed by running water. From Greek words meaning 'swallow' and 'hole'.

kathenotheism [kath-en-oh-thee-iz-um] a kind of polytheism where each god is single and supreme in turn. From a Greek word meaning 'one by one' and -*theism*.

kyriolexy [kye-ree-oh-leck-see] the use of literal expressions. From Greek words meaning 'proper' and 'speaking'.

lambdacism [lam-duh-siz-um] too frequent use of the letter *l* in speaking or writing. Also, pronouncing the letter *r* as the letter *l* (also called *lallation*.)

lethiferous [li-thif-er-us] causing death, deadly. From Latin words meaning 'death' and 'bring'.

limitanean [lim-i-tay-nee-un] an adjective meaning 'on the border'. A term from Roman antiquity, it usually refers to soldiers stationed on the border. Another similar word is *limitrophe*, an adjective meaning 'on the frontier'.

lucifugous [loo-sif-yuh-gus] an adjective meaning 'shunning the light'. From Latin words meaning 'light' and 'to flee'. A similar adjective is *lucifugal*.

machicolation [muh-chick-uh-lay-shun] the opening in a wall through which fire, molten lead, stones, etc., are dropped on besiegers or attackers. Also used to mean the action of putting such things out of a *machicolation*.

magirology [madj-uh-rah-luh-djee] a rare word meaning 'the art or science of cooking'. A *magirist* (or *magirologist*) is an expert cook; something that is *magiristic* is related to cooking or cookery, and someone that is *magirological* is skilled in cooking. From a Greek word meaning 'cook'.

mesonoxian [mezz-uh-**nock**-see-un] of or related to midnight.

morigerate [muh-**ridj**-er-it] a rare adjective meaning 'obedient'. The noun is *morigeration*, which had the extended meaning of 'obsequiousness'.

multatitious [mull-tuh-**tish**-us] a rare word meaning 'acquired by fine or forfeit'.

nidulation [nidj-oo-**lay**-shun] nesting or nest making. Also, *nidification*. A *nidifugous* bird is a bird that has young that are able to leave the nest immediately after birth. These words all come from a Latin word meaning 'nest'.

noceur [naw-sur] someone who stays up late at night. Also, 'a rake or libertine'. From a French word of the same meaning.

nullibicity [null-uh-**biss**-i-tee] a rare word meaning 'the condition of not existing anywhere'. The adjective is *nullibiquitous*. From a Latin word meaning 'nowhere'.

ombrifuge [ahm-bruh-**fyoodj**] a rare word meaning 'a rain shelter'. From a Greek word meaning 'a shower of rain'. A semantically related word is *paravent*, 'a wind shelter'.

omnifarious [ahm-ni-**fair**-ee-us] an adjective meaning 'dealing with all kinds of things' or 'of all kinds or forms'.

oneirocritical [oh-nye-roh-**krit**-i-cle] an adjective meaning 'expert in the interpretation of dreams'.

opsophagize [ahp-sah-**fug**-gize] to eat delicacies, especially fish. *Opsophagist* is the agent noun. From a Greek word of the same meaning.

osphresiology [ahs-free-see-ah-**luh**-djee] the study of the sense of smell, or a scientific paper about smelling and scents. From a Greek word meaning 'smell'.

parorexia [parr-uh-**reck**-see-uh] an unnatural appetite, or an unnatural lack of appetite. A near synonym for *anorexia*.

pathognomy [path-**ahg**-nuh-mee] the study of the emotions, or the physical signs or expressions of them. A nice word that could possibly be extended to mean 'the study of tantrums'.

percoarcted [per-koh-**ark**-tid] an obsolete and rare word meaning 'brought into a narrow room'. *Coarct* is an obsolete verb meaning 'kept within narrow limits, restricted'.

percontation [per-**kahn**-tay-shun] a rare word meaning 'an inquiry'. The adjective is *percontatorial*, meaning 'inquisitive'. From a Latin word meaning 'to interrogate'.

perculsion [per-**kull**-shun] a rare word meaning 'a severe shock, consternation'. From a Latin word meaning 'to upset'. Something that is *perculsive* gives you a shock.

phobanthropy [fah-**ban**-thruh-pee] the 'morbid dread of mankind'. From Greek words meaning 'fear' and 'man', influenced by *philanthropy*.

psychopomp [**sye**-koh-pomp] someone or something that leads souls to the place of the dead. Also, a spiritual guide for a (living) person's soul; a person who acts as a guide of a soul. From Greek words meaning 'soul' and 'guide'.

quadragenarian [kwah-druh-djuh-**nair**-ee-un] someone who is forty years old.

quadrumanous [kwah-**drum**-uh-nus] an adjective meaning 'apelike in destructiveness'. From a Latin word meaning 'four-handed' (like an ape).

racemation [rass-i-**may**-shun] an obsolete word meaning 'the gleaning of grapes'. Also, 'a small number of things still remaining'. From a Latin word meaning 'a cluster of grapes'.

rhyparaographer [rip-uh-rah-**gruh**-fer] a painter of unpleasant or sordid subjects. From Greek words meaning 'filthy' and 'writer'.

roucoulement [roo-cool-**mahn**] a rare word meaning 'the gentle cooing of doves', of course also extended to mean the soft voices of women. From a French word of the same meaning.

rupestral [roo-**pess**-trul] an adjective meaning 'growing on rocks'. Something that is *rupestrian* is done on rocks or on cave walls. From a Latin word meaning 'rock'.

salebrosity [sal-uh-**brah**-si-tee] 'unevenness, roughness'. From a Latin word of the same meaning.

satisdiction [sat-is-**dick**-shun] a word meaning 'saying enough'. From Latin words meaning 'enough' and 'saying', on the model of *satisfaction*.

scelestious [si-**less**-chus] a rare adjective meaning 'wicked'. Another form is *scelestic*. They both come from a Latin word with the same meaning.

scitament [**sit**-uh-munt] something pleasant, especially a nice or witty thing to say. From a Latin word meaning 'elegant'.

scoteography [skoh-tee-**ogg**-ruh-fee] the art of writing in the dark. From Greek words meaning 'darkness' and 'writing'.

scriniary [**skrye**-nee-err-ee] a keeper of the archives, an archivist. From a Latin word meaning 'a box for books and papers; a writing desk'.

singerie [san-zhuh-**ree**] a decorative style using pictures of monkeys, often wearing clothes or indulging in other anthropomorphic behavior. From a French word meaning 'monkey business; a collection of monkeys'.

testudineous [tes-t(y)oo-**din**-ee-us] an adjective meaning 'as slow as a tortoise'. From a Latin word meaning 'tortoise'.

tyrotoxism [tye-roh-**tock**-siz-um] cheese-poisoning. This particular ptomaine (diazobenzene hyrdroxide) can also be found in bad milk. From Greek words meaning 'cheese' and 'poison'.

ubiquarian [yoo-bi-**kwair**-ee-un] a rare word meaning 'a person who goes everywhere'.

uliginous [yoo-**lidj**-uh-nus] an adjective meaning 'swampy, slimy, oozy'. From a Latin word meaning 'full of moisture'.

visagiste [vee-zuh-**zheest**] a makeup artist. From a French word with the same meaning.

visceration [vis-uh-**ray**-shun] a rare word meaning 'a portion of raw flesh, especially one distributed at the death of a rich man'. It's assumed that the flesh is that of an animal, and not that of the rich man. Related to the word *viscera*.

volacious [voh-**lay**-shus] suitable for flying. Something that has the power of flight is *volitorial*. From a Latin word meaning 'to fly'.

widdiful [**wid**-i-full] someone who deserves hanging. Another word with this meaning is *waghalter*. From *widdy*, 'a rope for hanging'.

windlestraw [**win**-dle-straw] a tall, thin, unhealthy-looking person.

yaply [**yap**-lee] an adverb meaning 'eagerly, hungrily'. *Yapness* is a noun meaning 'hunger', and *yap*, obviously, means 'hungry'.

zabernism [**zab**-er-niz-um] an obsolete word meaning 'the abuse of military power or authority; unjustified aggression'. From the name *Zabern*, the German name for Saverne in Alsace, where in 1912 an overeager German subaltern killed a cobbler who smiled at him.

zeitgeber [**tsite**-gebb-er] a cyclical event in the environment, especially one that acts as a cue for biological rhythms in an organism. From German words meaning 'time' and 'giver'.

zenocratically [zee-nuh-**krat**-ik-lee] with the authority of Zeus or Jove.

CHAPTER 5

125 Synonym Studies

INTRODUCTION

One of the great virtues of the English language is its versatility. Take the basic matter of words and their synonyms. English has a hydra-like variety of ways of expressing one concept. Pick practically any word in our language, and you will commonly find from several to many alternative choices with which to communicate the same thing. *Angry*, for example. Some synonyms for *angry* in English are *irritated, fuming, irate, mad, heated, livid, cross, furious, incensed, enraged,* and *infuriated*. What a banquet! You cannot find this same consistent array of choices in, say, the romance languages. English has at least twice as many words as French does, for example. English is like that mutt you adopt in the pound. You know it's part shepherd, maybe a bit of collie thrown in, perhaps some boxer, and heaven knows what else. The pedigree of English is complex, wide-ranging, and hard to pin down. Its influences cover not only the European map, but the rest of the world as well. It's got German, Norse, Icelandic, French, Latin, Anglo Saxon, Italian, Greek, Norman, Dutch—and "Old" versions of all of these—in its blood. It's hard to imagine what Shakespeare's plays would have been like had he written them in Spanish, for instance, but it's lucky they weren't. His range of expression would have been narrower, that's for certain.

So, as writers, we need to be eternally grateful we have English as our tongue, just for the synonyms alone. Many comic writers are funny simply *because* of their choice of words. One of my pet theories is that there are fewer comic writers in French than in English, because the Gallic writers had, and have, fewer choices of words in which to couch their observations. Just a theory. No proof whatsoever.

Here are 125 studies of the rich alternatives we have in English.

ABSOLVE, ACQUIT, EXEMPT, EXONERATE, FORGIVE, PARDON, VINDICATE

To varying degrees, all of these words mean to free from guilt or blame, and some are most frequently heard in a legal or political context.

Absolve is the most general term, meaning to set free or release—not only from guilt or blame, but from a duty or obligation (*absolved from her promise to serve on the committee*) or from the penalties for a violation.

Pardon is usually associated with the actions of a government or military official (*President Gerald Ford pardoned Richard Nixon following his resignation in the wake of the Watergate scandal*) and specifically refers to a release from prosecution or punishment.

It is usually a legal official who decides to **acquit** someone— that is, release someone from a specific and formal accusation of wrongdoing (*the court acquitted the accused due to lack of evidence*).

Exonerate suggests relief (its origin suggests the lifting of a burden), often in a moral sense, from a definite charge so that not even the suspicion of wrongdoing remains (*completely exonerated from the accusation of cheating*).

A person who is **vindicated** is also off the hook, usually due to the examination of evidence (*she vindicated herself by producing the missing documents*).

Exempt has less to do with guilt and punishment and more to do with duty and obligation (*exempt from paying taxes*).

To **forgive**, however, is the most magnanimous act of all: It implies not only giving up on the idea that an offense should be punished, but also relinquishing any feelings of resentment or vengefulness (*"To err is human; to forgive divine"*).

ABSURD, FOOLISH, LUDICROUS, PREPOSTEROUS, RIDICULOUS, UNREASONABLE

We call something **absurd** when it is utterly inconsistent with what common sense or experience tells us (*she found herself in the absurd position of having to defend the intelligence of a cockroach*).

Ludicrous applies to whatever is so incongruous that it provokes laughter or scorn (*a ludicrous suggestion that he might escape unnoticed if he dressed up as a woman*), and **ridiculous** implies that ridicule or mockery is the only appropriate response (*she tried to look younger, but succeeded only in making herself look ridiculous*).

Foolish behavior shows a lack of intelligence or good judgment (*it was foolish to keep that much money under a mattress*), while **unreasonable** behavior implies that the person has intentionally acted contrary to good sense (*his response was totally unreasonable in view of the fact that he'd asked for their honest opinion*).

Preposterous should be reserved for those acts or situations that are glaringly absurd or ludicrous. For example, it might be *unreasonable* to judge an entire nation on the basis of one tourist's experience and *foolish* to turn down an opportunity to visit that country on those grounds alone, but it would be *preposterous* to suggest that everyone who comes to the U.S. will be robbed at gunpoint.

ACCIDENTAL, ADVENTITIOUS, CASUAL, CONTINGENT, FORTUITOUS, INCIDENTAL

Things don't always go as planned, but there are many ways to describe the role that chance plays.

Accidental applies to events that occur entirely by chance (*an accidental encounter with the candidate outside the men's room*); but it is so strongly influenced by the noun "accident" that it carries connotations of undesirable or possibly disastrous results (*an accidental miscalculation of the distance he had to jump*).

A **casual** act or event is one that is random or unpremeditated (*a casual conversation with her son's teacher in the grocery store*), in which the role that chance plays is not always clear.

Something that is **incidental** may or may not involve chance; it typically refers to what is secondary or nonessential (*incidental expenses in the budget*) or what occurs without design or regularity (*incidental lighting throughout the garden*).

Adventitious also implies the lack of an essential relationship, referring to something that is a mere random occurrence (*adventitious circumstances that led to victory*).

In contrast, **contingent** points to something that is entirely dependent on an uncertain event for its existence or occurrence (*travel plans that are contingent upon the weather*).

Fortuitous refers to chance events of a fortunate nature; it is about as far as one can get from *accidental* (*a fortuitous meeting with the candidate outside the men's room just before the press conference*).

ATTACK, ASSAIL, ASSAULT, BESET, BESIEGE, BOMBARD, CHARGE, MOLEST, STORM

There is no shortage of "fighting words." **Attack** is the most general verb, meaning to set upon someone or something in a violent, forceful, or aggressive way (*the rebels attacked at dawn*); but it can also be used figuratively (*attack the government's policy*).

Assault implies a greater degree of violence or viciousness and the infliction of more damage. As part of the legal term "assault and battery," it suggests an attempt or threat to injure someone physically.

Molest is another word meaning to *attack* and is used today almost exclusively of sexual molestation (*she had been molested as a child*).

Charge and **storm** are primarily military words, both suggesting a forceful assault on a fixed position. To *charge* is to make a violent onslaught (*the infantry charged the enemy camp*) and is often used as a command (*"Charge!" the general cried*). To *storm* means to take by force, with all the momentum and fury of a storm (*after days of planning, the soldiers stormed the castle*), but there is often the suggestion of a last-ditch, all-out effort to end a long siege or avoid defeat.

To **assail** is to attack with repeated thrusts or blows, implying that victory depends not so much on force as on persistence.

To **bombard** is to assail continuously with bombs or shells (*they bombarded the city without mercy for days*).

Besiege means to surround with an armed force (*to besiege the capital city*). When used figuratively, its meaning comes close to that of *assail*, but with an emphasis on being hemmed in and enclosed rather than punished repeatedly (*besieged with fears*).

Beset also means to attack on all sides (*beset by enemies*), but it is also used frequently in other contexts to mean set or placed upon (*a bracelet beset with diamonds*).

BEG, BESEECH, ENTREAT, IMPLORE, IMPORTUNE, PETITION, PLEAD, SOLICIT

How badly do you want something? You can **beg** for it, which implies a humble and earnest approach.

If you **entreat**, you're trying to get what you want by ingratiating yourself (*she entreated her mother to help her prepare for the exam*).

To **plead** involves more urgency (*he pleaded with the judge to spare his life*) and is usually associated with the legal system (*she was advised to plead guilty*).

Beseech also suggests urgency, as well as an emotional appeal (*he beseeched her to tell the truth*).

Implore is still stronger, suggesting desperation or great distress (*the look in his mother's eyes implored him to have mercy*).

If you really want to get your way, you can **importune**, which means to *beg* not only urgently but persistently and to risk making a pest of yourself (*he importuned her daily to accept his invitation*).

Petition suggests an appeal to authority (*to petition the government to repeal an unjust law*), while **solicit** suggests petitioning in a courteous, formal way (*soliciting financial support for the school carnival*).

BIAS, BIGOTRY, INTOLERANCE, NARROW-MINDEDNESS, PAROCHIALISM, PARTIALITY, PREJUDICE, PROVINCIALISM

Bias is a predisposition either for or against something; one can have a *bias* against police officers or a *bias* for French food and wines.

Partiality, on the other hand, is a favorable bias (*the partiality of parents for their own children; the partiality of Americans for fast food*), while **prejudice** implies a preconceived and usually negative judgment or opinion (*a decision motivated by racial prejudice*).

Bigotry is an even stronger term, referring to an intense dislike and often violent hatred for the members of a particular race, religion, or ethnic group.

Narrow-mindedness also points to rigidly preconceived ideas, but implies that they are the result of lack of education or understanding, rather than outright hostility (*her parents' narrow-mindedness prevented her from meeting any boys her age*).

Parochialism is another term meaning excessive narrowness of mind (from "parochial," pertaining to a parish or parishes; that is, concerned mainly about local issues), while **provincialism** is narrow-mindedness that results from lack of exposure to cultural or intellectual activity, characteristic of a province or non-urban area.

Intolerance is a broad term used to describe the inability to put up with almost anything (*parents' intolerance of their children's misbehavior*).

BOLD, AGGRESSIVE, AUDACIOUS, BRAZEN, BUMPTIOUS, INTREPID, PRESUMPTUOUS

Is walking up to an attractive stranger and asking him or her to have dinner with you tonight a **bold** move or merely an **aggressive** one?

Both words suggest assertive, confident behavior that is a little on the shameless side, but *bold* has a wider range of application. It can suggest self-confidence that borders on impudence (*to be so bold as to call the president by his first name*), but it can also be used to describe a daring temperament that is either courageous or defiant (*a bold investigator who would not give up*).

Aggressive behavior, on the other hand, usually falls within a narrower range, somewhere between menacing (*aggressive attacks on innocent villagers*) and just plain pushy (*an aggressive salesperson*).

Brazen implies a defiant lack of modesty (*a brazen stare*), and **presumptuous** goes even further, suggesting overconfidence to the point of causing offense (*a presumptuous request for money*).

Bumptious behavior can also be offensive, but it is usually associated with the kind of cockiness that can't be helped (*a bumptious young upstart*).

An **audacious** person is bold to the point of recklessness (*an audacious explorer*), which brings it very close in meaning to **intrepid**, suggesting fearlessness in the face of the unknown (*the intrepid settlers of the Great Plains*).

BRIGHT, BRILLIANT, EFFULGENT, LUMINOUS, LUSTROUS, RADIANT, REFULGENT, RESPLENDENT, SHINING

Looking for just the right word to capture the quality of the light on a moonlit night or a summer day? All of these adjectives describe an intense, steady light emanating (or appearing to emanate) from a source.

Bright is the most general term, applied to something that gives forth, reflects, or is filled with light (*a bright and sunny day; a bright star*).

Brilliant light is even more intense or dazzling (*the brilliant diamond on her finger*), and **resplendent** is a slightly more formal, even poetic, way of describing a striking brilliance (*the sky was resplendent with stars*).

Poets also prefer adjectives like **effulgent** and **refulgent**, both of which can be applied to an intense, pervading light, sometimes from an unseen source (*her effulgent loveliness*); but *refulgent* specifically refers to reflected light (*a chandelier of refulgent crystal pendants*).

Radiant is used to describe the power of giving off light, either literally or metaphorically (*a radiant June day; the bride's radiant face*); it describes a steady, warm light that is emitted in all directions.

Like *radiant*, **luminous** suggests sending forth light, but light of the glow-in-the-dark variety (*the luminous face of the alarm clock*).

While diamonds are known for being *brilliant*, fabrics like satin and surfaces like polished wood, which reflect light and take on a gloss or sheen, are often called **lustrous**.

If none of these words captures the exact quality of the light you're trying to describe, you can always join the masses and use shining, a word that has been overworked to the point of cliché (*my knight in shining armor*).

BURN, CAUTERIZE, CHAR, SCALD, SCORCH, SEAR, SINGE

If you're not an experienced cook, you're likely to **burn** your vegetables and **char** your meat, and, if you put your face too close to the stove, you might even **singe** your eyebrows. All of these verbs mean to injure or bring about a change in something by exposing it to fire or intense heat.

Burn, which is the most comprehensive term, can mean to change only slightly (*she burned her face by staying out in the sun*) or to destroy completely (*the factory was burned to the ground*).

To *char* is to reduce a substance to carbon or charcoal (*the beams in the ceiling were charred by the fire*).

Like *char*, **singe** and **scorch** mean to burn only partially or superficially (*scorched the blouse while ironing it; singe the chicken before cooking it*). *Singeing* is often done deliberately to remove the hair, bristles, or feathers from the carcass of an animal or bird.

Scald refers specifically to burning with, or as if with, a hot liquid or steam (*the cook scalded herself when she spilled the boiling water*); it can also mean to parboil or heat to a temperature just below boiling (*scald the milk to make the sauce*).

Sear is also a term used in cooking, where it means to brown the outside of a piece of meat by subjecting it briefly to intense heat to seal in the juices.

When it's human flesh that's being seared in surgery, the correct verb is **cauterize**, which means to burn for healing purposes (*the doctor cauterized the wound to ward off infection*).

CALM, HALCYON, PEACEFUL, PLACID, SERENE, TRANQUIL

We usually speak of the weather or the sea as **calm**, meaning free from disturbance or storm.

When applied to people and their feelings or moods, *calm* implies an unruffled state, often under disturbing conditions (*to remain calm in the face of disaster*).

Halcyon is another adjective associated with the weather (*the halcyon days of summer*); it comes from the name of a mythical bird, usually identified with the kingfisher, that builds its nest on the sea and possesses a magical power to calm the winds and waves.

Peaceful also suggests a lack of turbulence or disorder, although it is usually applied to situations, scenes, and activities rather than to people (*a peaceful gathering of protesters*; *a peaceful resolution to their problems*).

Serene, tranquil, and **placid** are more often used to describe human states of being. *Serene* suggests a lofty and undisturbed calmness (*he died with a serene look on his face*), while *tranquil* implies an intrinsic calmness (*they led a tranquil life in the country*).

Placid usually refers to a prevailing tendency and is sometimes used disparagingly to suggest a lack of responsiveness or a dull complacency (*with her placid disposition, she seldom got involved in family arguments*).

COMPEL, COERCE, CONSTRAIN, FORCE, NECESSITATE, OBLIGE

A parent faced with a rebellious teenager may try to **compel** him to do his homework by threatening to take away his allowance. *Compel* commonly implies the exercise of authority, the exertion of great effort, or the impossibility of doing anything else (*compelled to graduate from high school by her eagerness to leave home*). It typically requires a personal object, although it is possible to *compel* a reaction or response (*she compels admiration*).

Force is a little stronger, suggesting the exertion of power, energy, or physical strength to accomplish something or to subdue resistance (*his mother forced him to confess that he'd broken the basement window*).

Coerce can imply the use of force, but often stops short of using it (*she was coerced into obedience by the threat of losing her telephone privileges*).

Constrain means *compel*, but by means of restriction, confinement, or limitation (*constrained from dating by his parents' strictness*).

Necessitate and **oblige** make an action necessary by imposing certain conditions that demand a response (*her mother's illness* *obliged her to be more cooperative; it also necessitated her giving up her social life*).

CONVERSATION, CHAT, COLLOQUY, COMMUNION, DIALOGUE, PARLEY, TÊTE-À-TÊTE

It is nearly impossible for most people to get through a day without having a **conversation** with someone, even if it's only a **chat** with the mailman.

Although *conversation* can and does take place in all sorts of contexts, both formal and informal, the word usually implies a relaxed, casual exchange.

A *chat* is the least formal of all conversations, whether it's a father talking to his son about girls or two women having a **tête-à-tête** (French for "head to head," meaning a confidential conversation) about their wayward husbands.

Both men and women often complain that their partners don't understand the meaning of **dialogue**, which is a two-way conversation that may involve opposing points of view.

Argument is even more likely to play a role in a **parley**, which formally is a discussion between enemies regarding the terms of a truce.

A **colloquy** is the most formal of all conversations (*a colloquy on nuclear disarmament*); it can also be used to jocularly describe a guarded exchange (*a brief colloquy with the arresting officer*).

Communion may be a form of conversation as well, but sometimes it takes place on such a profound level that no words are necessary (*communion with nature*).

COURAGE, FORTITUDE, GUTS, NERVE, PLUCK, RESOLUTION, TENACITY

Courage is what makes someone capable of facing extreme danger and difficulty without retreating (*the courage to confront the enemy head-on*). It implies not only bravery and a dauntless spirit but the ability to endure in times of adversity (*a mother's courage in the face of her loss*).

Someone who has **guts**, a slang word indicating an admirable display of courage when it really counts (*having the guts to stand* *up to one's boss*), might also be described as having "intestinal fortitude," a cliché that is more formal and means the same thing.

Fortitude is the most formal of any of these words; it suggests firmness or strength of mind rather than physical bravery (*the fortitude to stand up for his beliefs*).

Resolution also implies firmness of mind rather than fearlessness, but the emphasis is on the determination to achieve a goal in spite of opposition or interference (*a woman of strong resolution, not easily held back by her male superiors*).

Tenacity goes one step beyond *resolution*, adding stubborn persistence and unwillingness to acknowledge defeat (*the tenacity of a bulldog*).

Nerve and **pluck** are informal words. *Pluck* connotes high spirits, conviction, and eagerness (*the pluck to volunteer her time even after she'd been laid off*), while *nerve* is the cool, unflappable daring with which someone takes a calculated risk (*the nerve to take over the controls and land the plane safely*).

Nerve can also refer to brashness or even rudeness in social situations (*She had the nerve to go to his house without calling first*).

CREATIVE, IMAGINATIVE, INGENIOUS, INVENTIVE, ORIGINAL, RESOURCEFUL

Everyone likes to think that he or she is **creative**, which is used to describe the active, exploratory minds possessed by artists, writers, and inventors (*a creative approach to problem-solving*). Today, however, *creative* has become an advertising buzzword (*creative cooking, creative hairstyling*) that simply means new or different.

Original is more specific and limited in scope. Someone who is *original* comes up with things that no one else has thought of (*an original approach to constructing a doghouse*), or thinks in an independent and creative way (*a highly original filmmaker*).

Imaginative implies having an active and creative imagination, which often means that the person visualizes things quite differently than the way they appear in the real world (*imaginative illustrations for a children's book*).

The practical side of *imaginative* is **inventive**; the *inventive* person figures out how to make things work (*an inventive solution to the problem of getting a wheelchair into a van*).

But where an *inventive* mind tends to comes up with solutions to problems it has posed for itself, a **resourceful** mind deals successfully with externally imposed problems or limitations (*A resourceful child can amuse herself with simple wooden blocks*).

Someone who is **ingenious** is both *inventive* and *resourceful*, with a dose of cleverness thrown in (*the ingenious idea of using recycled plastic to create a warm, fleecelike fabric*).

DEPRAVED, CORRUPT, DEBASED, DEGENERATE, PERVERTED, VILE

There are many terms to describe the dark side of human nature.

Someone who preys on young children would be considered **depraved**, a term that means totally immoral and implies a warped character or a twisted mind (*a depraved man who stole money from his own mother and eventually murdered her*).

While *depraved* suggests an absolute condition, **degenerate** is a relative term that implies deterioration from a mental, moral, or physical standard (*her degenerate habits eventually led to her arrest for possession of drugs*).

Corrupt also suggests a deterioration or loss of soundness, particularly through a destructive or contaminating influence. But unlike *depraved*, which usually applies to the lower end of the human spectrum, people in high positions are often referred to as *corrupt* (*a corrupt politician from a prominent family*).

To say that someone or something is **debased** suggests a lowering in quality, value, dignity, or character (*debased by having to spend time in prison*).

Perverted and **vile** are the strongest of these words describing lack of moral character.

Perverted suggests a distortion of someone or something from what is right, natural, or true; in a moral sense, it means to use one's appetites or natural desires for other ends than those which are considered normal or natural (*a perverted individual who never should have been left alone with young children*).

Most people find criminals who prey on either very old or very young victims to be **vile**, a more general term for whatever is loathsome, repulsive, or utterly despicable (*a vile killer who deserved the maximum sentence*).

DESPISE, ABHOR, CONTEMN, DETEST, DISDAIN, LOATHE, SCORN

It's one thing to dislike someone; it's quite another to **despise** or **detest** the person. Both are strong words, used to describe extreme dislike or hatred.

Detest is probably the purest expression of hatred (*she detested the woman who had raised her, and longed to find her own mother*), while *despise* suggests looking down with great contempt and regarding the person as mean, petty, weak, or worthless (*he despised men whose only concern was their own safety*).

Disdain carries even stronger connotations of superiority, often combined with self-righteousness (*to disdain anyone lacking a college education*).

Scorn is a stronger word for *disdain*, and it implies an attitude of not only contempt but of haughty rejection or refusal (*to scorn the woman he'd once loved*).

To **loathe** something is to feel utter disgust toward it (*he grew to loathe peanut butter and jelly sandwiches*) and to **abhor** it is to feel a profound, shuddering, repugnance (*she abhorred the very idea of asking her husband for the money*).

Contemn is a more literary word meaning to treat with disdain, scorn, or contempt.

DESTROY, ANNIHILATE, DEMOLISH, ERADICATE, EXTERMINATE, EXTIRPATE, RAZE

If you're interested in getting rid of something, you've got a number of options at your disposal.

Destroy is a general term covering any force that wrecks, ruins, kills, etc. (*to destroy an ant hill by pouring boiling water on it*).

If it's a building, you'll want to **demolish** or **raze** it, two words that are generally applied only to very large things.

Raze is used almost exclusively with structures; it means to bring something down to the level of the ground (*they razed the apartment building to make way for the new hospital*).

Demolish implies pulling or smashing something to pieces; when used with regard to buildings, it conjures up a vision of complete wreckage and often a heap of rubble (*their new house was demolished by the first hurricane of the season*). But unlike *raze*, *demolish* can also be applied to nonmaterial things (*to demolish the theory with a few simple experiments*).

If you **eradicate** something, you eliminate it completely, literally or figuratively, pull it out by the roots (*to eradicate smallpox with a vaccine*) and prevent its reappearance.

Extirpate, like *eradicate*, implies the utter destruction of something (*the species was extirpated from the park by the flooding*).

If you're dealing with cockroaches, you'll probably want to **exterminate** them, which means to wipe out or kill in great numbers.

Or better yet, you'll want to **annihilate** them, which is the most extreme word in this group and literally means to reduce to nothingness.

DRUNK, BLOTTO, DRUNKEN, INEBRIATED, INTOXICATED, TIGHT, TIPSY

Anyone who is obviously or legally under the influence of alcohol is said to be **drunk**.

Drunken means the same thing, but only *drunk* should be used predicatively—that is, after a linking verb (*she was drunk*)—while *drunken* is more often used to modify a noun (*a drunken sailor*) and, in some cases, to imply habitual drinking to excess. *Drunken* is also used to modify nouns that do not refer to a person (*a drunken celebration*).

To say **intoxicated** or **inebriated** is a more formal and less offensive way of calling someone *drunk*, with *intoxicated* implying that the person is only slightly drunk, and *inebriated* implying drunkenness to the point of excitement or exhilaration (*the streets were filled with inebriated revelers*).

Tight and **tipsy** are two of the more common slang expressions (there are dozens more) meaning *drunk*.

Like *intoxicated*, *tipsy* implies that someone is only slightly drunk, while *tight* implies obvious drunkenness but without any loss of muscular coordination. An elderly woman who has had one sherry too many might be described as *tipsy*, but someone who has been drinking all evening and is still able to stand up and give a speech might be described as *tight*.

Either condition is preferable to being **blotto**, a word that means drunk to the point of incomprehensibility or unconsciousness.

DRY, ARID, DEHYDRATED, DESSICATED, PARCHED, SERE

Almost anything lacking in moisture (in relative terms)—whether it's a piece of bread, the basement of a house, or the state of Arizona—may be described as **dry**, a word that also connotes a lack of life or spirit (*a dry lecture on cell division*).

Arid, on the other hand, applies to places or things that have been deprived of moisture and are therefore extremely or abnormally dry (*one side of the island was arid*); it is most commonly used to describe a desertlike region or climate that is lifeless or barren.

Desiccated is used as a technical term for something from which moisture has been removed, and in general use it suggests lifelessness, although it is applied very often to people who have lost their vitality (*a desiccated old woman who never left her house*) or to animal and vegetable products that have been completely deprived of their vital juices (*desiccated oranges hanging limply from the tree*).

Dehydrated is very close in meaning to *desiccated* and is often the preferred adjective when describing foods from which the moisture has been extracted (*they lived on dehydrated fruit*).

Dehydrated may also refer to an unwanted loss of moisture (*the virus had left him seriously dehydrated*), as may the less formal term **parched**, which refers to an undesirable or uncomfortable lack of water in either a human being or a place (*parched with thirst; the parched landscape*).

Sere is associated primarily with places and means *dry* or *arid* (*a harsh, sere land where few inhabitants could survive*).

EAGER, ARDENT, AVID, ENTHUSIASTIC, FERVENT, KEEN, ZEALOUS

You've heard of the "eager beaver"? Anyone who has a strong interest or an impatient desire to pursue or become involved in something is called eager (*eager to get started; an eager learner*).

Someone who is especially *eager* might be called **avid**, a word that implies greed or insatiable desire (*an avid golfer, he was never at home on weekends*).

Ardent combines eagerness with intense feelings of passion or devotion (*an ardent lover; an ardent theatergoer*), while **fervent** suggests an eagerness that is ready, at least figuratively, to boil over (*their fervent pleas could not be ignored*).

Anyone who is deeply interested in something or who shows a spirited readiness to act is called **keen** (*he was keen on bicycling*), while **zealous** implies the kind of eagerness that pushes all other considerations aside (*a zealous environmentalist*).

Enthusiastic may connote participation rather than expectation: One can be *eager* to take a trip to Switzerland, an *ardent* student of Swiss history, and an *avid* outdoorsperson who is *keen* on hiking, but one is usually called *enthusiastic* about a trip to Switzerland when it is under way. *Enthusiastic* also very often applies to someone who outwardly and forcefully expresses eagerness.

ECONOMICAL, FRUGAL, MISERLY, PARSIMONIOUS, PROVIDENT, PRUDENT, SPARING, THRIFTY

If you don't like to spend money unnecessarily, you may simply be **economical**, which means that you manage your finances wisely and avoid any unnecessary expenses.

If you're **thrifty**, you're both industrious and clever in managing your resources (*a thrifty shopper who never leaves home without her coupons*).

Frugal, on the other hand, means that you tend to be sparing with money—sometimes getting a little carried away in your efforts—by avoiding any form of luxury or lavishness (*too frugal to take a taxi, even at night*).

If you're **sparing**, you exercise such restraint in your spending that you sometimes deprive yourself (*sparing to the point where she allowed herself only one new item of clothing a season*).

If you're **provident**, however, you're focused on providing for the future (*never one to be provident, she spent her allowance the day she received it*).

Miserly and **parsimonious** are both used to describe frugality in its most extreme form. But while being *frugal* might be considered a virtue, being *parsimonious* is usually considered to be a fault or even a vice (*they could have been generous with their wealth, but they chose to lead a parsimonious life*).

And no one wants to be called *miserly*, which implies being stingy out of greed rather than need (*so miserly that he reveled in his riches while those around him were starving*).

EJECT, DISMISS, EVICT, EXPEL, OUST

Want to get rid of someone? You can **eject** him or her, which means to throw or cast out (*he was ejected from the meeting room*).

If you hope the person never comes back, use **expel**, a verb that suggests driving someone out of a country, an organization, etc., for all time (*to be expelled from school*); it can also imply the use of voluntary force (*to expel air from the lungs*).

If you exercise force or the power of law to get rid of someone or something, **oust** is the correct verb (*ousted after less than two years in office*).

If as a property owner you are turning someone out of a house or a place of business, you'll want to **evict** the person (*she was evicted for not paying the rent*).

Dismiss is by far the mildest of these terms, suggesting that you are rejecting or refusing to consider someone or something (*to dismiss a legal case*). It is also commonly used of loss of employment (*dismissed from his job for excessive tardiness*).

EMBLEM, ATTRIBUTE, IMAGE, SIGN, SYMBOL, TOKEN, TYPE

When it comes to representing or embodying the invisible or intangible, you can't beat a **symbol**. It applies to anything that serves as an outward sign of something immaterial or spiritual (*the* *cross as a symbol of salvation; the crown as a symbol of monarchy*), although the association between the symbol and what it represents does not have to be based on tradition or convention and may, in fact, be quite arbitrary (*the annual gathering at the cemetery became a symbol of the family's long and tragic history*).

An **emblem** is a visual symbol or pictorial device that represents the character or history of a family, a nation, or an office (*the eagle is an emblem of the U.S.*).

It is very close in meaning to **attribute**, which is an object that is conventionally associated with a person, a group, or an abstraction (*the spiked wheel as an attribute of St. Catherine; the scales as an attribute of Justice*).

An **image** is also a visual representation or embodiment, but in a much broader sense (*veins popping, he was the image of the angry father*).

Sign is often used in place of *symbol* to refer to a simple representation of an agreed-upon meaning (*the upraised fist as a sign of victory; the white flag as a sign of surrender*), but a *symbol* usually embodies a wider range of meanings, while a *sign* can be any object, event, or gesture from which information can be deduced (*her faltering voice was a sign of her nervousness*).

A **token**, on the other hand, is something offered as a symbol or reminder (*he gave her his class ring as a token of his devotion*) and a **type**, particularly in a religious context, is a symbol or representation of something not present (*Jerusalem as the type of heaven; the paschal lamb as the type of Christ*).

ENCOURAGE, EMBOLDEN, FOSTER, HEARTEN, INSPIRE, INSTIGATE, STIMULATE

To **encourage** is to give active help or to raise confidence to the point where one dares to do what is difficult (*encouraged by her teacher, she set her sights on attending Harvard*).

Embolden also entails giving confidence or boldness, but it implies overcoming reluctance or shyness (*success as a public speaker emboldened her to enter politics*).

To **hearten** is to put one's heart into or to renew someone's spirit (*heartened by the news of his recovery*), and to **inspire** is to infuse with confidence, resolution, or enthusiasm (*inspired by her mother's example, she started exercising regularly*).

To **foster** is to encourage by nurturing or extending aid (*to foster the growth of small businesses by offering low-interest loans*); in some contexts, *foster* suggests an unwise or controversial kind of help (*to foster rebellion among local farmers*).

Instigate also implies that what is being encouraged is not necessarily desirable (*to instigate a fight*), while **stimulate** is a more neutral term meaning to rouse to action or effort (*to stimulate the growth of crops; to stimulate an interest in literature*).

ESTEEM, ADMIRE, APPRECIATE, PRIZE, REGARD, RESPECT

If you're a classical music aficionado, you might **appreciate** a good symphony orchestra, **admire** someone who plays the oboe, and **esteem** the works of Beethoven above all other classical composers.

All three of these verbs are concerned with recognizing the worth of something, but in order to *appreciate* it, you have to understand it well enough to judge it critically.

If you *admire* something, you appreciate its superiority (*to admire a pianist's performance*), while *esteem* goes one step further, implying that your admiration is of the highest degree (*a musician esteemed throughout the music world*).

You **prize** what you value highly or cherish, especially if it is a possession (*she prized her Stradivarius violin*), while **regard** is a more neutral term meaning to look at or to have a certain mental view of something, either favorable or unfavorable (*to regard him as a great musician; to regard her as a ruthless competitor*).

To **respect** is to have a deferential regard for someone or something because of its worth or value (*to respect the conductor's interpretation of the music*).

FAULT, BLEMISH, DEFECT, FAILING, FLAW, FOIBLE, SHORTCOMING

No one is perfect. But when it comes to cataloging your own imperfections, it's best to start with your **foibles**—the slight weaknesses or eccentricities for which you will be most quickly forgiven.

You also have a good chance of being forgiven for your **short-comings**, which are not necessarily damaging to others (*his ardent devotion to his dog was a shortcoming that was readily overlooked*).

Failing suggests a more severe shortcoming, usually with more serious consequences (*chronic tardiness was one of her failings*), but a *failing* can also be a weakness of character that you're not responsible for and perhaps not even aware of (*pride is a common failing among those who have met with great success early in life*).

Fault also implies failure—but not necessarily a serious failure—to reach moral perfection (*his major fault was his outspokenness*).

While *fault* usually indicates something inherent in your nature rather than external to it, a **flaw** can be either superficial (*a flaw in his otherwise immaculate appearance*) or profound (*a personality flaw that made her impossible to work with*), and it can refer to things as well as people (*a flaw in the table's finish*).

A **blemish** is usually a physical flaw (*a facial blemish*), although it can be anything that disfigures or mars the perfection of someone or something (*a blemish on her otherwise spotless academic record*).

You can get rid of a blemish and even overcome your short-comings, but a **defect** is a flaw so serious that you may never be able to get rid of it (*a defect in his hearing*).

FICTION, DECEPTION, FABLE, FABRICATION, FALSEHOOD, FIGMENT

If a young child tells you there is a dinosaur under his bed, you might assume that his story is a **fiction**, but it is probably a **figment**. A *fiction* is a story that is invented either to entertain or to deceive (*her excuse was ingenious, but it was pure fiction*), while *figment* suggests the operation of fancy or imagination (*a figment of his imagination*).

If a child hides his sandwich under the sofa cushions and tells you that a dinosaur ate it, this would be a **fabrication**, which is a story that is intended to deceive. Unlike a *figment*, which is mostly imagined, a *fabrication* is a false but thoughtfully constructed story in which some truth is often interwoven (*the city's safety record was a fabrication designed to lure tourists downtown*).

A **falsehood** is basically a lie—a statement or story that one knows to be false but tells with intent to deceive (*a deliberate falsehood about where the money had come from*).

A **deception**, on the other hand, is an act that deceives but not always intentionally (*a foolish deception designed to prevent her parents from worrying*).

A **fable** is a fictitious story that deals with events or situations that are clearly fantastic, impossible, or incredible. It often gives animals or inanimate objects the power to speak and conveys a lesson of practical wisdom, as in *Aesop's Fables*.

FORMAL, CEREMONIAL, CEREMONIOUS, POMPOUS, PROPER, PUNCTILIOUS

Formal suggests a suit-and-tie approach to certain situations—reserved, conventional, obeying all the rules (*an engraved invitation to a formal dinner requiring black tie or evening gown*).

Proper, in this regard, implies scrupulously correct behavior that observes rules of etiquette (*the proper way to serve a guest; the proper spoon for dessert*).

Punctilious behavior observes all the proper formalities (a *"punctilio"* is a detail or fine point), but may verge on the annoying (*her punctilious attention to the correct placement of silverware made setting the table an ordeal*).

Someone (usually a man) who likes to show off just how *formal* and *proper* he can be runs the risk of becoming the most dreaded dinner guest of all: the **pompous** ass.

Pompous people may derive more than the normal amount of pleasure from participating in **ceremonial** acts or events, which are those performed according to set rules, but **ceremonious** suggests a less negative and more ritualized approach to formality (*the Japanese woman could not have been more ceremonious than when she was carrying out the ceremonial serving of tea*).

GATHER, ASSEMBLE, COLLECT, CONGREGATE, CONVENE, MARSHAL, MUSTER

Gather is the most general of these terms meaning to come or bring together. It implies bringing widely scattered things or people to one place but with no particular arrangement (*to gather shells at the beach; to gather the family in the living room*).

Collect, on the other hand, implies both selectivity (*to collect evidence for the trial*) and organization (*to collect butterflies as a hobby*). To *gather* one's thoughts means to bring them together because they have been previously scattered; to *collect* one's thoughts is to organize them.

Assemble pertains to objects or people who are brought together for a purpose (*to assemble data for a report; to assemble Congress so that legislation will be passed*), while **congregate** may be more spontaneous, done as a free choice (*people congregated in front of the palace, hoping to catch a glimpse of the queen*).

Convene is a formal word meaning to *assemble* or meet in a body (*to convene an international conference on the subject of global warming*).

Marshal and **muster** are usually thought of as military terms. *Muster* implies bringing together the parts or units of a force (*troops mustered for inspection*), and *marshal* suggests a very orderly and purposeful arrangement (*to marshal the allied forces along the battle front*).

GENUINE, ACTUAL, AUTHENTIC, BONA FIDE, LEGITIMATE, VERITABLE

A car salesperson might claim that the seats of that pricey sedan you're considering are made from **genuine** leather—*genuine* being a word that applies to anything that is really what it is claimed or represented to be.

If you're in the market for a Model T Ford, however, you'll want to make sure that the car is **authentic**, which emphasizes formal proof or documentation that an object is what it is claimed to be.

Use **bona fide** when sincerity is involved (*a bona fide offer*), and **legitimate** when you mean lawful or in accordance with established rules, principles, and standards (*a legitimate business*).

Veritable implies correspondence with the truth but not necessarily a literal or strict correspondence with reality (*a veritable supermarket for car-buyers*).

How will it feel to drive that Mercedes out of the showroom? You won't know until you're the **actual** owner of the car—because *actual* means existing in fact rather than in the imagination.

GET, ACQUIRE, ATTAIN, GAIN, OBTAIN, PROCURE, SECURE

Get is a very broad term meaning to come into possession of. You can *get* something by fetching it (*get some groceries*), by receiving it (*get a birthday gift*), by earning it (*get interest on a bank loan*), or by any of a dozen other familiar means.

Substituting **obtain** sounds less colloquial. But it can also sound pretentious (*all employees were required to obtain an annual physical exam*) and should be reserved for contexts where the emphasis is on seeking something out (*to obtain blood samples*).

Acquire often suggests a continued, sustained, or cumulative acquisition (*to acquire poise as one matures*), but it can also hint at deviousness (*to acquire the keys to the safe*).

Use **procure** if you want to emphasize the effort involved in bringing something to pass (*procure a mediated divorce settlement*) or if you want to imply maneuvering to possess something (*procure a reserved parking space*). [But beware: *Procure* is so often used to describe the act of obtaining partners to gratify the lust of others (*to procure a prostitute*) that it has acquired somewhat unsavory overtones.]

Gain also implies effort, usually in *getting* something advantageous or profitable (*gain entry; gain victory*).

In a similar vein, **secure** underscores the difficulty involved in bringing something to pass and the desire to place it beyond danger (*secure a permanent peace; secure a lifeline*).

Attain should be reserved for achieving a high goal or desirable result (*if she attains the summit of Mt. Everest, she will secure for herself a place in mountaineering history*).

GIVE, AFFORD, AWARD, BESTOW, CONFER, DONATE, GRANT

You *give* a birthday present, *grant* a favor, *bestow* charity, and *confer* an honor. While all of these verbs mean to convey something or transfer it from one's own possession to that of another, the circumstances surrounding that transfer dictate which word is the best one.

Give is the most general, meaning to pass over, deliver, or transmit something (*give him encouragement*).

Grant implies that a request or desire has been expressed, and that the receiver is dependent on the giver's discretion (*grant permission for the trip*).

Award suggests that the giver is in some sense a judge, and that the thing given is deserved (*award a scholarship*), while bestow implies that something is given as a gift and may imply condescension on the part of the giver (*bestow a large sum of money on a needy charity*).

To confer is to give an honor, a privilege, or a favor. It implies that the giver is a superior (*confer a knighthood; confer a college degree*).

Donate implies that the giving is to a public cause or charity (*donate a painting to the local art museum*), and to afford is to give or bestow as a natural consequence (*the window afforded a fine view of the mountains*).

GOODNESS, MORALITY, PROBITY, RECTITUDE, VIRTUE

Of all these words denoting moral excellence, goodness is the broadest in meaning. It describes an excellence so well established that it is thought of as inherent or innate and is associated with kindness, generosity, helpfulness, and sincerity (*she has more goodness in her little finger than most people have in their whole body*).

Morality, on the other hand, is moral excellence based on a code of ethical conduct or religious teaching (*his behavior was kept in line by fear of punishment rather than morality*).

Although it is often used as a synonym for *goodness*, virtue suggests moral excellence that is acquired rather than innate and that is consciously or steadfastly maintained, often in spite of temptations or evil influences (*her virtue was as unassailable as her noble character*).

Rectitude is used to describe strict adherence to the rules of just or right behavior and carries strong connotations of sternness and self-discipline (*he had a reputation for rectitude and insisted on absolute truthfulness*).

Probity describes an honesty or integrity that has been tried and proved (*as mayor, she displayed a probity that was rare in a politician*).

GREEDY, ACQUISITIVE, AVARICIOUS, COVETOUS, GLUTTONOUS, RAPACIOUS

The desire for money and the things it can buy is often associated with Americans. But not all Americans are **greedy**, which implies an insatiable desire to possess or acquire something, beyond what one needs or deserves (*greedy for profits*). *Greedy* is especially derogatory when the object of longing is itself evil or when it cannot be possessed without harm to oneself or others (*a reporter greedy for information*).

Someone who is *greedy* for food might be called **gluttonous**, which emphasizes consumption as well as desire (*a gluttonous appetite for sweets*).

A *greedy* child may grow up to be an **avaricious** adult, which implies a fanatical greediness for money or other valuables.

Rapacious is an even stronger term, with an emphasis on taking things by force (*so rapacious in his desire for land that he forced dozens of families from their homes*).

Acquisitive, on the other hand, is a more neutral word suggesting a willingness to exert effort in acquiring things (*an acquisitive woman who filled her house with antiques and artwork*), and not necessarily material things (*a probing, acquisitive mind*).

Covetous, in contrast to *acquisitive*, implies an intense desire for something as opposed to the act of acquiring or possessing it. It is often associated with the Ten Commandments (*Thou shalt not covet thy neighbor's wife*) and suggests a longing for something that rightfully belongs to another.

GULLIBLE, CALLOW, CREDULOUS, INGENUOUS, NAIVE, TRUSTING, UNSOPHISTICATED

Some people will believe anything. Those who are truly **gullible** are the easiest to deceive, which is why they so often make fools of themselves.

Those who are merely **credulous** might be a little too quick to believe something, but they usually aren't stupid enough to act on it.

Trusting suggests the same willingness to believe (*a trusting child*), but it isn't necessarily a bad way to be (*a person so trusting he completely disarmed his enemies*).

No one likes to be called **naive** because it implies a lack of street smarts (*she's so naive she'd accept a ride from a stranger*), but when applied to things other than people, it can describe a simplicity and absence of artificiality that is quite charming (*the naive style in which nineteenth-century American portraits were often painted*).

Most people would rather be thought of as **ingenuous**, meaning straightforward and sincere (*an ingenuous confession of the truth*), because it implies the simplicity of a child without the negative overtones.

Callow, however, comes down a little more heavily on the side of immaturity and almost always goes hand-in-hand with youth.

Whether young or old, someone who is **unsophisticated** lacks experience in worldly and cultural matters.

HARD, ARDUOUS, DIFFICULT, LABORIOUS, TRYING

For the student who doesn't read well, homework is **hard** work, which means that it demands great physical or mental effort.

An English assignment to write an essay might be particularly **difficult**, meaning that it not only requires effort but skill. Where *hard* suggests toil, *difficult* emphasizes complexity (*a difficult math problem*).

Memorizing long lists of vocabulary words would be **laborious**, which is even more restrictive than *hard* and suggests prolonged, wearisome toil with no suggestion of the skill required and no reference to the complexity of the task.

Reading *War and Peace*, however, would be an **arduous** task, because it would require a persistent effort over a long period of time.

A school assignment may be *difficult*, but is usually not *arduous*; that is, it may require skill rather than perseverance. It may also be *arduous* without being particularly *difficult*, as when a student is asked to write "I will not throw spitballs" five hundred times.

A student who is new to a school may find it especially **trying**, which implies that it taxes someone's patience, skill, or capabilities.

HEAVY, BURDENSOME, CUMBERSOME, MASSIVE, PONDEROUS, WEIGHTY

Trying to move a refrigerator out of a third-floor apartment is difficult because it is **cumbersome**, which means that it is so heavy and bulky that it becomes unwieldy or awkward to handle.

Cartons filled with books, on the other hand, are merely **heavy**, which implies greater density and compactness than the average load.

A huge oak dining table might be described as **massive**, which stresses largeness and solidity rather than weight, while something that is **ponderous** is too large or too massive to move, or to be moved quickly (*a ponderous printing press*).

Most of these terms can be used figuratively as well. *Heavy*, for example, connotes a pressing down on the mind, spirits, or senses (*heavy with fatigue; a heavy heart*), and *ponderous* implies a dull and labored quality (*a novel too ponderous to read*).

Burdensome, which refers to something that is not only *heavy* but must be carried or supported, is even more likely to be used in an abstract way to describe something that is difficult but can, with effort, be managed (*a burdensome task*).

Both a package and a problem may be described as **weighty**, meaning actually (as opposed to relatively) heavy; but it is more commonly used to mean very important or momentous (*weighty matters to discuss*).

HONOR, DEFERENCE, HOMAGE, OBEISANCE, REVERENCE

The Ten Commandments instruct us to "**Honor** thy father and mother." But what does *honor* entail? While all of these nouns describe the respect or esteem that one shows to another, *honor* implies acknowledgment of a person's right to such respect (*honor one's ancestors; honor the dead*).

Homage is honor with praise or tributes added, and it connotes a more worshipful attitude (*pay homage to the king*).

Reverence combines profound respect with love or devotion (*he treated his wife with reverence*), while **deference** suggests courteous regard for a superior, often by yielding to the person's status or wishes (*show deference to one's elders*).

Obeisance is a show of honor or reverence by an act or gesture of submission or humility, such as a bow or a curtsy (*the schoolchildren were instructed to pay obeisance when the queen arrived*).

HOSTILE, ADVERSE, BELLICOSE, BELLIGERENT, INIMICAL

Few people have trouble recognizing hostility when confronted with it. Someone who is **hostile** displays an attitude of intense ill will and acts like an enemy (*the audience grew hostile after waiting an hour for the show to start*).

Both **bellicose** and **belligerent** imply a readiness or eagerness to fight, but the former is used to describe a state of mind or temper (*after drinking all night, he was in a bellicose mood*), while the latter is normally used to describe someone who is actively engaged in hostilities (*the belligerent brothers were at it again*).

While *hostile* and *belligerent* usually apply to people, **adverse** and **inimical** are used to describe tendencies or influences. *Inimical* means having an antagonistic tendency (*remarks that were inimical to everything she believed in*), and *adverse* means turned toward something in opposition (*an adverse wind; under adverse circumstances*). Unlike *hostile*, *adverse* and *inimical* need not connote the involvement of human feeling.

IDEA, CONCEPT, CONCEPTION, IMPRESSION, NOTION, THOUGHT

If you have an **idea** it might refer to something perceived through the senses (*I had no idea it was so cold out*), to something visualized (*the idea of a joyous family outing*), or to something that is the product of the imagination (*a great idea for raising money*). *Idea* is a comprehensive word that applies to almost any aspect of mental activity.

A **thought**, on the other hand, is an idea that is the result of meditation, reasoning, or some other intellectual activity (*she hadn't given much thought to the possibility of losing*).

A **notion** is a vague or capricious idea, often without any sound basis (*he had a notion that he could get there by hitchhiking*).

A widely held idea of what something is or should be is a **concept** (*the concept of loyalty was beyond him*), while a **conception** is a concept that is held by a person or small group and that is often colored by imagination and feeling (*her conception of marriage as a romantic ideal*).

An idea that is triggered by something external is an **impression**, a word that suggests a half-formed mental picture or superficial view (*he made a good impression; she had the impression that everything would be taken care of*).

IMITATE, APE, COPY, IMPERSONATE, MIMIC, MOCK

A young girl might **imitate** her mother by answering the phone in exactly the same tone of voice, while a teenager who deliberately *imitates* the way her mother talks for the purpose of irritating her would more accurately be said to **mimic** her. *Imitate* implies following something as an example or model (*he imitated the playing style of his music teacher*), while *mimic* suggests imitating someone's mannerisms for fun or ridicule (*they liked to mimic the teacher's southern drawl*).

To **copy** is to imitate or reproduce something as closely as possible (*he copied the style of dress and speech used by the other gang members*).

When someone assumes another person's appearance or mannerisms, sometimes for the purpose of perpetrating a fraud, he or she is said to **impersonate** (*arrested for impersonating a police officer; a comedian well known for impersonating political figures*).

Ape and **mock** both imply an unflattering imitation. Someone who mimics in a contemptuous way is said to *ape* (*he entertained everyone in the office by aping the boss's phone conversations with his wife*), while someone who imitates with the intention of belittling or irritating is said to *mock* (*the students openly mocked their teacher's attempt to have a serious discussion about sex*).

IMPERTINENT, IMPUDENT, INSOLENT, INTRUSIVE, MEDDLESOME, OBTRUSIVE

All of these adjectives mean 'exceeding the bounds of propriety'; the easiest way to distinguish **impertinent** from the others is to think of its root: *impertinent* behavior is not pertinent—in other words, it is out of place. The *impertinent* person has a tendency to be rude or presumptuous toward those who are entitled to deference or respect (*it was an impertinent question to ask a woman who had just lost her husband*).

The **intrusive** person is unduly curious about other people's affairs (*her constant questions about the state of their marriage were intrusive and unwelcome*), while **obtrusive** implies objectionable actions rather than an objectionable disposition. The *obtrusive* person has a tendency to thrust himself or herself into a position where he or she is conspicuous and apt to do more harm than good (*they tried to keep him out of the meeting because his presence would be obtrusive*).

To be **meddlesome** is to have a prying or inquisitive nature and a tendency to interfere in an annoying way in other people's affairs (*a meddlesome neighbor*).

Impudent and **insolent** are much stronger words for inappropriate behavior. Young people are often accused of being *impudent*, which means to be impertinent in a bold and shameless way (*an impudent young man who had a lot to learn about tact*).

Anyone who is guilty of insulting and contemptuously arrogant behavior might be called *insolent* (*he was so insolent to the arresting officer that he was handcuffed*).

INCITE, AROUSE, EXHORT, FOMENT, INSTIGATE, PROVOKE

The best way to start a riot is to **incite** one, which means to urge or stimulate to action, either in a favorable or an unfavorable sense.

If you **instigate** an action, however, it implies that you are responsible for initiating it and that the purpose is probably a negative or evil one (*the man who instigated the assassination plot*).

Foment suggests agitation or incitement over an extended period of time (*foment a discussion; foment the rebellion that leads to war*). An instigator, in other words, is someone who initiates the idea, while a fomenter is someone who keeps it alive.

You can **provoke** a riot in the same way that you instigate one, but the emphasis here is on spontaneity rather than on conscious design (*her statement provoked an outcry from animal rights activists*).

To **arouse** is to awaken a feeling or elicit a response (*my presence in the junkyard aroused suspicion*), or to open people's eyes to a situation (*we attempted to arouse public awareness*).

But once you've aroused people, you may have to **exhort** them, meaning to urge or persuade them, by appealing to their sympathy or conscience, to take constructive action.

INHERENT, CONGENITAL, ESSENTIAL, INBORN, INGRAINED, INNATE, INTRINSIC

A quality that is **inherent** is a permanent part of a person's nature or essence (*an inherent tendency to fight back*).

If it is **ingrained**, it is deeply wrought into his or her substance or character (*ingrained prejudice against women*).

Inborn and **innate** are nearly synonymous, sharing the basic sense of existing at the time of birth, but *innate* is usually preferred in an abstract or philosophical context (*innate defects; innate ideas*), while *inborn* is reserved for human characteristics that are so deep-seated they seem to have been there from birth (*an inborn aptitude for the piano*).

Congenital also means from the time of one's birth, but it is primarily used in medical contexts and refers to problems or defects (*congenital color-blindness; a congenital tendency toward schizophrenia*).

Intrinsic and **essential** are broader terms that can apply to things as well as people. Something that is *essential* is part of the essence or constitution of something (*an essential ingredient; essential revisions in the text*), while an *intrinsic* quality is one that belongs naturally to a person or thing (*her intrinsic fairness; an intrinsic weakness in the design*).

INTEND, AIM, DESIGN, MEAN, PLAN, PROPOSE, PURPOSE

If you **intend** to do something, you may or may not be serious about getting it done (*I intend to clean out the garage some day*), but at least you have a goal in mind.

Although **mean** can also imply either a firm resolve (*I mean to go, with or without her permission*) or a vague intention (*I've been meaning to write her for weeks*), it is a less formal word that usually connotes a certain lack of determination or a weak resolve.

Plan, like *mean* and *intend,* may imply a vague goal (*I plan to tour China some day*), but it is often used to suggest that you're taking active steps (*I plan to leave as soon as I finish packing*).

Aim indicates that you have an actual goal or purpose in mind and that you're putting some effort behind it (*I aim to be the first woman president*), without the hint of failure conveyed by *mean.*

If you **propose** to do something, you declare your intention ahead of time (*I propose that we set up a meeting next week*), and if you **purpose** to do it, you are even more determined to achieve your goal (*I purpose to write a three-volume history of baseball in America*).

Design suggests forethought in devising a plan (*design a strategy that will keep everyone happy*).

JEALOUS, COVETOUS, ENVIOUS

Envious implies wanting something that belongs to another and to which one has no particular right or claim (*envious of her good fortune*).

Jealous may refer to a strong feeling of envy (*it is hard not to be jealous of a man with a job like his*), or it may imply an intense effort to hold on to what one possesses (*jealous of what little time she has to herself*); it is often associated with distrust, suspicion, anger, and other negative emotions (*a jealous wife*).

Someone who is **covetous** has fallen prey to an inordinate or wrongful desire, usually for a person or thing that rightfully belongs to another.

In other words, a young man might be *jealous* of the other men who flirt with his girlfriend, while they might be *envious* of her obvious preference for him. But the young man had better not be *covetous* of his neighbor's wife.

JOURNEY, EXCURSION, EXPEDITION, JAUNT, PILGRIMAGE, TRIP, VOYAGE

While all of these nouns refer to a course of travel to a particular place, usually for a specific purpose, there is a big difference between a **jaunt** to the nearest beach and an **expedition** to the rain forest.

While a **trip** may be either long or short, for business or pleasure, and taken at either a rushed or a leisurely pace (*a ski trip; a trip to Europe*), a **journey** suggests that a considerable amount of time and distance will be covered and that the travel will take place over land (*a journey into the Australian outback*).

A long trip by water or through air or space is a **voyage** (*a voyage to the Galapagos Islands; a voyage to Mars*), while a short, casual trip for pleasure or recreation is a *jaunt* (*a jaunt to the local shopping mall*).

Excursion also applies to a brief pleasure trip, usually no more than a day in length, that returns to the place where it began (*an afternoon excursion to the zoo*).

Unlike the rest of these nouns, *expedition* and **pilgrimage** apply to *journeys* that are undertaken for a specific purpose. An *expedition* is usually made by an organized group or company (*a scientific expedition; an expedition to locate new sources of oil*), while a *pilgrimage* is a journey to a place that has religious or emotional significance (*the Muslims' annual pilgrimage to Mecca; a pilgrimage to the place where her father died*).

JUMBLE, CONFUSION, CONGLOMERATION, DISARRAY, FARRAGO, HODGEPODGE, MÉLANGE, MUDDLE

Confusion is a very broad term, applying to any indiscriminate mixing or mingling that makes it difficult to distinguish individual elements or parts (*a confusion of languages*).

The typical teenager's bedroom is usually a **jumble** of books, papers, clothing, CDs, and soda cans—the word suggests physical disorder and a mixture of dissimilar things.

If the disorder exists on a figurative level, it is usually called a **hodgepodge** (*a hodgepodge of ideas, opinions, and quotations, with a few facts thrown in for good measure*).

Conglomeration refers to a collection of dissimilar things, but with a suggestion that the collection is random or inappropriate (*a conglomeration of decorating styles*).

A **mélange** can be a mixture of foods (*add peppers or zucchini to the mélange*), but it can also be used in a derogatory way (*an error-filled mélange of pseudoscience, religion, and fanciful ideas*).

A **farrago** is an irrational or confused mixture of elements and is usually worse than a *conglomeration* (*a farrago of doubts, fears, hopes, and desires*), while a **muddle** is less serious and suggests confused thinking and lack of organization (*their bank records were in a complete muddle*).

Disarray implies disarrangement and is most appropriately used when order or discipline has been lost (*his unexpected appearance threw the meeting into disarray*).

KEEN, ACUTE, ASTUTE, PENETRATING, PERSPICACIOUS, SHARP, SHREWD

A knife can be **sharp**, even **keen**, but it can't be **astute**. While *keen* and *sharp* mean having a fine point or edge, they also pertain to mental agility and perceptiveness.

You might describe someone as having a *keen* mind, which suggests the ability to grapple with complex problems, or to observe details and see them as part of a larger pattern (*a keen appreciation of what victory would mean for the Democratic*

Party), or a *keen* wit, which suggests an incisive or stimulating sense of humor.

Someone who is *sharp* has an alert and rational mind, but is not necessarily well grounded in a particular field and may in some cases be cunning or devious (*sharp enough to see how the situation might be turned to her advantage*).

An **astute** mind, in contrast, is one that has a thorough and profound understanding of a given subject or field (*an astute understanding of the legal principles involved*).

Like *sharp*, shrewd implies both practicality and cleverness, but with an undercurrent of self-interest (*a shrewd salesperson*).

Acute is close in meaning to *keen*, but with more emphasis on sensitivity and the ability to make subtle distinctions (*an acute sense of smell*).

While a keen mind might see only superficial details, a **penetrating** mind would focus on underlying causes (*a penetrating analysis of the plan's feasibility*).

Perspicacious is the most formal of these terms, meaning both perceptive and discerning (*a perspicacious remark; perspicacious judgment*).

KILL, ASSASSINATE, DISPATCH, EXECUTE, MASSACRE, MURDER, SLAUGHTER, SLAY

When it comes to depriving someone or something of life, the options are seemingly endless.

To **kill** is the most general term, meaning to cause the death of a person, animal, or plant, with no automatic implication of a method or cause (*killed in a car accident*). Even inanimate things may be killed (*Congress killed the project when they vetoed the bill*).

To **slay** is to kill deliberately and violently; it is used more often in written than in spoken English (*a novel about a presidential candidate who is slain by his opponent*).

Murder implies a malicious and premeditated killing of one person by another (*a gruesome murder carried out by the son-in-law*), while **assassinate** implies that a politically important person has been murdered, often by someone hired to do the job (*assassinate the head of the guerrilla forces*).

Someone who is put to death by a legal or military process is said to be **executed** (*execute by lethal injection*), but if someone is killed primarily to get rid or him or her, the appropriate verb is **dispatch**, which also suggests speed or promptness (*after delivering the secret documents, the informer was dispatched*).

While **slaughter** is usually associated with the killing of animals for food, it can also apply to a mass killing of humans (*the slaughter of innocent civilians provoked a worldwide outcry*).

Massacre also refers to the brutal murder of large numbers of people, but it is used more specifically to indicate the wholesale destruction of a relatively defenseless group of people (*the massacre of Bethlehem's male children by King Herod*).

KNOWLEDGE, ERUDITION, INFORMATION, LEARNING, PEDANTRY, SCHOLARSHIP, WISDOM

How much do you know?

Knowledge applies to any body of facts gathered by study, observation, or experience, and to the ideas inferred from these facts (*an in-depth knowledge of particle physics; firsthand knowledge about the company*).

Information may be no more than a collection of data or facts (*information about vacation resorts*) gathered through observation, reading, or hearsay, with no guarantee of their validity (*false information that led to the arrest*).

Scholarship emphasizes academic knowledge or accomplishment (*a special award for scholarship*), while **learning** is knowledge gained not only by study in schools and universities but by individual research and investigation (*a man of great learning*), which puts it on a somewhat higher plane.

Erudition is on a higher plane still, implying bookish knowledge that is beyond the average person's comprehension (*exhibit extraordinary erudition in a doctoral dissertation*).

Pedantry, on the other hand, is a negative term for a slavish attention to obscure facts or details or an undue display of learning (*the pedantry of modern literary criticism*).

You can have extensive *knowledge* of a subject and even exhibit *erudition*, however, without attaining **wisdom**, the superior judgment and understanding that is based on both knowledge and experience.

LACK, ABSENCE, DEARTH, PRIVATION, SHORTAGE, WANT

To suffer from a **lack** of food means to be partially or totally without it; to be in **want** of food also implies a *lack*, but with an emphasis on the essential or desirable nature of what is lacking; for example, you may experience a complete *lack* of pain following surgery, but you would be in *want* of medication if pain were suddenly to occur.

Absence, on the other hand, refers to the complete nonexistence of something or someone. A *lack* of dairy products in your diet implies that you're not getting enough; an *absence* of dairy products implies that you're not getting any at all.

If the scarcity or lack of something makes it costly, or if something is in distressingly low supply, the correct word is **dearth** (*a dearth of water in the desert; a dearth of nylon stockings during World War II*).

A **shortage** of something is a partial insufficiency of an established, required, or accustomed amount (*a shortage of fresh oranges after the late-season frost*), while **privation** is the negative state or absence of a corresponding positive (*they suffered from hunger, cold, and other privations*).

LIE, EQUIVOCATE, FABRICATE, FIB, PREVARICATE, RATIONALIZE

If your spouse asks you whether you remembered to mail the tax forms and you say "Yes," even though you know they're still sitting on the passenger seat of your car, you're telling a **lie**, which is a deliberately false statement.

If you launch into a lengthy explanation of the day's frustrations and setbacks, the correct word would be **prevaricate**, which is to quibble, dodge the point, or confuse the issue so as to avoid telling the truth.

If you tell your spouse that you would have mailed the taxes, but then you started thinking about an important deduction you might be entitled to take and decided it would be unwise to mail them without looking into it, you're **rationalizing**, which is to come up with reasons that put your own behavior in the most favorable possible light.

If you say that there was an accident in front of the post office that prevented you from finding a parking space and there really wasn't, **fabricate** is the correct verb, meaning that you've invented a false story or excuse without the harsh connotations of *lie* (*she fabricated an elaborate story about how they got lost on their way home*).

Equivocate implies saying one thing and meaning another; it usually suggests the use of words that have more than one meaning, or whose ambiguity may be misleading. For example, if your spouse says, "Did you take care of the taxes today?" you might equivocate by saying "Yes," you took care of them—meaning that you finished completing the forms and sealing them in the envelope, but that you didn't actually get them to the post office.

To **fib** is to tell a falsehood about something unimportant; it is often used as a euphemism for *lie* (*a child who fibs about eating his vegetables*).

LOITER, DALLY, DAWDLE, IDLE, LAG

Someone who hangs around downtown after the stores are closed and appears to be deliberately wasting time is said to **loiter**, a verb that connotes improper or sinister motives (*the police warned the boys not to loiter*).

To **dawdle** is to pass time leisurely or to pursue something half-heartedly (*dawdle in a stationery shop; dawdle over a sinkful of dishes*).

Someone who **dallies** dawdles in a particularly pleasurable and relaxed way, with connotations of amorous activity (*he dallied with his girlfriend when he should have been delivering papers*).

Idle suggests that the person makes a habit of avoiding work or activity (*idle away the hours of a hot summer day*), while **lag** suggests falling behind or failing to maintain a desirable rate of progress (*she lagged several yards behind her classmates as they walked to the museum*).

MALIGN, CALUMNIATE, DEFAME, LIBEL, SLANDER, VILIFY

Do you want to ruin someone's life? You can **malign** someone, which is to say or write something evil without necessarily lying (*she was maligned for her past association with radical causes*).

To **calumniate** is to make false and malicious statements about someone; the word often implies that you have seriously damaged that person's good name (*after leaving his job, he spent most of his time calumniating and ridiculing his former boss*).

To **defame** is to cause actual injury to someone's good name or reputation (*he defamed her by accusing her of being a spy*).

If you don't mind risking a lawsuit, you can **libel** the person, which is to write or print something that defames him or her (*the tabloid libeled the celebrity and ended up paying the price*).

Slander, which is to defame someone orally, is seldom a basis for court action but can nevertheless cause injury to someone's reputation (*after a loud and very public argument, she accused him of slandering her*).

If all else fails, you can **vilify** the person, which is to engage in abusive name-calling (*even though he was found innocent by the jury, he was vilified by his neighbors*).

MERCY, BENEVOLENCE, CHARITY, CLEMENCY, COMPASSION, LENIENCY

If you want to win friends and influence people, it's best to start with **benevolence**, a general term for goodwill and kindness (*a grandfather's benevolence*).

Charity is even better, suggesting generous giving (*the baker gave him bread out of charity*) but also meaning tolerance and understanding of others (*she viewed his selfish behavior with charity*).

Compassion is a feeling of sympathy or sorrow for someone else's misfortune (*he has shown compassion for the homeless*), and often includes showing **mercy**.

Aside from its religious overtones, *mercy* means compassion or kindness in our treatment of others, especially those who have offended us or who deserve punishment (*mercy toward the pickpocket*).

Clemency is mercy shown by someone whose duty or function it is to administer justice or punish offenses (*the judge granted clemency*), while leniency emphasizes gentleness, softness, or lack of severity, even if it isn't quite deserved (*a father's leniency in punishing his young son*).

MISTAKE, BLOOPER, BLUNDER, ERROR, FAUX PAS, GOOF, SLIP

It would be a mistake to argue with your boss the day before he or she evaluates your performance, but to forget an important step in an assigned task would be an error.

Although these nouns are used interchangeably in many contexts, a *mistake* is usually caused by poor judgment or a disregard of rules or principles (*it was a mistake not to tell the truth at the outset*), while an *error* implies an unintentional deviation from standards of accuracy or right conduct (*a mathematical error*).

A blunder is a careless, stupid, or blatant mistake involving behavior or judgment; it suggests awkwardness or ignorance on the part of the person who makes it (*his blunder that ruined the evening*).

A slip is a minor and usually accidental mistake that is the result of haste or carelessness (*her slip of the tongue spoiled the surprise*), while a faux pas (which means "false step" in French) is an embarrassing breach of etiquette (*it was a faux pas to have meat at the table when so many of the guests were vegetarians*).

Goofs and bloopers are humorous mistakes. A *blooper* is usually a mix-up in speech, while to *goof* is to make a careless error that is honestly admitted (*she shrugged her shoulders and said, "I goofed!"*)

MORAL, ETHICAL, HONORABLE, RIGHTEOUS, SANCTIMONIOUS, VIRTUOUS

You can be an ethical person without necessarily being a moral one, since *ethical* implies conformity with a code of fair and honest behavior, particularly in business or in a profession (*an ethical legislator who didn't believe in cutting deals*), while *moral* refers to

generally accepted standards of goodness and rightness in character and conduct—especially sexual conduct (*the moral values she'd
learned from her mother*).

In the same way, you can be **honorable** without necessarily being
virtuous, since *honorable* suggests dealing with others in a decent
and ethical manner, while *virtuous* implies the possession of moral
excellence in character (*many honorable businesspeople fail to live a
virtuous private life*).

Righteous is similar in meaning to **virtuous** but also implies
freedom from guilt or blame (*righteous anger*); when the righteous
person is also somewhat intolerant and narrow-minded, *self-right-
eous* might be a better adjective.

Someone who makes a hypocritical show of being righteous is
often described as **sanctimonious**—in other words, acting like a
saint without having a saintly character.

MOVING, AFFECTING, PATHETIC, POIGNANT, TOUCHING

A movie about the Holocaust might be described as **moving**, since it
arouses emotions or strong feelings, particularly feelings of pathos.

A movie about a young girl's devotion to her dog might more
accurately be described as **touching**, which means arousing tenderness or compassion, while a movie dealing with a young girl's
first experience with love would be **poignant**, since it pierces
one's heart or keenly affects one's sensibilities.

While *poignant* implies a bittersweet response that combines
pity and longing or other contradictory emotions, **pathetic** means
simply moving one to pity (*a pathetic scene in which the dog strug-
gled to save his drowning mistress*).

Almost any well-made film can be **affecting**, a more general term
that suggests moving one to tears or some other display of feeling
(*the affecting story of a daughter's search for her birth mother*).

NATIVE, ABORIGINAL, ENDEMIC, INDIGENOUS

A **native** New Yorker is probably not **indigenous**, although both
words apply to persons or things that belong to or are associated
with a particular place by birth or origin.

Native means born or produced in a specific region or country (*native plants; native dances*), but it can also apply to persons or things that were introduced from elsewhere some time ago—which is the case with most New Yorkers who consider themselves natives.

Indigenous, on the other hand, is more restricted in meaning; it applies only to someone or something that is not only native but was not introduced from elsewhere (*the pumpkin is indigenous to North America*). Generally speaking, *native* applies to individual organisms, while *indigenous* applies to races or species.

Something that is endemic is prevalent in a particular region because of special conditions there that favor its growth or existence (*heather is endemic in the Scottish Highlands; malaria is endemic in Central America*).

There are no longer any aboriginal New Yorkers, a word that refers to the earliest known inhabitants of a place or to ancient peoples who have no known ancestors and have inhabited a region since its earliest historical time. Australia is known for its *aboriginal* culture, which was preserved for centuries through geographical isolation.

NECESSARY, ESSENTIAL, INDISPENSABLE, REQUISITE

Food is essential to human life, which means that we must have it to survive. *Essential* can also apply to something that makes up the *essence*, or necessary qualities or attributes, of a thing (*a good safecracker is essential to our plan*).

Clothing is indispensable in northern climates, which means that it cannot be done without if the specified or implied purpose—in this case, survival—is to be achieved.

Necessary applies to something without which a condition cannot be fulfilled (*cooperation was necessary to gather the harvest*), although it generally implies a pressing need rather than absolute indispensability.

Requisite refers to that which is required by the circumstances (*the requisite skills for a botanist*) and generally describes a requirement that is imposed from the outside rather than an inherent need.

NEGLECT, DISREGARD, IGNORE, OVERLOOK, SLIGHT

One of the most common reasons why people fail to arrive at work on time is that they **neglect** to set their alarm clocks, a verb that implies a failure to carry out some expected or required action, either intentionally or through carelessness.

Some people, of course, choose to **disregard** their employer's rules pertaining to tardiness, which implies a voluntary, and sometimes deliberate, inattention.

Others hear the alarm go off and simply **ignore** it, which suggests not only a deliberate decision to *disregard* something but a stubborn refusal to face the facts.

No doubt they hope their employers will **overlook** their frequent late arrivals, which implies a failure to see or to take action, which can be either intentional or due to haste or lack of care (*to overlook minor errors*).

But they also hope no one will **slight** them for their conduct when it comes to handing out raises and promotions, which means to *disregard* or *neglect* in a disdainful way.

NONSENSE, BULL, BUNK, DRIVEL, POPPYCOCK, TWADDLE

If you write or speak in an obscure, senseless, or unintelligible manner, you'll probably be accused of producing **nonsense**. It is the most general of these nouns and may refer to behavior as well as to what is said (*the demonstrators were told in no uncertain terms to stop this nonsense or leave the room*).

Twaddle refers to silly, empty utterances from people who know nothing about a subject but who write or talk about it anyway (*I was sick of her twaddle about the dangers of electromagnetic fields*).

Bunk (short for bunkum) applies to an utterance that strikes the popular fancy even though it is lacking in worth or substance (*the speech, which received enthusiastic applause, was pure bunk*).

Poppycock applies to nonsense that is full of complex, confused, or clichéd ideas (*the report was a strange combination of logical thinking and outright poppycock*).

Bull is a slang term for deceitful and often boastful writing or speech (*he gave them a line of bull*).

Perhaps the most insulting of these terms is **drivel**, which implies a steady flow of inane, idle, or nonsensical speech or writing similar to what might be expected from a very young child or an idiot (*his first novel was full of romantic drivel*).

NORMAL, AVERAGE, NATURAL, ORDINARY, REGULAR, TYPICAL, USUAL

Most people want to be regarded as **normal**, an adjective that implies conformity with established norms or standards and is the opposite of abnormal (*a normal body temperature; normal intelligence*).

Regular, like *normal*, is usually preferred to its opposite (irregular) and implies conformity to prescribed standards or established patterns (*their regular monthly meeting; a regular guy*), but *normal* carries stronger connotations of conformity within prescribed limits and sometimes allows for a wider range of differences.

Few of us think of ourselves as **ordinary**, a term used to describe what is commonplace or unexceptional (*an ordinary person wearing ordinary clothes*), although many people are ordinary in some ways and extraordinary in others.

Average also implies conformity with what is regarded as *normal* or *ordinary* (*a woman of average height*), although it tends to emphasize the middle ground and to exclude both positive and negative extremes.

Typical applies to persons or things possessing the representative characteristics of a type or class (*a typical teenager*).

Someone or something described as **natural** behaves or operates in accordance with an inherent nature or character (*his fears were natural for one so young*), while **usual** applies to that which conforms to common or ordinary use or occurrence (*we paid the usual price*).

NOTICEABLE, CONSPICUOUS, OUTSTANDING, PROMINENT, REMARKABLE, STRIKING

A scratch on someone's face might be **noticeable**, while a scar that runs from cheekbone to chin would be **conspicuous**. When it comes to describing the things that attract our attention, *noticeable* means readily noticed or unlikely to escape observation (*a noticeable facial tic; a noticeable aversion to cocktail parties*), while *conspicuous* implies that the eye (or mind) cannot miss it (*her absence was conspicuous*).

Use **prominent** when you want to describe something that literally or figuratively stands out from its background (*a prominent nose; a prominent position on the committee*). It can also apply to persons or things that stand out so clearly they are generally known or recognized (*a prominent citizen*).

Someone or something that is **outstanding** rises above or beyond others and is usually superior to them (*an outstanding student*).

Remarkable applies to anything that is noticeable because it is extraordinary or exceptional (*remarkable blue eyes*).

Striking is an even stronger word, used to describe something so out of the ordinary that it makes a deep and powerful impression on the observer's mind or vision (*a striking young woman over six feet tall*).

OBEDIENT, BIDDABLE, COMPLIANT, DOCILE, DUTIFUL

Children and animals may be expected to obey, but nowadays obedient is seldom used to describe adult human beings without a suggestion that they are allowing someone else to assume too great a degree of authority (*are we to believe that Cinderella became the prince's demure, obedient wife?*).

The critical note is stronger in biddable. A *biddable* person is excessively meek and ready to obey any instruction, without questioning either its wisdom or the authority of the person giving it (*he could barely think for himself, having been so biddable to his domineering parents*).

Docile (from Latin *docilis* 'teachable') has similar implications, but in addition to unquestioning obedience it suggests a general reluctance to complain or rebel, even where such behavior would be justified (*employers depended on the regime for a cheap and docile workforce*).

Dutiful may evoke a sneer, suggesting the virtuous, yet dull (*his dutiful niece spent most of her life caring for him*), or the perfunctory fulfillment of an obligation (*a dutiful postcard to his mother*).

One of the oldest (and still living) meanings of compliant is 'reshaping under pressure' (*conversion of the gel to a much less compliant glass*). This helps to explain the principal modern sense of the adjective, '(excessively) disposed to agree with others or obey rules' (*compliant legislators loyally followed party policy*). In the computer age a further sense, 'technically compatible,' has developed (*the system is Windows compliant*).

OBSEQUIOUS, SERVILE, SLAVISH, SUBSERVIENT

If you want to get ahead with your boss, you might trying being **obsequious**, which suggests an attitude of inferiority that may or may not be genuine, but that is assumed in order to placate a superior in hopes of getting what one wants (*a "goody two shoes" whose obsequious behavior made everyone in the class cringe*).

While **subservient** may connote similar behavior, it is more often applied to those who are genuinely subordinate or dependent and act accordingly (*a timid, subservient child who was terrified of making a mistake*).

Servile is a stronger and more negative term, suggesting a cringing submissiveness (*the dog's servile obedience to her master*).

Slavish, suggesting the status or attitude of a slave, is often used to describe strict adherence to a set of rules or a code of conduct (*a slavish adherence to the rules of etiquette*).

OFFENSIVE, ABHORRENT, ABOMINABLE, DETESTABLE, ODIOUS, REPUGNANT

Looking for just the right word to express your dislike, distaste, disgust, or aversion to something? **Offensive** is a relatively mild adjective, used to describe anyone or anything that is unpleasant or disagreeable (*she found his remarks offensive; the offensive sight of garbage piled in the alley*).

If you want to express strong dislike for someone or something that deserves to be disliked, use **detestable** (*a detestable man who never had a kind word for anyone*).

If something is so offensive that it provokes a physical as well as a moral or intellectual response, use **odious** (*the odious treatment of women during the war in Bosnia*), and if you instinctively draw back from it, use **repugnant** (*the very thought of piercing one's nose was repugnant to her*).

If your repugnance is extreme, go one step further and use **abhorrent** (*an abhorrent act that could not go unpunished*).

Persons and things that are truly loathsome or terrifying can be called **abominable** (*an abominable act of desecration; the abominable snowman*), although this word is often used as an overstatement to mean "awful" (*abominable taste in clothes*).

OLD, AGED, ANCIENT, ANTEDILUVIAN, ANTIQUATED, ARCHAIC, OBSOLETE

Almost no one likes to be thought of as **old**, which means having been in existence or use for a relatively long time (*an old washing machine*).

But those who are **aged**, indicating a longer life span than *old* and usually referring to persons of very advanced years, are often proud of the fact that they have outlived most of their peers.

Children may exaggerate and regard their parents as **ancient**, which means dating back to the remote past, often specifically the time before the end of the Roman Empire (*ancient history*), and their attitudes as **antediluvian**, which literally means dating back to the period before the biblical Great Flood and Noah's ark (*an antediluvian transportation system*).

Some people seem older than they really are, simply because their ideas are **antiquated**, which means out of vogue or no longer practiced (*antiquated ideas about dating*).

Things rather than people are usually described as **archaic**, which means having the characteristics of an earlier, sometimes primitive, period (*archaic words like "thou" and "thine"*).

Obsolete also refers to things, implying that they have gone out of use or need to be replaced by something newer (*an obsolete textbook; a machine that will be obsolete within the decade*).

OPINION, BELIEF, CONVICTION, PERSUASION, SENTIMENT, VIEW

When you give your **opinion** on something, you offer a conclusion or a judgment that, although it may be open to question, seems true or probable to you at the time (*she was known for her strong opinions on women in the workplace*).

A **view** is an opinion that is affected by your personal feelings or biases (*his views on life were essentially optimistic*), while a **sentiment** is a more or less settled opinion that may still be colored by emotion (*her sentiments on aging were shared by many other women approaching fifty*).

A **belief** differs from an *opinion* or a *view* in that it is not necessarily the creation of the person who holds it; the emphasis here is on the mental acceptance of an idea, a proposition, or a doctrine and on the assurance of its truth (*religious beliefs; his belief in the power of the body to heal itself*).

A **conviction** is a firmly held and unshakable belief whose truth is not doubted (*she could not be swayed in her convictions*), while a **persuasion** (in this sense) is a strong belief that is unshakable because you want to believe that it's true rather than because there is evidence proving it so (*she was of the persuasion that he was innocent*).

ORIGIN, INCEPTION, PROVENANCE, ROOT, SOURCE

The **origin** of something is the point from which it starts or sets out, or the person or thing from which it is ultimately derived (*the origin of the custom of carving pumpkins at Halloween; the origin of a word*). It often applies to causes that were in operation before the thing itself was brought into being.

Source, on the other hand, applies to that which provides a first and continuous supply (*the source of the river; an ongoing source of inspiration and encouragement*).

Root, more often than *source*, applies to what is regarded as the first or final cause of something; it suggests an origin so fundamental as to be the ultimate cause from which something stems (*money is the root of all evil*).

Inception refers specifically to the beginning of an undertaking, project, institution, or practice (*she was in charge of the organization from its inception*).

Provenance is similarly restricted in meaning, referring to thespecific place, or sometimes the race or people, from which something is derived or by whom it was invented or constructed (*in digging, they uncovered an artifact of unknown provenance*).

PACIFY, APPEASE, CONCILIATE, MOLLIFY, PLACATE, PROPITIATE

You might try to **pacify** a crying baby, to **appease** a demanding boss, to **mollify** a friend whose feelings have been hurt, and to **placate** an angry crowd. While all of these verbs have something to do with quieting people who are upset, excited, or disturbed, each involves taking a slightly different approach.

Pacify suggests soothing or calming (*the mother made soft cooing noises in an attempt to pacify her child*).

Appease implies that you've given in to someone's demands or made concessions in order to please (*she said she would visit his mother just to appease him*), while *mollify* stresses minimizing anger or hurt feelings by taking positive action (*her flattery failed to mollify him*).

Placate suggests changing a hostile or angry attitude to a friendly or favorable one, usually with a more complete or long-lasting effect than *appease* (*they were able to placate their enemies by offering to support them*).

You can **propitiate** a superior or someone who has the power to injure you by allaying or forestalling their anger (*they were able to propitiate the trustees by holding a dinner party in their honor*).

Conciliate implies the use of arbitration or compromise to settle a dispute or to win someone over (*the company made every effort to conciliate its angry competitor*).

PLEASANT, AGREEABLE, ATTRACTIVE, CONGENIAL, ENJOYABLE, GRATIFYING, PLEASING

One might have a **pleasant** smile and a **pleasing** personality, since the former suggests something that is naturally appealing while the latter suggests a conscious attempt to please.

Something that is **enjoyable** is able to give enjoyment or pleasure (*a thoroughly enjoyable evening*), while **agreeable** describes something that is in harmony with one's personal mood or wishes (*an agreeable afternoon spent relaxing in the sun*).

Gratifying is more intense, suggesting that deeper expectations or needs have been met (*the awards ceremony was particularly gratifying for parents*).

Something that is **attractive** gives pleasure because of its appearance or manner (*an attractive house in a wooded setting*), while **congenial** has more to do with compatibility (*a congenial couple*).

PLOT, CABAL, CONSPIRACY, INTRIGUE, MACHINATION

If you come up with a secret plan to do something, especially with evil or mischievous intent, it's called a **plot** (*a plot to seize control of the company*).

If you get other people or groups involved in your plot, it's called a **conspiracy** (*a conspiracy to overthrow the government*).

Cabal usually applies to a small group of political conspirators (*a cabal of right-wing extremists*), while **machination** (usually plural) suggests deceit and cunning in devising a plot intended to harm someone (*the machinations of the would-be assassins*).

An **intrigue** involves more complicated scheming or maneuvering than a plot and often employs underhanded methods in an attempt to gain one's own ends (*she had a passion for intrigue, particularly where romance was involved*).

POLLUTE, ADULTERATE, CONTAMINATE, DEFILE, TAINT

When a factory pours harmful chemicals or wastes into the air or water, it is said to **pollute** the environment. But *pollute* may also refer to impairing the purity, integrity, or effectiveness of something (*a campaign polluted by allegations of sexual impropriety*).

To **contaminate** is to spread harmful or undesirable impurities throughout something. Unlike *pollute*, which suggests visible or noticeable impurities, *contaminate* is preferred where the change is unsuspected or not immediately noticeable (*milk contaminated by radioactive fallout from a nuclear plant accident*).

Adulterate often refers to food products to which harmful, low-quality, or low-cost substances have been added in order to defraud the consumer (*cereal adulterated with sawdust*), although this word can apply to any mixture to which the inferior or harmful element is added deliberately and in the hope that no one will notice (*a report adulterated with false statistics*).

To **defile** is to pollute something that should be kept pure or sacred (*a church defiled by vandals*), while **taint** implies that a trace of something toxic or corrupt has been introduced (*he contracted the disease from a tainted blood transfusion; the book is tainted by gratuitous violence*).

POSTPONE, ADJOURN, DEFER, DELAY, SUSPEND

All of these verbs have to do with putting things off.

Defer is the broadest in meaning; it suggests putting something off until a later time (*defer payment; defer a discussion*).

If you **postpone** an event or activity, you put it off intentionally, usually until a definite time in the future (*we postponed the party until the next weekend*).

If you **adjourn** an activity, you postpone its completion until another day or place; *adjourn* is usually associated with meetings or other formal gatherings that are brought to an end and then resumed (*the judge adjourned the hearing until the following morning*).

If you **delay** something, you postpone it because of obstacles (*delayed by severe thunderstorms and highway flooding*) or because you are reluctant to do it (*delay going to the dentist*).

Suspend suggests stopping an activity for a while, usually for a reason (*forced to suspend work on the bridge until the holiday weekend was over*).

PRAISE, ACCLAIM, COMMEND, EULOGIZE, EXTOL, LAUD

If your dog sits when you tell him to sit, you'll want to **praise** him for his obedience. *Praise* is a general term for expressing approval, esteem, or commendation that usually suggests the judgment of a superior (*the teacher's praise for her students*).

If a salesperson goes out of his way to help you, you may want to **commend** him to his superior, which is a more formal, public way of praising someone, either verbally or in writing.

If you're watching a performance and want to express your approval verbally or with applause, **acclaim** is the verb you're looking for.

Laud and **extol** suggest the highest of praise, although *laud* may imply that the praise is excessive (*the accomplishments for which she was lauded were really nothing out of the ordinary*).

Extol, which comes from the Latin meaning to raise up, suggests that you're trying to magnify whatever or whomever you're praising (*to extol her virtues so that everyone would vote for her*).

If you want to praise someone who has died recently, you will **eulogize** him or her, which means to speak or write your praise for a special occasion, such as a funeral.

PREDICT, AUGUR, DIVINE, FORECAST, FORESHADOW, FORETELL, PROGNOSTICATE, PROPHESY

While all of these words refer to telling something before it happens, **predict** is the most commonly used and applies to the widest variety of situations. It can mean anything from hazarding a guess (*they predicted he'd never survive the year*) to making an astute inference based on facts or statistical evidence (*predict that the Republicans would win the election*).

When a meteorologist tells us whether it will rain or snow tomorrow, he or she is said to **forecast** the weather, a word that means *predict* but is used particularly in the context of weather and other phenomena that cannot be predicted easily by the general public (*statistics forecast an influx of women into the labor force*).

Divine and **foreshadow** mean to suggest the future rather than to predict it, especially by giving or evaluating subtle hints or clues. To *divine* something is to perceive it through intuition or insight (*to divine in the current economic situation the disaster that lay ahead*), while *foreshadow* can apply to anyone or anything that gives an indication of what is to come (*her abrupt departure that night foreshadowed the breakdown in their relationship*).

Foretell, like *foreshadow*, can refer to the clue rather than the person who gives it and is often used in reference to the past (*evidence that foretold the young girl's violent end*).

Augur means to foreshadow a favorable or unfavorable outcome for something (*the turnout on opening night augured well for the play's success*).

Prophesy connotes either inspired or mystical knowledge of the future and suggests more authoritative wisdom than *augur* (*a baseball fan for decades, he prophesied the young batter's rise to stardom*).

Although anyone who has inside information or knowledge of signs and symptoms can **prognosticate**, it is usually a doctor who does so by looking at the symptoms of a disease to predict its future outcome.

PRESENT, BONUS, DONATION, GIFT, GRATUITY, LAGNIAPPE, LARGESSE

What's the difference between a birthday **present** and a Christmas **gift**? Both words refer to something given as an expression of friendship, affection, esteem, etc.

But *gift* is a more formal term, often suggesting something of monetary value that is formally bestowed on an individual, group, or institution (*a gift to the university*).

Present, on the other hand, implies something of less value that is an expression of goodwill (*a housewarming present; a present for the teacher*).

Largesse is a somewhat pompous term for a very generous gift that is conferred in an ostentatious or condescending way, often on many recipients (*the king's largesse; the largesse of our government*).

A **gratuity** is associated with tipping and other forms of voluntary compensation for special attention or service above and beyond what is included in a charge (*known for her generous gratuities, the duchess enjoyed watching the waiters compete with each other to serve her*), while a **lagniappe** is a Southern word, used chiefly in Louisiana and southeast Texas, for either a gratuity or a small gift given to a customer along with a purchase.

If you give money or anything else as a gift to a philanthropic, charitable, or religious organization, it is known as a **donation** (*donations for the poor*).

But if your employer gives you money at the end of the year in addition to your regular salary, it isn't a Christmas *gift*; it's a Christmas **bonus**.

PRIDE, ARROGANCE, CONCEIT, EGOTISM, SELF-ESTEEM, VAINGLORY, VANITY

If you take **pride** in yourself or your accomplishments, it means that you believe in your own worth, merit, or superiority—

whether or not that belief is justified (*she took pride in her accomplishments*).

When your opinion of yourself is exaggerated, you're showing **conceit**, a word that combines *pride* with self-obsession.

If you like to be noticed and admired for your appearance or achievements, you're revealing your **vanity**, and if you show off or boast about your accomplishments, you're likely to be accused of **vainglory**, a somewhat literary term for a self-important display of power, skill, or influence.

Arrogance is an overbearing pride combined with disdain for others (*his arrogance led him to assume that everyone else would obey his orders*), while **egotism** implies self-centeredness or an excessive preoccupation with yourself (*blinded by egotism to the suffering of others*).

While no one wants to be accused of *arrogance* or *egotism*, there's a lot to be said for **self-esteem**, which may suggest undue pride but is more often used to describe a healthy belief in oneself and respect for one's worth as a person (*she suffered from low self-esteem*).

PROFUSE, EXTRAVAGANT, LAVISH, LUSH, LUXURIANT, PRODIGAL

Something that is **profuse** is poured out or given freely, often to the point of exaggeration or excess (*profuse apologies*).

Extravagant also suggests unreasonable excess, but with an emphasis on wasteful spending (*her gift was much too extravagant for the occasion*).

Someone who is **prodigal** is so recklessly extravagant that his or her resources will ultimately be exhausted (*the prodigal heir to the family fortune*).

Another way to end up impoverished is through **lavish** spending, a word that combines extravagance with generosity or a lack of moderation (*lavish praise; lavish furnishings*).

While *lavish, extravagant* and *prodigal* are often used to describe human behavior, **lush** and **luxuriant** normally refer to things. What is *luxuriant* is produced in great quantity, suggesting that it is not only profuse but gorgeous (*luxuriant auburn hair*). Something described as *lush* is not only luxuriant but has reached a peak of perfection (*the lush summer grass*).

PROHIBIT, BAN, DISALLOW, ENJOIN, FORBID, HINDER, INTERDICT, PRECLUDE

There are a number of ways to prevent something from happening. You can **prohibit** it, which assumes that you have legal or other authority and are willing to back up your prohibition with force (*prohibit smoking*); or you can simply **forbid** it and hope that you've got the necessary clout (*forbid teenagers to stay out after midnight*).

Ban carries a little more weight—both legal and moral—and **interdict** suggests that church or civil authorities are behind the idea.

To **enjoin** (in this sense) is to prohibit by legal injunction (*the truckers were enjoined from striking*), which practically guarantees that you'll get what you want.

A government or some other authority may **disallow** an act it might otherwise have permitted (*the IRS disallowed the deduction*), but anyone with a little gumption can **hinder** an activity by putting obstacles in its path (*hinder the thief's getaway by tripping him on his way out the door*).

Of course, the easiest way to prohibit something is to **preclude** it, which means stopping it before it even gets started.

QUACK, CHARLATAN, DISSEMBLER, FAKE, IMPOSTOR, MOUNTEBANK

There are many different ways to describe a **fake**, a colloquial term for anyone who knowingly practices deception or misrepresentation.

Someone who sells a special tonic that claims to do everything from curing the common cold to making hair grow on a bald man's head is called a **quack**, a term that refers to any fraudulent practitioner of medicine or law.

Mountebank sometimes carries implications of quackery, but more often it refers to a self-promoting person who resorts to cheap tricks or undignified efforts to win attention (*political mountebanks*).

A **charlatan** is usually a writer, speaker, preacher, professor, or some other "expert" who tries to conceal his or her lack of skill or knowledge by resorting to pretentious displays (*supposedly a leading authority in his field, he turned out to be nothing but a charlatan*).

Someone who tries to pass himself or herself off as someone else is an **impostor** (*an impostor who bore a close physical resemblance to the king*), although this term can also refer to anyone who assumes a title or profession that is not his or her own.

Although all of these deceivers are out to fool people, it is the **dissembler** who is primarily interested in concealing his or her true motives or evil purpose (*he is a dissembler who weaves a tangled web of lies*).

QUARREL, ALTERCATION, DISPUTE, FEUD, ROW, SPAT, SQUABBLE, WRANGLE

Fighting is an unfriendliness that comes in a variety of shapes and sizes.

A husband and his wife may have a **quarrel**, which suggests a heated verbal argument, with hostility that may persist even after it is over (*it took them almost a week to patch up their quarrel*).

Siblings tend to have **squabbles**, which are childlike disputes over trivial matters, although they are by no means confined to childhood (*frequent squabbles over who would pick up the check*).

A **spat** is also a petty quarrel, but unlike *squabble*, it suggests an angry outburst followed by a quick ending without hard feelings (*another spat in an otherwise loving relationship*).

A **row** is more serious, involving noisy quarreling and the potential for physical violence (*a row that woke the neighbors*).

Neighbors are more likely to have an **altercation**, which is usually confined to verbal blows but may involve actual or threatened physical ones (*an altercation over the location of the fence*).

A **dispute** is also a verbal argument, but one that is carried on over an extended period of time (*an ongoing dispute over who was responsible for taking out the garbage*).

Two families who have been enemies for a long time are probably involved in a **feud**, which suggests a bitter quarrel that lasts for years or even generations (*the feud between the Hatfields and the McCoys*).

There is no dignity at all in being involved in a **wrangle**, which is an angry, noisy, and often futile dispute in which both parties are unwilling to listen to the other's point of view.

RANGE, COMPASS, GAMUT, LATITUDE, REACH, SCOPE, SWEEP

To say that someone has a wide **range** of interests implies that these interests are not only extensive but varied.

Another way of expressing the same idea would be to say that the person's interests run the **gamut** from TV quiz shows to nuclear physics, a word that suggests a graduated scale or series running from one extreme to another.

Compass implies a range of knowledge or activity that falls within very definite limits reminiscent of a circumference (*within the compass of her abilities*), while **sweep** suggests more of an arc-shaped range of motion or activity (*the sweep of the searchlight*) or a continuous extent or stretch (*a broad sweep of lawn*).

Latitude and **scope** both emphasize the idea of freedom, although *scope* implies great freedom within prescribed limits (*the scope of the investigation*), while *latitude* means freedom from such limits (*she was granted more latitude than usual in interviewing the disaster victims*).

Even someone who has a wide *range* of interests and a broad *scope* of authority will sooner or later come up against something that is beyond his or her **reach**, which suggests the furthest limit of effectiveness or influence.

RAVAGE, DESPOIL, DEVASTATE, PILLAGE, PLUNDER, SACK, WASTE

Ravage, **pillage**, **sack**, and **plunder** are all verbs associated with the actions of a conquering army during wartime.

Ravage implies violent destruction, usually in a series of raids or invasions over an extended period of time (*the invading forces ravaged the countryside*).

Plunder refers to the roving of soldiers through recently conquered territory in search of money and goods (*they plundered the city and left its inhabitants destitute*), while *pillage* describes the act of stripping a conquered city or people of valuables (*churches pillaged by ruthless invaders*).

Sack is even more extreme than *pillage*, implying not only the seizure of all valuables, but total destruction as well (*the army sacked every village along the coast*).

Despoil also entails the stripping of valuables, but with less violence than *sack*; it is more common in nonmilitary contexts, where it describes a heedless or inadvertent destruction (*forests despoiled by logging companies*).

Devastate emphasizes ruin and desolation, whether it happens to buildings, forests, or crops (*fields of corn devastated by flooding*).

Waste comes close in meaning to *devastate*, but it suggests a less violent or more gradual destruction (*a region of the country wasted by years of drought and periodic fires*).

REBUKE, ADMONISH, CENSURE, REPRIMAND, REPROACH, SCOLD

All of these verbs mean to criticize or express disapproval, but which one you use depends on how upset you are.

If you want to go easy on someone, you can **admonish** or **reproach**, both of which indicate mild and sometimes kindly disapproval. To *admonish* is to warn or counsel someone, usually because a duty has been forgotten or might be forgotten in the future (*admonish her about leaving the key in the lock*), while *reproach* also suggests mild criticism aimed at correcting a fault or pattern of misbehavior (*he was reproved for his lack of attention in class*).

If you want to express your disapproval formally or in public, use **censure** or **reprimand**. You can *censure* someone either directly or indirectly (*the judge censured the lawyer for violating court-*

room procedures; a newspaper article that censured "deadbeat dads"), while *reprimand* suggests a direct confrontation (*reprimanded by his parole officer for leaving town without reporting his whereabouts*).

If you're irritated enough to want to express your disapproval quite harshly and at some length, you can **scold** (*to scold a child for jaywalking*).

Rebuke is the harshest word of this group, meaning to criticize sharply or sternly, often in the midst of some action (*rebuke a carpenter for walking across an icy roof*).

RELINQUISH, ABANDON, CEDE, SURRENDER, WAIVE, YIELD

Of all these verbs meaning to let go or give up, relinquish is the most general. It can imply anything from simply releasing one's grasp (*she relinquished the wheel*) to giving up control or possession reluctantly (*after the defeat, he was forced to relinquish his command*).

Surrender also implies giving up, but usually after a struggle or show of resistance (*the villagers were forced to surrender to the guerrillas*).

Yield is a milder synonym for *surrender*, implying some concession, respect, or even affection on the part of the person who is surrendering (*she yielded to her mother's wishes and stayed home*).

Waive means to give up voluntarily a right or claim to something (*she waived her right to have a lawyer present*), while cede is to give up by legal transfer or according to the terms of a treaty (*the French ceded the territory that is now Louisiana*).

If one *relinquishes* something finally and completely, often because of weariness or discouragement, the correct word is **abandon** (*they were told to abandon all hope of being rescued*).

RESOLUTE, CONSTANT, DECISIVE, DETERMINED, FAITHFUL, STAUNCH

Any of the above adjectives might apply to you if you take a stand on something and stick to it, or show your loyalty to a person, country, or cause.

If you show unswerving loyalty to someone or something you are tied to (as in marriage, friendship, etc.), you would be described as **faithful** (*a faithful wife; a faithful Republican*).

Constant also implies a firm or steady attachment to someone or something, but with less emphasis on vows, pledges, and obligations; it is the opposite of fickleness rather than of unfaithfulness (*my grandfather's constant confidant*).

To be described as **staunch** carries loyalty one step further, implying an unwillingness to be dissuaded or turned aside (*a staunch friend who refused to believe the rumors that were circulating*).

To be called **resolute** means that you are both staunch and steadfast, but the emphasis here is on character and a firm adherence to your own goals and purposes rather than to those of others (*resolute in insisting upon her right to be heard*).

Determined and **decisive** are less forceful words. You can be *decisive* in almost any situation, as long as you have a choice among alternatives and don't hesitate in taking a stand (*decisive as always, she barely glanced at the menu before ordering*).

Determined, unlike *resolute*, suggests a stubborn will rather than a conscious adherence to goals or principles (*he was determined to be home before the holidays*).

REVERE, ADMIRE, ADORE, IDOLIZE, VENERATE, WORSHIP

We might **admire** someone who walks a tightrope between two skyscrapers, **idolize** a rock star, **adore** our mothers, and **revere** a person like Martin Luther King, Jr. Each of these verbs conveys the idea of regarding someone or something with respect and honor, but they differ considerably in terms of the feelings they connote.

Admire suggests a feeling of delight and enthusiastic appreciation (*admire the courage of the mountain climber*), while *adore* implies the tenderness and warmth of unquestioning love (*he adored babies*).

Idolize is an extreme form of adoration, suggesting a slavish, helpless love, (*he idolized the older quarterback*).

We *revere* individuals and institutions that command our respect for their accomplishments or attributes (*he revered his old English professor*).

Venerate and **worship** are usually found in religious contexts (*venerate saints and worship God*) but both words may be used in other contexts as well.

Venerate is usually associated with dignity and advanced age (*venerate the old man who had founded the company more than 50 years ago*), while *worship* connotes an excessive and uncritical respect (*the young girls who waited outside the stage door worshiped the ground he walked on*).

RIDDLE, CONUNDRUM, ENIGMA, MYSTERY, PARADOX, PUZZLE

All of these terms imply something baffling or challenging.

A **mystery** is anything that is incomprehensible to human reason, particularly if it invites speculation (*the mystery surrounding her sudden disappearance*).

An **enigma** is a statement whose meaning is hidden under obscure or ambiguous allusions, so that we can only guess at its significance; it can also refer to a person of puzzling or contradictory character (*he remained an enigma throughout his long career*).

A **riddle** is a mystery involving contradictory statements, with a hidden meaning designed to be guessed at (*the old riddle about how many college graduates it takes to change a light bulb*).

Conundrum applies specifically to a riddle phrased as a question, the answer to which usually involves a pun or a play on words, such as "What is black and white and read all over?"; *conundrum* can also refer to any puzzling or difficult situation.

A **paradox** is a statement that seems self-contradictory or absurd, but in reality expresses a possible truth (*Francis Bacon's well-known paradox, "The most corrected copies are commonly the least correct"*).

A **puzzle** is not necessarily a verbal statement, but it presents a problem with a particularly baffling solution or tests one's ingenuity or skill in coming up with a solution (*a crossword puzzle*).

RUDE, CALLOW, CRUDE, ILL-MANNERED, ROUGH, UNCIVIL, UNCOUTH

Someone who lacks consideration for the feelings of others and who is deliberately insolent is **rude** (*It was rude of you not to introduce me to your friends*).

Ill-mannered suggests that the person is ignorant of the rules of social behavior rather than deliberately rude (*an ill-mannered child*), while **uncivil** implies disregard for even the most basic rules of social behavior among civilized people (*his uncivil response resulted in his being kicked out of the classroom*).

Rough is used to describe people who lack polish and refinement (*he was a rough but honest man*), while **crude** is a more negative term for people and behavior lacking culture, civility, and tact (*he made a crude gesture*).

Uncouth describes what seems strange, awkward, or unmannerly rather than rude (*his uncouth behavior at the wedding*).

Although people of any age may be rude, crude, ill-mannered, or uncouth, **callow** almost always applies to those who are young or immature; it suggests naiveté and lack of sophistication (*he was surprisingly callow for a man of almost 40*).

SAME, EQUAL, EQUIVALENT, IDENTICAL, SELFSAME, TANTAMOUNT

All of these adjectives describe something that is not significantly different from something else.

Same may imply, and **selfsame** always implies, that what is referred to is one thing and not two or more distinct things (*they go to the same restaurant every Friday night; this is the selfsame house in which the family once lived*).

In one sense, **identical** is synonymous with *selfsame* (*the identical place where we first met*); but it can also imply exact correspondence in quality, shape, and appearance (*wearing identical raincoats*).

Equivalent describes things that are interchangeable or that amount to the same thing in value, force, or significance (*the equivalent of a free hotel room at a luxury resort*), while **equal**

implies exact correspondence in quantity, value, or size (*equal portions of food*).

Tantamount is used to describe one of a pair of things, usually intangible, that are in effect equivalent to each other (*her tears were tantamount to a confession of guilt*).

SAYING, ADAGE, APHORISM, APOTHEGM, EPIGRAM, EPIGRAPH, MAXIM, PROVERB

"Once burned, twice shy" is an old **saying** about learning from your mistakes. In fact, *sayings*—a term used to describe any current or habitual expression of wisdom or truth—are a dime a dozen.

Proverbs—sayings that are well known and often repeated, usually expressing metaphorically a truth based on common sense or practical experience—are just as plentiful (*her favorite proverb was "A stitch in time saves nine"*).

An **adage** is a time-honored and widely known proverb, such as "Where's there's smoke, there's fire."

A **maxim** offers a rule of conduct or action in the form of a proverb, such as "Neither a borrower nor a lender be."

Epigram and **epigraph** are often confused, but their meanings are quite separate. An *epigram* is a terse, witty, or satirical statement that often relies on a paradox for its effect (*Oscar Wilde's well-known epigram that "The only way to get rid of temptation is to yield to it"*). An *epigraph*, on the other hand, is a brief quotation used to introduce a piece of writing (*he used a quote from T. S. Eliot as the epigraph to his new novel*).

An **aphorism** requires a little more thought than an *epigram*, since it aims to be profound rather than witty (*as one of Solomon's aphorisms warn, "Better is a living dog than a dead lion"*).

An **apothegm** is a pointed and often startling aphorism, such as Samuel Johnson's remark that "Patriotism is the last refuge of a scoundrel."

SCOLD, BERATE, CHIDE, REVILE, UPBRAID, VITUPERATE

A mother might **scold** a child who misbehaves, which means to rebuke in an angry, irritated, and often nagging way, whether or not such treatment is justified.

Chide is a more formal term than *scold*, and it usually implies disapproval for specific failings (*she was chided by her teacher for using "less" instead of "fewer"*).

Berate suggests a prolonged scolding, usually aimed at a pattern of behavior or way of life rather than a single misdeed and often combined with scorn or contempt for the person being criticized (*he berated his parents for being too protective and ruining his social life*).

Upbraid also implies a lengthy expression of displeasure or criticism, but usually with more justification than *scold* and with an eye toward encouraging better behavior in the future (*the tennis coach upbraided her players for missing so many serves*).

Revile and **vituperate** are reserved for very strong or even violent displays of anger. To *revile* is to use highly abusive and contemptuous language (*revile one's opponent in the press*), while **vituperate** connotes even more violence in the attack (*the angry hockey players were held apart by their teammates, but they continued to vituperate each other with the foulest possible language*).

SECRET, CLANDESTINE, COVERT, FURTIVE, STEALTHY, SURREPTITIOUS, UNDERHANDED

While all of these adjectives describe an attempt to do something without attracting attention or observation, **secret** is the most general term, implying that something is being concealed or kept from the knowledge of others (*a secret pact; a secret passageway*).

Covert suggests that something is being done under cover, or concealed as if with a veil or disguise (*a covert attack; a covert threat*), while **clandestine** suggests that something illicit or immoral is being concealed (*a clandestine meeting between the two lovers*).

Someone who is deliberately sneaking around and trying to do something without attracting notice is best described as **stealthy** (*the cat moved toward the bird with a slow, stealthy pace*), and **furtive** connotes even more slyness and watchfulness, as revealed not only by movements but by facial expressions (*a furtive glance; a furtive movement toward the door*).

Surreptitious connotes guilt on the part of the person who is acting in a stealthy or furtive manner (*a surreptitious attempt to hide the book before it was noticed*).

Underhanded is the strongest of these words, implying fraud, deceit, or unfairness (*underhanded business dealings*).

SENSUOUS, EPICUREAN, LUXURIOUS, SYBARITIC, VOLUPTUOUS

Sensuous implies gratification of the senses for the sake of aesthetic pleasure, or delight in the color, sound, or form of something (*a dress made from a soft, sensuous fabric*).

Luxurious implies indulgence in sensuous pleasures, especially those that induce a feeling of physical comfort or satisfaction (*a luxurious satin coverlet*), while **epicurean** refers to taking delight in the pleasures of eating and drinking (*the epicurean life of a king and his courtiers*).

To be **voluptuous** is to give oneself up to the pleasures of the senses (*the symphony is voluptuous in its scoring*), but it carries a suggestion of physical pleasure and can refer to a curvaceous and sexually attractive woman (*he was seen with a voluptuous blonde*).

Sybaritic implies an overrefined luxuriousness, also suggesting indulgence in good food and drink and the presence of things designed to soothe and charm the senses (*he lived alone, in sybaritic splendor*).

SENTIMENTAL, EFFUSIVE, MAUDLIN, MAWKISH, MUSHY, ROMANTIC

If you are moved to tears by a situation that does not necessarily warrant such a response, you're likely to be called **sentimental**, an adjective used to describe a willingness to get emotional at the slightest prompting (*a sentimental man who kept his dog's ashes in an urn on the mantel*).

Effusive applies to excessive or insincere displays of emotion, although it may be used in an approving sense (*effusive in her gratitude for the help she had received*).

Maudlin derives from the name Mary Magdalene, who was often shown with her eyes swollen from weeping. It implies a lack of self-restraint, particularly in the form of excessive tearfulness.

Mawkish carries sentimentality a step further, implying emotion so excessive that it provokes loathing or disgust (*mawkish attempts to win the audience over*).

Although **romantic** at one time referred to an expression of deep feeling, nowadays it is often used disapprovingly to describe emotion that has little to do with the way things actually are and that is linked to an idealized vision of the way they should be (*she had a romantic notion of what it meant to be a "starving artist"*).

Mushy suggests both excessive emotion or sentimentality and a contempt for romantic love (*a mushy love story*).

SHAKE, QUAKE, QUIVER, SHIVER, SHUDDER, TREMBLE

Does a cool breeze make you shiver, quiver, shudder, or tremble? All of these verbs describe vibrating, wavering, or oscillating movements that, in living creatures, are often involuntary expressions of strain or discomfort.

Shake, which refers to abrupt forward-and-backward, side-to-side, or up-and-down movements, is different from the others in that it can be done to a person or object as well as by one (*shake a can of paint; shake visibly while lifting a heavy load*).

Tremble applies specifically to the slight and rapid shaking motion the human body makes when it is nervous, frightened, or uneasy (*his hands trembled when he picked up the phone*).

To *shiver* is to make a similar movement with the entire body, but the cause is usually a sensation of cold or fear (*shiver in the draft from an open door*).

Quiver suggests a rapid and almost imperceptible vibration resulting from disturbed or irregular surface tension; it refers more often to things (*the leaves quivered in the breeze*), although people may quiver when they're under emotional tension (*her lower lip quivered and her eyes were downcast*).

Shudder suggests a more intense shaking, usually in response to something horrible or revolting (*shudder at the thought of eating uncooked meat*).

Quake implies a violent upheaval or shaking, similar to what occurs during an earthquake (*the boy's heart quaked at his father's approach*).

SIGN, AUGURY, INDICATION, MANIFESTATION, OMEN, SIGNAL, SYMPTOM, TOKEN

What's the difference between a **sign** and a **signal**? The former (in this sense) is a general term for anything that gives evidence of an event, a mood, a quality of character, a mental or physical state, or a trace of something (*a sign of approaching rain; a sign of good breeding; a sign that someone has entered the house*).

While a sign may be involuntary or even unconscious, a *signal* is always voluntary and is usually deliberate. A ship that shows signs of distress may or may not be in trouble; but one that sends a distress *signal* is definitely in need of help.

Indication, like *sign*, is a comprehensive term for anything that serves to indicate or point out (*he gave no indication that he was lying*).

A **manifestation** is an outward or perceptible indication of something (*the letter was a manifestation of his guilt*), and a **symptom** is an indication of a diseased condition (*a symptom of pneumonia*).

An object that proves the existence of something abstract is called a **token** (*she gave him a locket as a token of her love*).

Omen and **augury** both pertain to foretelling future events, with *augury* being the general term for a prediction of the future and *omen* being a definite sign foretelling good or evil (*they regarded the stormy weather as a bad omen*).

SIN, CRIME, FAULT, INDISCRETION, OFFENSE, TRANSGRESSION, VICE

If you've ever driven through a red light or chewed with your mouth open, you've committed an **offense**, which is a broad term covering any violation of the law or of standards of propriety and taste.

A **sin**, on the other hand, is an act that specifically violates a religious, ethical, or moral standard (*to marry someone of another faith was considered a sin*).

Transgression is a weightier and more serious word for *sin*, suggesting any violation of an agreed-upon set of rules (*their behavior was clearly a transgression of the terms set forth in the treaty*).

A crime is any act forbidden by law and punishable upon conviction (*a crime for which he was sentenced to death*).

A vice has less to do with violating the law and more to do with habits and practices that debase a person's character (*alcohol was her only vice*).

Fault and indiscretion are gentler words, although they may be used as euphemisms for *sin* or *crime*.

A *fault* is an unsatisfactory feature in someone's character (*she is exuberant to a fault*), while *indiscretion* refers to an unwise or improper action (*speaking to the media was an indiscretion for which she was chastised*). In recent years, however, *indiscretion* has become a euphemism for such sins as adultery, as if to excuse such behavior by attributing it to a momentary lapse of judgment (*his indiscretions were no secret*).

SMALL, DIMINUTIVE, LITTLE, MINIATURE, MINUTE, PETITE, TINY

Why do we call a house small and a woman petite?

Small and little are used interchangeably to describe people or things of reduced dimensions, but *small* is preferred when describing something concrete that is of less than the usual size, quantity, value, or importance (*a small matter to discuss; a small room; a small price to pay*).

Little more often refers to concepts (*through little fault of his own; an issue of little importance*) or to a more drastic reduction in scale (*a little shopping cart just like the one her mother used*).

Diminutive and *petite* intensify the meaning of *small*, particularly with reference to women's figures that are very trim and compact (*with her diminutive figure, she had to shop in stores that specialized in petite sizes*).

Tiny is used to describe what is extremely small, often to the point where it can be seen only by looking closely (*a tiny flaw in the material; a tiny insect*), while minute not only describes what is seen with difficulty but may also refer to a very small amount of something (*minute traces of gunpowder on his glove*).

Miniature applies specifically to a copy, a model, or a representation of something on a very small scale (*a child's mobile consisting of miniature farm animals*).

SMELL, AROMA, BOUQUET, FRAGRANCE, ODOR, PERFUME, SCENT, STENCH, STINK

Everyone appreciates the **fragrance** of fresh-cut flowers, but the **stench** from the paper mill across town is usually unwelcome.

Both have a distinctive **smell**, which is the most general of these words for what is perceived through the nose, but there is a big difference between a pleasant smell and a foul one.

An **odor** may be either pleasant or unpleasant, but it suggests a smell that is clearly recognizable and can usually be traced to a single source (*the pungent odor of onions*).

An **aroma** is a pleasing and distinctive odor that is usually penetrating or pervasive (*the aroma of fresh-ground coffee*), while **bouquet** refers to a delicate aroma, such as that of a fine wine (*after swirling the wine around in her glass, she sniffed the bouquet*).

A **scent** is usually delicate and pleasing, with an emphasis on the source rather than on an olfactory impression (*the scent of balsam associated with Christmas*).

Fragrance and **perfume** are both associated with flowers, but *fragrance* is more delicate. A *perfume* may be so rich and strong that it is repulsive or overpowering (*the air was so dense with the perfume of lilacs that I had to go indoors*).

Stench and **stink** are reserved for smells that are foul, strong, and pervasive, although *stink* implies a sharper sensation, while *stench* refers to a more sickening one (*the stink of sweaty gym clothes; the stench of a rotting carcass*).

SMILE, GRIN, SIMPER, SMIRK

The facial expression created by turning the corners of the mouth upward is commonly known as a **smile**. It can convey a wide range of emotion, from pleasure, approval, or amusement to insincerity and disinterest (*his complaint was met with a blank smile*).

A **grin** is a wide smile that suggests spontaneous cheerfulness, warmth, pleasure, or amusement (*her teasing provoked an affectionate grin*).

But *grin* may also describe a ferocious baring of the teeth or an angry grimace (*the grin of a skeleton*).

A **simper**, on the other hand, is an expression of smugness and self-righteousness (*her simper of superiority*) as well as a silly or affected smile (*she curtsied with a girlish simper*).

Smirk also implies an affected or self-conscious smile, but one that expresses derision or hostility (*after he tricked them, he smirked and made a fool of himself*).

SPONTANEOUS, IMPROMPTU, IMPROVISED, IMPULSIVE, OFFHAND, UNPREMEDITATED

If you're the kind of person who acts first and thinks about it later, your friends are likely to describe you as **spontaneous**, which means that you behave in a very natural way, without prompting or premeditation (*a spontaneous embrace; a spontaneous burst of applause*).

Or they may call you **impulsive**, which has somewhat less positive connotations, suggesting someone who is governed by his or her own moods and whims without regard for others. Although *impulsive* behavior may be admirable (*his impulsive generosity prompted him to empty his pockets*), it is just as likely to be ugly or disruptive (*impulsive buying; an impulsive temper*).

Offhand also has negative overtones, implying behavior that is spontaneous to the point of being cavalier or brusque (*her offhand remarks offended them*).

Unpremeditated is a more formal term, often used in a legal context to describe an impulsive crime committed without forethought (*unpremeditated murder*).

In the world of public speaking, an **extemporaneous** speech is one that is delivered without referring to a written text, although the speaker may have been aware that he or she would be called upon to speak, while an **impromptu** speech is one that the speaker was not expecting to give.

Improvised is often used in the context of a musical or theatrical performance, suggesting a basic structure within which the performers are free to play in a spontaneous manner (*by its very nature, jazz is improvised*). But it has broader applications as well; in fact, anything that is devised on the spur of the moment may be described as *improvised*.

STUBBORN, DOGGED, INTRACTABLE, OBDURATE, OBSTINATE, PERTINACIOUS

If you're the kind of person who takes a stand and then refuses to back down, your friends might say you have a **stubborn** disposition, a word that implies an innate resistance to any attempt to change one's purpose, course, or opinion.

People who are stubborn by nature exhibit this kind of behavior in most situations, but they might be obstinate in a particular instance (*a stubborn child, he was obstinate in his refusal to eat vegetables*). *Obstinate* implies sticking persistently to an opinion, purpose, or course of action, especially in the face of persuasion or attack.

While *obstinate* is usually a negative term, **dogged** can be either positive or negative, implying both tenacious, often sullen, persistence (*dogged pursuit of a college degree, even though he knew he would end up in the family business*) and great determination (*dogged loyalty to a cause*).

Obdurate usually connotes a stubborn resistance marked by harshness and lack of feeling (*obdurate in ignoring their pleas*), while **intractable** means stubborn in a headstrong sense and difficult for others to control or manage (*intractable pain*).

No matter how stubborn you are, you probably don't want to be called **pertinacious**, which implies persistence to the point of being annoying or unreasonable (*a pertinacious panhandler*).

STUPID, ASININE, DENSE, DULL, DUMB, OBTUSE, SLOW, UNINTELLIGENT

If you want to impugn someone's intelligence, the options are almost limitless.

You can call the person **stupid**, a term that implies a sluggish, slow-witted lack of intelligence.

Asinine is a harsher word, implying asslike or foolish behavior rather than slow-wittedness (*a woman her age looked asinine in a miniskirt*).

Calling someone **dumb** is risky, because it is not only an informal word (*you dumb bunny!*), but because it also means mute and is associated with the offensive expression "deaf and dumb," used to describe people who cannot hear or speak.

Dense implies an inability to understand even simple facts or instructions (*too dense to get the joke*), while **dull** suggests a sluggishness of mind unrelieved by any hint of quickness, brightness, or liveliness (*a dull stare*).

Slow also implies a lack of quickness in comprehension or reaction and is often used as a euphemistic substitute for *stupid* (*he was a little slow intellectually*).

Obtuse is a more formal word for slow-wittedness, but with a strong undercurrent of scorn (*it almost seemed as though he were being deliberately obtuse*).

You can't go wrong with a word like **unintelligent**, which is probably the most objective term for low mental ability and the least likely to provoke an angry response (*unintelligent answers to the teacher's questions*).

SUPERFICIAL, CURSORY, HASTY, SHALLOW, SLAPDASH

No one wants to be accused of being **superficial** or **shallow**, two adjectives that literally indicate a lack of depth (*a superficial wound; a shallow grave*).

Superficial suggests too much concern with the surface or obvious aspects of something, and it is considered a derogatory term because it connotes a personality that is not genuine or sincere.

Shallow is even more derogatory because it implies not only a refusal to explore something deeply but an inability to feel, sympathize, or understand. It is unlikely that a *shallow* person, in other words, will ever have more than superficial relationships with his or her peers.

Cursory, which may or may not be a derogatory term, suggests a lack of thoroughness or attention to detail (*a cursory glance at the newspaper*), while hasty emphasizes a refusal or inability to spend the necessary time on something (*a hasty review of the facts*).

If you are slapdash in your approach, it means that you are both careless and hasty (*a slapdash job of cleaning up*).

TANGIBLE, APPRECIABLE, CORPOREAL, PALPABLE, PERCEPTIBLE, SENSIBLE

Anything that can be grasped, either with the hand or with the mind, is tangible (*tangible assets; tangible objects*).

Palpable, like *tangible*, means capable of being touched or felt (*a palpable mist*), but it is often applied to whatever evokes a tactile response from the body (*a palpable chill in the room*).

Perceptible is used to describe something that just crosses the border between invisibility and visibility or some other sense barrier (*a perceptible change in her tone of voice; a perceptible odor of garlic*).

Sensible (in this sense) describes that which can clearly be perceived through the senses or which makes a strong impression on the mind through the medium of sensations. In contrast to *perceptible*, something that is *sensible* is more obvious or immediately recognized (*a sensible shift in the tenor of the conversation*).

Corporeal means bodily or material, in contrast to things that are immaterial or spiritual (*corporeal goods*).

Something that is appreciable is large enough to be measured, valued, estimated, or considered significant.

An *appreciable* change in temperature, for example, can be determined by looking at a thermometer; a *palpable* change in temperature may be slight, but still great enough to be felt; and a *perceptible* change in temperature might be so slight that it almost—but not quite—escapes notice.

TEMERITY, AUDACITY, EFFRONTERY, FOOLHARDINESS, GALL, IMPETUOSITY, RASHNESS

The line that divides boldness from foolishness or stupidity is often a fine one.

Someone who rushes hastily into a situation without thinking about the consequences might be accused of **rashness**, while **temerity** implies exposing oneself needlessly to danger while failing to estimate one's chances of success (*she had the temerity to criticize her teacher in front of the class*).

Audacity describes a different kind of boldness, one that disregards moral standards or social conventions (*he had the audacity to ask her if she would mind paying for the trip*).

Someone who behaves with **foolhardiness** is reckless or downright foolish (*climbing the mountain after dark was foolhardiness and everyone knew it*), while **impetuosity** describes an eager impulsiveness or behavior that is sudden, rash, and sometimes violent (*his impetuosity had landed him in trouble before*).

Gall and **effrontery** are always derogatory terms. *Effrontery* is a more formal word for the flagrant disregard of the rules of propriety and courtesy (*she had the effrontery to call the president by his first name*), while *gall* is more colloquial and suggests outright insolence (*he was the only one with enough gall to tell the boss off*).

TEMPT, ALLURE, BEGUILE, ENTICE, INVEIGLE, LURE, SEDUCE

When we are under the influence of a powerful attraction, particularly to something that is wrong or unwise, we are **tempted**.

Entice implies that a crafty or skillful person has attracted us by offering a reward or pleasure (*she was enticed into joining the group by a personal plea from its handsome leader*), while **inveigle** suggests that we are enticed through the use of deception or cajolery (*inveigled into supporting the plan*).

If someone **lures** us, it suggests that we have been tempted or influenced for fraudulent or destructive purposes or attracted to something harmful or evil (*lured by gang members*).

Allure may also suggest that we have been deliberately tempted against our will, but the connotations here are often sexual (*allured by her dark green eyes*).

Seduce carries heavy sexual connotations (*seduced by an older woman*), although it can simply mean prompted to action against our will (*seduced by a clever sales pitch*).

While **beguile** at one time referred exclusively to the use of deception to lead someone astray, nowadays it can also refer to the use of subtle devices to engage someone's attention (*a local festival designed to beguile the tourists*).

THIN, GAUNT, LEAN, SKINNY, SLENDER, SPARE, SVELTE

Like a strict dieter's menu, all of these adjectives are nonfat, but that's not to say that they necessarily describe a healthy ideal.

Thin describes someone whose healthy weight is naturally low in proportion to his or her height, although it may also imply that the person is underweight (*she looked pale and thin after her operation*). **Skinny** is a more blunt and derogatory term for someone who is too thin, and it often implies underdevelopment (*a skinny little boy; a tall, skinny fashion model*).

Most people would rather be called **slender**, which combines thinness with gracefulness and good proportions (*the slender legs of a Queen Anne table*), or better yet, **svelte**, a complimentary term that implies a slim, elegant figure (*after six months of dieting, she looked so svelte I hardly recognized her*).

Lean and **spare** are used to describe people who are naturally thin, although *spare* suggests a more muscular leanness (*a tall, spare man who looked like Abraham Lincoln*).

Gaunt, on the other hand, means so thin that the angularity of the bones can be seen beneath the skin (*looking gaunt after her latest bout with cancer*).

THWART, BAFFLE, BALK, FOIL, FRUSTRATE, INHIBIT

These verbs refer to the various ways in which we can outwit or overcome opposing forces.

Thwart suggests using cleverness rather than force to bring about the defeat of an enemy or to block progress toward an objective (*thwart a rebellion; have one's goals thwarted by lack of education*).

Balk also emphasizes setting up barriers (*a sudden reversal that balked their hopes for a speedy resolution*), but it is used more often as an intransitive verb meaning to stop at an obstacle and refuse to proceed (*he balked at appearing in front of the angry crowd*).

To **baffle** is to cause defeat by bewildering or confusing (*the police were baffled by the lack of evidence*), while **foil** means to throw off course so as to discourage further effort (*her plan to arrive early was foiled by heavy traffic*).

Frustrate implies rendering all attempts or efforts useless (*frustrated by the increasingly bad weather, they decided to work indoors*), while **inhibit** suggests forcing something into inaction (*to inhibit wage increases by raising corporate taxes*).

Both *frustrate* and *inhibit* are used in a psychological context to suggest barriers that impede normal development or prevent the realization of natural desires (*he was both frustrated by her refusal to acknowledge his presence and inhibited by his own shyness*).

TIRED, EXHAUSTED, FATIGUED, TUCKERED, WEARY

Tired is what you are after you've cleaned the house, spent two hours reading a dull report, or trained for a marathon; it means that your strength and energy are diminished, without giving any indication of degree.

Weary, on the other hand, is how you feel after you've had to interrupt your dinner five or six times to answer the phone. It implies not only a depletion of energy but also the vexation that accompanies having to put up with something that is, or has become, disagreeable.

Exhausted means that you are totally drained of strength and energy, a condition that may even be irreversible (*exhausted by battling a terminal disease*).

Fatigued is a more precise word than either *tired* or *weary*; it implies a loss of energy through strain, illness, or overwork to the point where rest or sleep is essential (*fatigued after working a 24-hour shift*).

Tuckered is an informal word that comes close in meaning to *fatigued* or *exhausted*, but often carries the suggestion of loss of breath (*tuckered out after running up six flights of stairs*).

TOOL, APPARATUS, APPLIANCE, IMPLEMENT, INSTRUMENT, UTENSIL

A wrench is a **tool**, meaning that it is a device held in and manipulated by the hand and used by a mechanic, plumber, carpenter, or other laborer to work, shape, move, or transform material (*he couldn't fix the drawer without the right tools*).

An **implement** is a broader term referring to any tool or mechanical device used for a particular purpose (*agricultural implements*).

A washing machine is an **appliance**, which refers to a mechanical or power-driven device, especially for household use (*the newlyweds went shopping for appliances*).

A utensil is a hand-held implement for domestic use (*eating utensils*), while an **instrument** is used for scientific or artistic purposes (*musical instrument; surgical instrument*).

Apparatus refers to a collection of distinct instruments, tools, or other devices that are used in connection or combination with one another for a certain purpose (*the gym was open, but the exercise apparatus had not been set up*).

UNCERTAINTY, DOUBT, DUBIETY, SKEPTICISM

If you're not sure about something, you're probably experiencing a degree of **uncertainty**, which is a general term covering everything from a mere lack of absolute certainty (*uncertainty about the time of the dinner party*) to an almost complete lack of knowledge that makes it impossible to do more than guess at the result or outcome (*uncertainty about the country's future*).

Doubt implies both uncertainty and an inability to make a decision because the evidence is insufficient (*considerable doubt as to her innocence*).

Dubiety comes closer in meaning to *uncertainty* than to *doubt*, because it stresses a lack of sureness rather than an inability to reach a decision; but unlike *uncertainty*, it connotes wavering or fluctuating between one conclusion and another (*no one could fail to notice the dubiety in his voice*).

If you exhibit **skepticism**, you are not so much uncertain as unwilling to believe. It usually refers to a habitual state of mind or to a customary reaction (*she always listened to his excuses with skepticism*).

UNIVERSAL, CATHOLIC, COMMON, ECUMENICAL, GENERAL, GENERIC

Something that is **universal** applies to every case or individual in a class or category (*a universal practice among aboriginal tribesmen; a universal truth*).

General, on the other hand, is less precise; it implies applicability to all or most of a group or class, whether the members of that group are clearly defined or only casually associated (*a drug that has come into general use among women but has not yet won the universal acceptance of doctors*).

Generic is often used in place of *general* when referring to every member of a genus or clearly defined scientific category (*a generic characteristic of insects*); with reference to language, it means referring to both men and women (*a generic pronoun*).

Common implies participation or sharing by all members of a class (*a common interest in French culture*) or frequently occurring (*a common complaint*).

Catholic implies a wide-ranging or inclusive attitude (*known for his catholic tastes in music*), while **ecumenical** means pertaining to the whole Christian church or promoting unity among religious groups or divisions (*an ecumenical marriage ceremony*).

URBANE, COSMOPOLITAN, GENTEEL, SOPHISTICATED, SUAVE

In his long career as a film star, Cary Grant was known for playing urbane, sophisticated roles. *Urbane* in this context suggests the social poise and polished manner of someone who is well-traveled and well-bred, while *sophisticated* means worldly-wise as opposed to naive (*a sophisticated young girl who had spent her childhood in Paris and London*).

Cosmopolitan describes someone who is at home anywhere in the world and is free from provincial attitudes (*a cosmopolitan man who could charm women of all ages and nationalities*), while **suave** suggests the gracious social behavior of *urbane* combined with a certain glibness or superficial politeness (*she was taken in by his expensive clothes and suave manner*).

At one time **genteel** meant well-bred or refined, but nowadays it has connotations of self-consciousness or pretentiousness (*too genteel to drink wine from a juice glass*).

VIGILANT, ALERT, CAREFUL, CAUTIOUS, CIRCUMSPECT, WARY, WATCHFUL

All of these adjectives connote being on the lookout for danger or opportunity.

Watchful is the most general term, meaning closely observant (*a watchful young man who noticed everything*).

If you're **vigilant**, you are watchful for a purpose (*to be vigilant in the presence of one's enemies*), and **wary** suggests being on the lookout for treachery or trickery (*wary of his neighbor's motives in offering to move the fence*).

If you're **alert**, you are quick to apprehend a danger, an opportunity, or an emergency (*she was much more alert after a good night's sleep*), and if you're **careful**, you may be able to avoid danger or error altogether.

Cautious and **circumspect** also emphasize the avoidance of danger or unpleasant situations. To be *circumspect* is to be watchful in all directions and with regard to all possible consequences (*these journalists have to be circumspect, not criticizing anyone too harshly*); to be *cautious* is to guard against contingencies (*a cautious approach to treating illness*).

VINDICTIVE, RANCOROUS, SPITEFUL, VENGEFUL, VENOMOUS

Someone who is motivated by a desire to get even might be described as **vindictive**, a word that suggests harboring grudges for perceived wrongs (*a vindictive person who had alienated friends and neighbors alike*).

Spiteful is a stronger term, implying a bitter or vicious vindictiveness (*a spiteful child who broke the toy she had been forced to share*).

Vengeful implies a strong urge to actually seek vengeance (*vengeful after losing her husband in a hit-and-run accident*).

Someone who is **rancorous** suffers from a deep-seated and lasting bitterness, although it does not imply a desire to hurt or to be vindictive (*his rancorous nature made him difficult to befriend*).

Venomous takes its meaning from "venom," referring to someone or something of a spiteful, malignant nature and suggesting a poisonous sting (*a critic's venomous attack on the author's first novel*).

VOID, ABROGATE, ANNUL, INVALIDATE, NEGATE, NULLIFY

To **void** a check, to **invalidate** a claim, to **abrogate** a law, and to **annul** a marriage all refer to the same basic activity, which is putting an end to something or depriving it of validity, force, or authority. But these verbs are not always interchangeable.

Annul is the most general term, meaning to end something that exists or to declare that it never really existed (*the charter was annulled before it could be challenged*).

Abrogate implies the exercise of legal authority (*Congress abrogated the treaty between the two warring factions*), while **nullify** means to deprive something of its value or effectiveness (*nullify the enemy's attempt to establish communications*).

Void and *invalidate* are often used interchangeably as they both mean to make null or worthless (*void a legal document by tearing it up; invalidate a check by putting the wrong date on it*).

Negate means to prove an assertion false (*her version of the story negated everything her brother had said*) or to nullify or make something ineffective (*the study's findings were negated by its author's arrest for fraud*).

WEALTHY, AFFLUENT, FLUSH, OPULENT, PROSPEROUS, RICH, WELL-TO-DO

If you have an abundance of money, you are **rich**.

Another term for *rich* is **wealthy**, which may further imply that you are an established and prominent member of the community whose lifestyle is in keeping with your income (*a wealthy family whose influence on public opinion could not be ignored*).

Affluent comes from a Latin word meaning to flow, and it connotes a generous income (*an affluent neighborhood*), while **opulent** suggests lavish spending or an ostentatious display of wealth (*an opulent mansion with every imaginable luxury*). One may come from an *affluent* family, in other words, and not have a particularly *opulent* lifestyle.

If you're **prosperous**, you are thriving or flourishing (*a prosperous merchant; a prosperous business*).

While *prosperous* suggests an economic situation that is on the rise, **flush** means having plenty of money on hand at a particular time (*she was feeling flush after receiving her first paycheck*).

Well-to-do implies prosperity, enough to support more-than-comfortable living but not necessarily enough to be considered among the world's richest (*they were known as a well-to-do family with a strong commitment to educating their children*).

WIT, HUMOR, IRONY, REPARTEE, SARCASM, SATIRE

If you're good at perceiving analogies between dissimilar things and expressing them in quick, sharp, spontaneous observations or remarks, you have **wit**.

Humor, on the other hand, is the ability to perceive what is comical, ridiculous, or ludicrous in a situation or character, and to express it in a way that makes others see or feel the same thing. It suggests more sympathy, tolerance, and kindliness than *wit* (*she maintained a sense of humor in the midst of trying circumstances*).

Irony is the implicit humor in the contradiction between what is meant and what is expressed, or in the discrepancy between appearance and reality. An example would be to shout, in the midst of a hurricane, "What a perfect day for a wedding!"

Although **sarcasm** may take the form of irony, it is less subtle and is often used harshly or bitterly to wound or ridicule someone. Unlike irony, however, *sarcasm* depends on tone of voice for its effect (*"a fine friend you turned out to be!" he said, with obvious sarcasm*).

Satire usually implies the use of sarcasm or irony for the purpose of ridicule or criticism, often directed at institutions or political figures (*she wrote political satire for the comedy team*).

If you are good at making quick, witty replies, you will be known for your **repartee**, which is the art of responding pointedly and skillfully with wit or humor in a conversational exchange (*no one could compete with her witty repartee*).

YOUTHFUL, ADOLESCENT, CALLOW, IMMATURE, JUVENILE, PUERILE

Everyone wants to look **youthful**, an adjective that means possessing, or appearing to possess, the qualities associated with youth (*she is remarkably more youthful than her twin*).

But no one wants to be called **immature**, which means childish or emotionally underdeveloped and usually pertains to behavior and attitudes rather than to physical appearance (*still immature despite the fact that he was almost thirty*).

Juvenile suggests immaturity of mind or body and is applied especially to things that are designed for boys and girls in their early teens (*juvenile books*), while **adolescent** applies to the period between puberty and maturity and suggests the physical awkwardness and emotional instability associated with the teenage years (*an adolescent response to criticism*).

Young men in particular are often described as **callow**, which means immature in terms of experience (*a callow youth who had never lived away from his family*).

Of all these words, **puerile** is probably the most insulting, because it is so often used to describe adults who display the immature behavior of a child (*a puerile piece of writing; a puerile revolt against his aging parents*).

ZEALOT, BIGOT, ENTHUSIAST, EXTREMIST, FANATIC

An **enthusiast** displays an intense and eager interest in something (*a sky-diving enthusiast*).

A **fanatic** is not only intense and eager but possibly irrational in his or her enthusiasm; *fanatic* suggests extreme devotion and a willingness to go to any length to maintain or carry out one's beliefs (*a fly-fishing fanatic who hired a helicopter to reach his favorite stream*).

A **zealot** exhibits not only extreme devotion but vehement activity in support of a cause or goal (*a feminist zealot who spent most of her time campaigning for women's rights*).

An **extremist** is a supporter of extreme doctrines or practices, particularly in a political context (*a paramilitary extremist who anticipated the overthrow of the government*).

But it is the **bigot** who causes the most trouble, exhibiting obstinate and often blind devotion to his or her beliefs and opinions. In contrast to *fanatic* and *zealot*, the term *bigot* implies intolerance and contempt for those who do not agree (*a bigot who could not accept his daughter's decision to marry outside her religion*).

CHAPTER 6

Proofreader's Marks and What They Mean

INTRODUCTION

In the course of your career as a writer, you will inevitably get back some page proofs from a copy editor and/or proofreader. With any luck, these will be for the novel you have just sold to a publisher for an obscenely large advance. Then it will be a most happy occasion. Of course, you will want to be able to understand what the proofreader and/or copy editor is telling you. They do not mark manuscripts in the same way as your high school or college English teacher did. Proofreaders and copy editors have their own language, and while it looks a lot like shorthand sometimes, it's actually a quite old and honored form of communication. The good thing about it is that it's standardized. You don't—unlike style citation—have to know three or four different ways of expressing the same thing.

And let's not forget freelancing. Knowing what these marks mean and how to use them might get you a gig or two with a publishing house when you really could use one.

Proofreader's Marks

℘	delete	❝ ❞	quotation marks
ℰ	delete and close up	{ }	parentheses
℘#	delete and leave space	[ ]	square brackets
∧	insert	=	hyphen
#	space	1/M	em-dash
⊙	period	1/N	en-dash
⌃	comma	¶	new paragraph
⌃;	semicolon	dictionary	break line or word
:⌄ or ⊙	colon	⌃	set as superscript
⌄	apostrophe	⌄	set as subscript

diction**ary**	transpose
(tr)	transpose (note in margin)
(3)	spell out
(SP)	spell out (note in margin)
d̲i̲c̲t̲i̲o̲n̲a̲r̲y̲	capitalize
(cap)	set as capitals (note in margin)
Ðictionary	make lower case
(lc)	set in lower case (note in margin)
dictionary	make boldface
(bf)	set in boldface (note in margin)
dictionary	make italic
(ital)	set in italic (note in margin)
dictionary	small caps
(sc)	set in small caps (note in margin)
(lf)	lightface (note in margin)
(rom)	set in roman (note in margin)

CHAPTER 7

Common Citation Styles

INTRODUCTION

Why, you ask, are there so many different methods of citation? Why this Babel of ways of doing the same thing? Why can't they all get together and settle it, simplify it, make it easy on the writer and, really, on the proofreader, too? It's worse than having different electrical currents in Europe and America. *These* differences of citation all occur in the same country and in the same environment—yours. I have no sane answer as to why there exists an MLA, a Chicago Manual of Style, and an AP style (not to be confused with the APA style) of citation. The answer, of course, is turf. Because there is, in the end, absolutely no reason why MLA style and Chicago style should coexist and be used. It's as if half the country used the metric system and half didn't. But so far there has been no Bernard Shaw–like effort to standardize citation style. Books have been written about each method, are regularly updated, and sell consistently. *The Chicago Manual of Style* is in its 15th edition. *The MLA Handbook* is in its 6th. When you consider all the colleges and universities—not to mention the newspapers, journals, and magazine and book publishers—that purchase these guides, well, it becomes more than just a standardization issue. In the meantime, all we can do is show you the differences between the two main rivals.

Note: Always check the publisher you are submitting to for what citation system they employ before you do any of this cumbersome stuff.

For all intents and purposes, this is a duel between the *Chicago Manual of Style* and the *MLA Handbook*. (Both these books cover many more issues than just how to cite written, spoken, and electronic matter, especially in the case of the *Chicago Manual of Style*.) So, here we go.

MLA style

All the information about citation in the 6th and latest edition of the *MLA Handbook* is in Chapter 5. When in doubt, head there.

To cite a book by a single author, first put the author's name, last name first; then title of the book, underlined, followed by publication information. Example (always theirs, along with proper formatting):

> Fukuyama, Francis. <u>Our Posthuman Future: Consequences of the Biotechnology Revolution</u>. New York: Farrar, 2002.

Notice one of the omnipresent subtleties? The underline does *not* include the period after the title. Can this sort of thing drive you crazy? Of course. Is there a logic to it? Somewhere, perhaps. How do you deal with it? Deal with it.

To cite an anthology, begin with the editor:

> Lopate, Philip, ed. <u>The Art of the Personal Essay: An Anthology from the Classical Era to the Present</u>. New York: Anchor-Doubleday, 1994.

To cite two or more books by the same author:

> Frye, Northrop. <u>Anatomy of Criticism: Four Essays</u>. Princeton: Princeton UP, 1957.
>
> ———. <u>The Double Vision: Language and Meaning in Religion</u>. Toronto: U of Toronto P, 1991.

To cite a book by two or more authors, give their names in the same order as they appear on the title page, even if they are not in alphabetical order. Reverse only the name of the first author:

Eggins, Suzanne, and Diana Slade. <u>Analysing Casual Conversation</u>. London: Cassell, 1997.

If there are more than three authors, you can simply put "et al" after the first author.

Citing a book by a corporate author:

American Medical Association. <u>The American Medical Association Encyclopedia of Medicine</u>. Ed. Charles B. Clayman. New York: Random, 1989.

Citing a work in an anthology. Here, you want to make sure to put the page numbers at the end:

More, Hannah. "The Black Slave Trade: A Poem." <u>British Women Poets of the Romantic Era</u>. Ed. Paula R. Feldman. Baltimore: Johns Hopkins UP, 1997. 472–82.

To cite an introduction or preface. Notice that Introduction is not surrounded by quotation marks or in italics:

Hamill, Pete. Introduction. <u>The Brooklyn Reader: Thirty Writers Celebrate America's Favorite Borough</u>. Ed. Andrea Wyatt Sexton and Alice Leccese Powers. New York: Harmony, 1994. xi–xiv.

Citing a government publication:

United States Dept. of Labor. <u>Child Care: A Workforce Issue</u>. Washington: GPO, 1988.

Citing an article in a scholarly publication. This is much the same as the citation for a book, except that your information is of a slightly different kind—date and volume number—and you also must give page numbers:

Trumpener, Katie. "Memories Carved in Granite: Great War Memorials and Everyday Life." <u>PMLA</u> 115 (2000): 1096–103.

How to cite an article in a newspaper. Note: Do not put in the beginning article, as in "The" <u>Wall Street Journal</u>. Letters serve to represent sections of the paper:

Jeromack, Paul. "This Once, a David of the Art World Does Goliath a Favor." <u>New York Times</u> 13 July 2002, late ed.: B7+.

How to cite an article in a magazine:

> Mehta, Pratap Bhanu. "Exploding Myths." <u>New Republic</u> 6
> June 1998: 17–19.

How to cite a television or radio program. Notice where you can abbreviate, where you need periods, and where you do not need commas:

> "<u>Frankenstein</u>: The Making of the Monster." <u>Great Books</u>.
> Narr. Donald Sutherland. Writ. Eugenie Vink. Dir. Jonathan
> Ward. Learning Channel. 8 Sept. 1993.

How to cite an interview:

> Breslin, Jimmy. Interview with Neal Conan. <u>Talk of the Nation</u>.
> Natl. Public Radio. WBUR, Boston. 26 Mar. 2002.

Citing electronic publications. By now, this may be familiar to many of you. In the formal citation of electronic resources, you have to be practical. It's not really safe to cite an enormously long URL, and they certainly exist, just because the chance for error and getting lost is high, even with copying and pasting. In that case, simply put in the main address of the site. Then you might want to give the path. Notice that the two dates represent the date on the document and the date of access. The date of access is important because, as we all know, some sites can change daily, if not hourly. Again, see the *MLA* for expanded explanations and directions about citing electronic materials.

> "This Day in Technology History: August 20." <u>History
> Channel.com</u>. 2002. History Channel. 14 May 2002
> http://historychannel.com/. Path: Technology History; This
> Day in Technology History.

Citing an online book:

> Austen, Jane. <u>Pride and Prejudice</u>. Ed. Henry Churchyard.
> 1996. <u>Jane Austen Information Page</u>. 6 September. 2002
> <http://www.pemberley.com/janeinfo/ Prideprej.html>.

Notice that you are required to put in the "http://" or "http://www."

Citing a CD-ROM:

> <u>Encyclopedia of Islam</u>. CD-ROM. Leiden: Brill, 1999.

Now, let's look at the same issues from The **Chicago Manual of Style**'s point of view. All of this information is in Chapter 16 and Chapter 17 of the 15th Edition. The *CMS* is by far the more complex and difficult text to follow. It is somewhat stodgy, probably the result of strict old-school copy editors and the weight they feel as Designated Authorities. Nowhere is this more clearly displayed than in the fact that they present not one, but *two* complete systems of citation. The first is called the "notes and bibliography" system, and the second is the "author-date" system. The first is "the system favored by many writers in literature, history, and the arts." Here, "bibliographic citations are provided in notes . . . preferably supplemented by a bibliography."

In other words, if you have ever used the *CMS* system, this is the one you probably worked with. The "author-date" system is one that has been traditionally used by scientists.

This cumbersomeness is enhanced by the *CMS*'s presentation of the systems in four formats. They even had to give them initials so you can keep track.

Here's how to cite materials using the **Notes and Bibliography** system, using (*CMS*) bibliographic examples.

To cite a book by a single author:

Davies, Paul. *The Fifth Miracle: The Search for the Origin of Life*. New York: Simon & Schuster, 1999.

To cite two or more books by the same author. Notice the line length difference between this and *MLA* to indicate the author's name:

Beck, Lewis White. *A Commentary on Kant's* Critique of Practical Reason. Chicago: University of Chicago Press, 1960.

———. *Early German Philosophy*. Cambridge: Harvard University Press, Belknap Press, 1969.

To cite a book by two or more authors:

Harnack, Andrew, and Eugene Kleppinger. *Online! A Reference Guide to Using Internet Sources*. 3rd ed. New York: St. Martin's Press, 2000.

Citing a book by a corporate author:

University of Chicago Press. *The Chicago Manual of Style.* 15th ed. Chicago: University of Chicago Press, 2003.

Citing a work in an anthology. Compare placement of page numbers and abbreviations with *MLA* style:

Anscombe, G.E.M. "Thought and Action in Aristotle." In *New Essays on Plato and Aristotle*, edited by Renford Bambrough, 143–58. London: Routledge and Kegan Paul, 1965.

To cite an introduction or preface:

Harris, Mark. Introduction to *With the Procession*, by Henry B. Fuller. Chicago: University of Chicago Press, 1986.

Citing a government publication. Here, it's essential you check *CMS* itself for elaboration, because they have many subcategories:

Congressional Record. 71st Cong., 2d sess., 1930. Vol. 72, pt. 10.

Citing an article in a scholarly publication:

McMillen, Sally G. "Antebellum Southern Fathers and the Health Care of Children." *Journal of Southern History* 60, no. 3 (1994): 513–32.

How to cite an article in a newspaper. *CMS* prefers to list references to newspapers in the bibliography rarely. This information should be contained in a footnote or endnote.

How to cite an article in a magazine:

Lacey, Stephen. "The New German Style." *Horticulture*, March 2000, 44.

How to cite an interview:

Singer, Isaac Bashevis. Interview by Harold Flender. In *Writers at Work: The "Paris Review" Interviews*, edited by George Plimpton. 5th ser., 81–92. New York: Viking Press, 1981.

Citing electronic publications. Here's an example using multimedia. They ask that you include the type of medium. "Not only is such information more relevant by definition when it is a question of "multi*media*," they say, "but, given the wide variety of medium types, such information will give some indication of what software or hardware may be needed to gain access to the source." Also notice how they spell out the accession information:

Weed, A. E. *At the Foot of the Flatiron.* American Mutoscope and Biograph Co., 1903; 2 min., 19 sec; 35 mm. From Library of Congress, *The Life of a City: Early Films of New York, 1898–1906.* MPEG, http://lcweb2.loc.gov/ammem/Papr/nychome.html (accessed August 14, 2001).

Citing an online magazine:

Reaves, Jessica. "A Weighty Issue: Ever-Fatter Kids." Interview with James Rosen. Time, March 14, 2001. http://www.time.com/time/nation/article 0,8599,102443,00.html.

Citing a CD-ROM:

Complete National Geographic: 110 Years of National Geographic Magazine. CD-ROM. Mindscape, 2000.

Some examples from the **Author-Date** system:

To cite a book by a single author. You'll notice right away the advantages of this system. It immediately signals the pertinent information. Notice the italics for the title versus the underlining in *MLA.* Indentations are different, too:

Blinksworth, Roger. 1987. *Converging on the evanescent.* San Francisco: Threshold Publications.

To cite an anthology or book with an editor:

Collins, Geoffry, and Matthew Q. Wortmaster, eds. 1953. *The collected works of G. Farthington Pennyloss.* Boston: G. F. Pennyloss.

To cite two or more books by the same author:

Allen, G. M. 1939. *Bats.* Cambridge: Harvard University Press.

———. 1925. *Birds and their attributes.* Boston: Marshall Jones.

To cite a book by two or more authors:

Myerson, Martin, and Edward C. Banfield. 1955. *Politics, planning and the public interest: The case of public housing in Chicago.* Glencoe, IL: Free Press.

Citing a book by a corporate author:

International Monetary Fund (IMF). 1977. *Surveys of African economies.* Vol. 7, *Algeria, Mali, Morocco, and Tunisia.* Washington, D.C.: International Monetary Fund.

To cite an introduction or preface:

Zimring, Franklin E. 1989. Foreward to *Drunk driving: An American dilemma,* by James B. Jacobs. Chicago: University of Chicago Press.

Citing an article in a scholarly publication. Notice the lack of quotation marks around the article title:

Bennett, John W. 1946. The interpretation of Pueblo culture: A question of values. *Southwestern Journal of Anthropology* 2: 361-74.

How to cite an article in a newspaper:

Finnonian, Albert. 1990. The Iron Curtain rises. *Wilberton Journal,* 7 February, final edition.

How to cite an article in a magazine. This method has its appeal in terms of being streamlined:

Karen, Robert. 1990. Becoming attached. *Atlantic,* February 35-70.

How to cite an interview. Notice the very small differences between this and the Notes and Bibliography system for the same entry.

Singer, Isaac Bashevis. 1981. Interview by Harold Flender. In *Writers at work: The "Paris Review" interviews,* edited by George Plimpton. 5th ser., 81-92. New York: Viking Press.

CHAPTER 8

A List of Clichés to Avoid

INTRODUCTION

Khaled Hosseini, in his wonderful novel, *The Kite Runner,* writes, "A creative writing teacher at San Jose State used to say about clichés: 'Avoid them like the plague.' Then he'd laugh at his own joke. The class laughed along with him, but I always thought clichés got a bum rap. Because, often, they're dead-on. But the aptness of the clichéd saying is overshadowed by the nature of the saying as a cliché."

It's true that one of the more singularly arresting moments in life is experiencing a cliché come to life before your eyes—back from the dead, as it were. When, for example, you're trying to get over a love affair gone wrong, someone may mutter, "Time heals all wounds," and lo and behold, in a few months you find it *does*. What a remarkable saying!

Well, the fact is that clichés are truth, but a truth that has been squeezed bone dry. It's not that these little aphorisms weren't creative or startling when they were first spoken or written. It's just that now, many thousands of utterances later, such an expression has lost its power to surprise, delight, or inform. The words are numb. Of course, clichés appear in good writing, but they are normally reserved for dialogue, where they are used to illustrate the personality of a character. There *are* people who speak in clichés. We use them, too, probably far more often than we imagine.

Nevertheless, to consciously choose a cliché to express an emotion or state in writing that strives to be good is generally not a good idea. You don't serve stale bread at a dinner party, so why serve stale words to your readers? Find something fresher. Here's a list of clichés it would be prudent to avoid.

CLICHÉS TO AVOID

Achilles heel
acid test
to go against the grain
to be all ears
all hell breaks/broke loose
for all intents and purposes
all time high/low
the American dream
and then some
A-OK
the apple of one's eye
armed to the teeth
as luck would have it
as the crow flies
at a snail's pace
to be at loggerheads
at one's beck and call
at the crossroads
at the drop of a hat
an ax to grind
back to the salt mines
one's back to the wall
baldfaced lie
ballpark figure
bane of one's existence
basket case
beat a dead horse
beat around the bush
off the beaten track
beg, borrow, or steal
believe (with) one's own eyes
to go belly up

below the belt
beside oneself
best/worst case scenario
best/greatest thing since sliced
    bread
be that as it may
between a rock and a hard place
big fish in a little pond
big picture
birds of a feather
bite off more than one can chew
bite the bullet
black sheep
blessed event
blind as a bat
blithering idiot
blow your stack
blow the whistle on someone
blow to smithereens
boil down to
bone dry
bone of contention
boon companion
bore to tears
bottom line
boys will be boys
get down to brass tacks
breath of fresh air
bright and early
win brownie points
burning desire
burn the midnight oil

bury one's head in the sand
business as usual
busy as a bee
open a can of worms
can't hit the broad side of a barn
can't hold a candle to
can't see the forest for the trees
cardinal sin
cast in stone
catch someone napping
to champ at the bit
a change of heart
to change one's tune
cite chapter and verse
easy as child's play
chilled to the bone
chill out
chip off the old block
when the chips are down
clean as a whistle
to clear the air
cliffhanger
a close call
to coin a phrase
to give the cold shoulder to
come on board
come out of one's shell
come to a head
cool as a cucumber
cramp someone's style
crazy like a fox
crystal clear
cut and dried
cutting edge
a dark horse
to dawn on someone
dead in the water
dead set against
den of thieves
play devil's advocate
dime a dozen

to do a number on
dog eat dog
don't hold your breath
doom and gloom
double-edged sword
dressed to kill
drive someone up the/a wall
drunk as a skunk
dull as dishwater
eager beaver
easy as pie
eat like a bird
eat one's heart out
ego trip
elbow room
everything but the kitchen sink
to face the music
fair and square
fall by the wayside
famous last words
a far cry
fast and furious
feast one's eyes on
to have a field day
fifth wheel
fight fire with fire
a fighting chance
fight tooth and nail
figment of the imagination
to go over with a fine-toothed
    comb
at first blush
a fish out of water
fit like a glove
fly-by-night
to come off/out with flying colors
to foam at the mouth
food for thought
for better or worse
from bad to worse
to lead down the garden path

to get a handle on something
to get a kick out of something
to get down to brass tacks
to get into hot water
to get one's act together
to get one's feet wet
give and take
to give the shirt off one's back to
glutton for punishment
to go around in circles
to go ballistic
to go hog wild
to go overboard
the gory details
to go with the flow
to grasp at straws
the great unwashed
grist for the mill
hand in glove
hands down
happy as a clam
hard act to follow
hard as nails
head and shoulders above
have a heart of stone
hell freezes over
hit below the belt
hit or miss
hit the ground running
hit the hay
hit the nail on the head
cannot hold a candle to
hook, line and sinker
hot under the collar
ignorance is bliss
in a heartbeat
in a nutshell
in a pinch
in no uncertain terms
in one ear and out the other
in over one's head

in the cards
in the driver's seat
in the long run
in this day and age
in your face
jump down someone's throat
jump the gun
jump to conclusions
keep a straight face
keep your eyes peeled
keep your shirt on
to handle with kid gloves
kill two birds with one stone
a kindred spirit
know someone like a book
know the ropes
labor of love
lap of luxury
larger than life
last but not least
last laugh
last straw
leave out in the cold
leave well enough alone
leave to one's own devices
lesser of two evils
letter perfect
lie through one's teeth
life of the party
light as a feather
like a ton of bricks
like it was going out of style
like taking candy from a baby
lion's share
pay lip service to
lock horns with
a loose cannon
lost in the shuffle
make a beeline for
make a long story short
make heads or tails of something

make no bones about it
make one's hair stand on end
make one's mouth water
make waves
mind over matter
moment of truth
money talks
more than meets the eye
more than one bargained for
in the nick of time
nip in the bud
nodding acquaintance with
no great shakes
no ifs ands or buts
no laughing matter
nose out of joint
not all black and white
nothing to write home about
no two ways about it
nuts and bolts
off the wall
old hat
on an even keel
one foot in the grave
one/a picture is worth a thousand
   words
on pins and needles
on the level
on the ropes
on the sly
on/at the spur of the moment
on the tip of one's tongue
on the warpath
out of a/the clear blue sky
out on a limb
out to lunch
over the hill
paid one's dues
par for the course
pay through the nose
pick a bone with someone

pick someone's brain
piece of cake
plain as day
play with fire
plumb the depths of
powers that be
praise to the skies
pretty as a picture
pride and joy
prime of life
pull no punches
pure and simple
push the envelope
put one's foot down
put on hold
quantum leap
rack one's brain
rain or shine
read between the lines
red carpet treatment
red herring
red-letter day
rest is history
right off the bat
be on the right track
right up one's alley
ring of truth
risk life and limb
rock the boat
roll with the punches
rub elbows with
rub the wrong way
ruffle someone's feathers
run like clockwork
run out of steam
sacred cow
salt of the earth
saving grace
scratch the surface
scream bloody murder
see eye to eye

see the light
sell like hotcakes
separate the men from the boys
set one's sights on
shadow of one's former self
sharp as a tack
shed light on
short and sweet
show one's true colors
sight for sore eyes
sign of the times
sink one's teeth into
sink or swim
sitting pretty
skin and bones
sleep like a log
smart as a whip
smoke like a chimney
smooth as silk
soaked to the skin
spanking new
spread like wildfire
start from scratch
stiff as a board
stubborn as a mule
take a shine to
take by storm
take it in stride
take the bull by the horns
take the wind out of one's sails
talk one's head off

tall, dark, and handsome
tear one's hair out
tight as a drum
tip of the iceberg
tongue in cheek
tough nut to crack
towering rage
turn a blind eye to
ugly as sin
under one's belt
under the weather
unvarnished truth
up in arms
up to snuff
vanish into thin air
vicious circle
walking encyclopedia
wall-to-wall
war of nerves
wet blanket
what goes around comes around
whole new ball game
whole nine yards
window of opportunity
with a grain of salt
without batting an eye
work one's fingers to the bone
worth one's salt
you can't make an omelet without
   breaking eggs

CHAPTER 9

A List of Common Rhetorical Devices, Poetic Meters, and Forms

INTRODUCTION

Writers, like carpenters, have tools. Instead of hammer, wrench, screwdriver, level, and nails, we have meter, alliteration, repetition, metaphor, and irony, to name a few. Like a carpenter's tools, these writerly tools have been employed by others—the masters—with great skill, for hundreds of years. In fact, writing is often more like carpentry than anything else. Skill is what is wanted rather than talent. Skill comes from experience, from trial and error, and from observing what others have done with the same tools you have in your hands or mind.

One of the inspiring things about writing is that these tools have not changed very much over the centuries. Yes, some have gone out of favor, and a few new ones have been created—free verse comes to mind—but all in all, we writers have at our disposal the same devices as did the writers of the past. It's how well we know them and employ them that counts. Somerset Maugham used to painstakingly copy long passages from well-regarded writers. This is the way he sought to absorb their skills, their music. Other writers have done this, too. Here are some of the tools that he sought, and, presumably, you now seek, to master.

alexandrine: a line of verse having six iambic feet.

allegory: a story, poem, or picture that can be interpreted to reveal a hidden meaning, typically a moral or political one.

alliteration: the occurrence of the same letter or sound at the beginning of adjacent or closely connected words.

analogy: a comparison between two things, typically on the basis of their structure, for the purpose of explanation or clarification.

anapest: a metrical foot consisting of two short or unstressed syllables followed by one long or stressed syllable.

anthropomorphism: the attribution of human characteristics or behavior to a god, animal, or object.

assonance: in poetry, the repetition of the sound of a vowel or diphthong in nonrhyming stressed syllables near enough to each other for the echo to be discernible.

ballade: a poem normally composed of three stanzas and an envoy; the last line of the opening stanza is used as a refrain, and the same rhymes, strictly limited in number, recur throughout.

blank verse: verse without rhyme, esp. that which uses iambic pentameter.

caesura: in Greek and Latin verse, a break between words within a metrical foot; in modern verse, a pause near the middle of a line.

couplet: two lines of verse, usually in the same meter and joined by rhyme, that form a unit.

dactyl: a metrical foot consisting of one stressed syllable followed by two unstressed syllables; or (in Greek and Latin) one long syllable followed by two short syllables.

didactic: intended to teach, particularly in having moral instruction as an ulterior motive.

enjambment (also enjambement): in verse, the continuation of a sentence without a pause beyond the end of a line, couplet, or stanza.

envoi (also envoy): a short stanza concluding a ballade.

feminine rhyme: a rhyme between stressed syllables followed by one or more unstressed syllables (e.g., stocking/shocking, glamorous/amorous).

foot: a group of syllables constituting a metrical unit. In English poetry, it consists of stressed and unstressed syllables, while in ancient classical poetry, it consists of long and short syllables.

free verse: poetry that does not rhyme or have a regular meter.

heroic couplet: a pair of rhyming iambic pentameters, much used by Chaucer and the poets of the 17th and 18th centuries, such as Alexander Pope.

iamb: a metrical foot consisting of one short (or unstressed) syllable followed by one long (or stressed) syllable.

internal rhyme: a rhyme involving a word in the middle of a line and another at the end of the line or in the middle of the next.

irony: the expression of one's meaning by using language that normally signifies the opposite, typically for humorous or emphatic effect.

masculine rhyme: a rhyme of final stressed syllables (e.g., blow/flow, confess/redress).

metaphor: a figure of speech in which a word or phrase is applied to an object or action to which it is not literally applicable.

meter: the rhythm of a piece of poetry, determined by the number and length of feet in a line.

ode: a lyric poem in the form of an address to a particular subject, often elevated in style or manner and written in varied or irregular meter.

onomatopoeia: the formation of a word from a sound associated with what is named (e.g., cuckoo, sizzle); the use of such words for rhetorical effect.

oxymoron: a figure of speech in which apparently contradictory terms appear in conjunction (e.g., faith unfaithful kept him falsely true).

ottava rima: a form of poetry consisting of stanzas of eight lines of ten or eleven syllables, rhyming abababcc.

parody: an imitation of the style of a particular writer, artist, or genre with deliberate exaggeration for comic effect.

pathetic fallacy: the attribution of human feelings and responses to inanimate things or animals, esp. in art and literature.

pentameter: a line of verse consisting of five metrical feet, or (in Greek and Latin verse) of two halves each of two feet and a long syllable.

personification: the attribution of a personal nature or human characteristics to something nonhuman, or the representation of an abstract quality in human form.

Petrarchan: denoting a sonnet of the kind used by the Italian poet Petrarch, with an octave rhyming abbaabba, and a sestet typically rhyming cdcdcd or cdecde.

prosody: the patterns of rhythm and sound used in poetry; the theory or study of these patterns, or the rules governing them; the patterns of stress and intonation in a language.

quatrain: a stanza of four lines, esp. one having alternate rhymes.

rhetoric: the art of effective or persuasive speaking or writing, esp. the use of figures of speech and other compositional techniques.

satire: the use of humor, irony, exaggeration, or ridicule to expose and criticize people's stupidity or vices, particularly in the context of contemporary politics and other topical issues; a play, novel, film, or other work that uses satire.

sestina: a poem with six stanzas of six lines and a final triplet, all stanzas having the same six words at the line-ends in six different sequences that follow a fixed pattern, and with all six words appearing in the closing three-line envoi.

simile: a figure of speech involving the comparison of one thing with another thing of a different kind, used to make a description more emphatic or vivid (e.g., as brave as a lion).

sonnet: a poem of fourteen lines using any of a number of formal rhyme schemes; in English typically having ten syllables per line.

Spenserian stanza: the type of stanza used by Spenser in the *Faerie Queene*, consisting of eight iambic pentameters and an alexandrine, with the rhyming scheme ababbcbcc.

spondee: a foot consisting of two long (or stressed) syllables.

stanza: a group of lines forming the basic recurring metrical unit in a poem; a verse.

tercet: a set or group of three lines of verse rhyming together or connected by rhyme with an adjacent tercet.

trochee: a foot consisting of one long or stressed syllable followed by one short or unstressed syllable.

villanelle: a nineteen-line poem with two rhymes throughout, consisting of five tercets and a quatrain, with the first and third lines of the opening tercet recurring alternately at the end of the other tercets and with both repeated at the close of the concluding quatrain.

CHAPTER 10

A Quick Guide to All the Plays of Shakespeare

INTRODUCTION

Shakespeare. How do you introduce him? How about the simple fact that he is the most admired writer in the world. He is the standard by which all other writers—in most any language—is judged. As Stanley Wells says in the introduction to Oxford University Press's *Complete Works*, "No other secular imaginative writer has exerted so great an influence over so large a proportion of the world's population." Verdi worshiped him—and wrote three operas based on his plays, including his very last. Boris Pasternak translated him. Jean Cocteau claimed he could sense Shakespeare's greatness even without being able to read English. Keats was in awe of his "negative capability." Hemingway's goal as a writer was "to knock Mr. Shakespeare on his ass." He didn't, and no one else has, either. Can we say he was the greatest writer who ever lived? Do you have anyone who would like to go ten rounds with Will?

The simple fact is, whether you worship Shakespeare or not—and there *are* good writers who do not—he is unavoidable, and essential.

As for books about his plays, it would be impossible to list even single percentage point of how many have been written since his death. Scores of articles and books appear every year, and there will be hundreds more—thousands probably—you can be sure, emerging in 2016, the 400th anniversary of his death. There is a very good general bibliography at the end of the *Norton Shakespeare* (1997)—which is based on the Oxford edition. It's broken down by subjects, such as "Shakespeare's World," "London Theaters," "Shakespeare's Life," and, of course, "Criticism." It's an excellent resource.

Shakespeare is on the Internet, of course, and one of the better sites is www.bardweb.net. From there, you can journey all over the web. You might want to check out the website for the Globe Theater in London, http://www.shakespeares-globe.org/. This theater is, as best as was possible, a recreation of Shakespeare's own Globe.

One of the benefits of *not* living in Shakespeare's time is that you can see his plays on film. If you go to any large film database and type in Shakespeare, you'll get scores of results. Just for *Hamlet* alone, for example, you'll find productions with, in the leading role, Kevin Kline, Kenneth Branagh, Laurence Olivier, Mel Gibson, Richard Burton, Ethan Hawke (with Bill Murray as Polonius), Patrick Stewart and Richard Chamberlain. His plays were meant to be acted. Even if you can't get see one of his plays live—and it's hard not to if you have a child in school—you can still see them via DVDs. Only recently, a film version of *The Merchant of Venice* was released, starring Al Pacino. By the way, it seems almost every state in the Union has a Shakespeare Festival, so you should be able to see some live theater.

Which leads us to one final note. If you ever get the chance to act in a Shakespeare play yourself, seize the day. It doesn't matter what kind of production—junior high, college, community theater, professional stage. When you actually speak the words Shakespeare wrote, and use them in the way he intended they be used—on the stage— you will get an insight into his work unavailable in any other way.

The plays are presented in the order of their composition, according to *William Shakespeare: The Complete Works* (edited by Stanley Wells and Gary Taylor. Oxford University Press, 1986), along with their cast of characters. (There will be a new edition of this work coming out in July, 2005.) Other editions have variances for this chronology, but in the end this is a concern for scholars. We have also put some of the more well-known lines from each of the plays with them. Often, we may know the lines, but not their origin.

THE TWO GENTLEMEN OF VERONA (1590-1)

This is a play whose main theme is friendship. This lovely song comes from Act IV, "Who is Silvia? What is she, / That all our swains commend her? / Holy, fair, and wise is she; / The heaven such grace did lend her, / That she might admired be." You may remember Gwyneth Paltrow reciting it in *Shakespeare in Love*.

Dramatis Personae:

Duke of Milan
Valentine, a gentleman of Verona
Proteus, a gentleman of Verona
Antonio, father of Proteus
Thurio, Valentine's rival
Eglamour, a knight
Speed, Valentine's servant
Launce, Proteus's servant

Panthino, Antonio's servant
Host, where Julia lodges
Outlaws, with Valentine
Julia, beloved of Proteus
Silvia, beloved of Valentine
Lucetta, Julia's woman
Servants, Musicians

THE TAMING OF THE SHREW (1590-1)

The conflict here is one of a very strong-willed woman who, in the end, needs to be shown what she really wants—a loving marriage. Cole Porter obviously knew his Shakespeare and read this from Act II, "Kiss me, Kate, we will be married o' Sunday." From Act IV, we have, "And thereby hangs a tale."

Dramatis Personae:

A Lord
Hostess, Page, Players, Huntsmen, and Servants
Christopher Sly, a tinker
Baptista Minola, of Padua
Vincentio, old gentleman of Pisa
Hortensio, suitor to Bianca
Tranio, servant to Lucentio
Biondello, servant to Lucentio
Grumio, servant to Petruchio
Curtis, servant to Petruchio
A Pedant

Lucentio, son of Vincentio, in love with Bianca
Petruchio, gentleman of Verona, suitor to Katherina
Gremio, suitor to Bianca
Katherina, the shrew, daughter of Baptista
Bianca, daughter of Baptista
Widow
Tailor, Haberdasher, and Servants

2 HENRY VI (1591)

This play shows us how a strong king is needed when we only have a weak one. And how contemporary is this thought from Act IV, "The first thing we do, let's kill all the lawyers."

Dramatis Personae:

King Henry the Sixth
Humphrey, Duke of Gloucester
Cardinal Beaufort
Richard Plantagenet, Duke of York
Edward, Earl of March
Richard, Duke of Gloucester
Duke of Somerset
Duke of Suffolk
Duke of Buckingham
Lord Clifford
Young Clifford
Earl of Salisbury
Earl of Warwick
Lord Scales
Lord Say
Sir Humphrey Stafford
Sir John Stanley
Sir William Vaux
Matthew Goffe
Walter Whitmore
A Sea Captain, Master, and Master's Mate
Two Gentlemen, prisoners with Suffolk

John Hume and John Southwell
Bolingbroke
Thomas Horner
Peter
Clerk of Chatham
Mayor of St. Alban's
Simpcox
Jack Cade
George Bevis, John Holland, Dick the Butcher, Smith the Weaver, Michael, etc.
Alexander Iden
Two Murderers
Margaret, Queen of King Henry
Margery Jourdain
Wife of Simpcox
Lords, Ladies, and Attendants
Herald, Petitioner, Aldermen
A Beadle, Sheriff, and Officers
Citizens, Prentices, Falconers, Guards, Soldiers, Messengers, etc.
A Spirit

3 HENRY VI (1591)

It is here we have the foreboding of the future Richard III's ruthlessness. From Act V, "Suspicion always haunts the guilty mind; / The thief doth fear each bush an officer."

Dramatis Personae:

King Henry the Sixth	Sir John Mortimer
Edward, Prince of Wales, his son	Sir Hugh Mortimer
Lewis the Eleventh, King of France	Henry, Earl of Richmond
Duke of Somerset	Earl Rivers
Duke of Exeter	Sir William Stanley
Earl of Oxford	Sir John Montgomery
Earl of Northumberland	Sir John Somerville
Earl of Westmoreland	Tutor to Rutland
Lord Clifford	Mayor of York
Richard Plantagenet, Duke of York	Lieutenant of the Tower
Edward, Earl of March, afterwards	A Nobleman
King Edward the Fourth	Two Keepers
Edmund, Earl of Rutland	A Huntsman
George, Duke of Clarence	A Son, who has killed his father
Richard, Duke of Gloucester	A Father, who has killed his son
Duke of Norfolk	Queen Margaret
Marquess of Montague	Lady Grey, afterwards Queen to
Earl of Warwick	Edward the Fourth
Earl of Pembroke	Bona
Lord Hastings	Soldiers and other Attendants,
Lord Stafford	Messengers, Watchmen

TITUS ANDRONICUS (1592)

This is perhaps Shakespeare's bloodiest play and has one of his most evil characters as well. This is not a play renowned for its quotable lines, but this from Act I could be etched in stone, "These words are razors to my wounded heart."

Dramatis Personae:

Saturnius, Emperor of Rome	Young Lucius, son of Lucius
Bassianus, brother of Saturnius	Publius, son of Marcus
Titus Andronicus, Roman general	Sempronius, kinsman of Titus
Marcus Andronicus, a tribune	Caius, kinsman of Titus
Lucius, son of Titus	Valentine, kinsman of Titus
Quintus, son of Titus	Aemilius, a noble Roman
Martius, son of Titus	Alarbus, son of Tamora
Mutius, son of Titus	Demetrius, son of Tamora

Chiron, son of Tamora
Aaron, a moor; Tamora's lover
Tamora, Queen of the Goths
Lavinia, daughter of Titus
Captain, Tribune, Messenger,
    and Clown

Goths and Romans
A Nurse and Black Child
Senators, Tribunes, Officers,
Soldiers, and Attendants

1 HENRY VI (1592)

In this play, we see the beginnings of the War of the Roses. In all
his plays, Shakespeare had not just the gift of sterling language
but the ability to pen proverbs, maxims, and memorable adages.
They are often cautionary in tone. Here we have, from Act II,
"Unbidden guests / Are often welcomest when they are gone,"
and from Act III, "Delays have dangerous ends."

Dramatis Personae:

King Henry the Sixth
Humphrey of Gloucester
Duke of Bedford
Thomas Beaufort, Duke of Exeter
Henry Beaufort, Bishop of
    Winchester
John Beaufort, Earl of Somerset
Richard Plantagenet, Duke of York
Earl of Warwick
Earl of Salisbury
Earl of Suffolk
Lord Talbot
John Talbot
Edmund Mortimer
Sir John Fastolf, Sir William Lucy,
    Sir William Glansdale, Sir
    Thomas Gargrave
Mayor of London
Woodvile
Vernon
Basset
Mortimer's Keepers

A Lawyer
Charles Dauphin, afterwards King
    of France
Reignier, Duke of Anjou
Duke of Burgundy
Duke of Alençon
Bastard of Orleans
Governor of Paris
Master-Gunner of Orleans and
    his son
General of French Forces in
    Bordeaux
A French Sergeant
A Porter
An Old Shepherd, father to Joan
Margaret
Countess of Auvergne
Joan la Pucelle (called Joan of Arc)
Lords, Warders of the Tower, Heralds
Officers, Soldiers, Messengers, and
    Attendants
Fiends, to appear before Joan

RICHARD III (1592-93)

Readers might want to look at Al Pacino's splendid documentary, *Looking for Richard*, in which much of the complicated action is broken down, not to mention ably dramatized. Richard, in his plotting villainy, is akin to that other great plotter, Iago. This, of course, has what are probably the most famous opening lines of any of Shakespeare's plays, "Now is the winter of our discontent / Made glorious summer by this son of York." John Steinbeck used them as inspiration for the title of his novel, *The Winter of Our Discontent.* In fact, the whole opening soliloquy is wonderful. This surely is one of Shakespeare's most cynical plays, and Richard is very clear about this when in Act I he says, "And thus I clothe my naked villany / With odd old ends stol'n forth of holy writ, / And seem a saint when most I play the devil." And of course, in the final moments of the play, Richard, helpless on the ground in battle, cries out, "My kingdom for a horse!"

Dramatis Personae:

King Edward the Fourth
Edward, Prince of Wales, afterwards
    King Edward the Fifth
Richard, Duke of York
George, Duke of Clarence
Richard, Duke of Gloucester,
    afterwards King Richard
    the Third
A Young Son of Clarence
Henry, Earl of Richmond,
    afterwards King Henry
    the Seventh
Cardinal Bourchier
Thomas Rotherham, Archbishop
    of York
John Morton
Duke of Buckingham
Duke of Norfolk
Earl of Surrey
Earl Rivers

Marquess of Dorset
Lord Grey
Earl of Oxford
Lord Hastings
Lord Stanley, Earl of Derby
Lord Lovel
Sir Thomas Vaughan
Sir Richard Ratcliff
Sir William Catesby
Sir James Tyrell
Sir James Blunt
Sir Walther Herbert
Sir Robert Brakenbury
Christopher Urswick, a priest
Another Priest
Tressel and Berkeley
Lord Mayor of London
Sheriff of Wiltshire
Elizabeth, Queen of King
    Edward the Fourth

Margaret, widow of King Henry
  the Sixth
Duchess of York
Lady Anne
Margaret Plantagenet

Lords and other Attendants
A Pursuivant, Scrivener, Citizens
Murderers, Messengers, Soldiers
Ghosts of Richard III's victims

THE COMEDY OF ERRORS (1594)

This is a complicated play, in which not one, but two sets of twins are separated and reunited after years of being apart. Though not so known for famous lines, it does have the jarring, "A needy, hollow-ey'd, sharp-looking wretch, / A living-dead man."

Dramatis Personae:

Solinus, Duke of Ephesus
Aegeon, a merchant of Syracuse
Antipholus of Ephesus, Antipholus
  of Syracuse, twin brothers
Dromio of Ephesus, Dromio of
  Syracuse, twin brothers and
  servants
Balthasar, a merchant
Angelo, a goldsmith
Dr. Pinch, schoolmaster
Aemilia, Abbess of Ephesus and
  Aegeon's wife

Adriana, wife of Antipholus of
  Ephesus
Luce, her maid
Luciana, sister of Adriana
Two merchants
Courtesan
Jailer
Officers
Headsman
Attendants

LOVE'S LABOUR'S LOST (1594–95)

Ferdinand, the king, decides to abjure love and passion and lead an intellectual life for a year. He calls all to join him. It doesn't work. In this play you find the lovely song in Act V about winter that ends with, "When roasted crabs hiss in the bowl." Some memorable lines are, "When icicles hang by the wall, / And Dick, the shepherd, blows his nail, / And Tom bears logs into the hall / And milk comes frozen home in pail."

Dramatis Personae:

Ferdinand, King of Navarre
Lords of Navarre: Berowne,
    Longaville, Dumaine
Princess of France
Ladies of France: Rosaline,
    Maria, Katherine
Lords of France: Boyet and Marcade
Don Armado, a Spaniard

Moth, page to Armado
Costard, a clown
Jacquenetta, a country wench
Sir Nathaniel, a curate
Holofernes, a schoolmaster
Dull, a constable
Forester
Lords, attendants, etc.

A MIDSUMMER NIGHT'S DREAM (1595)

One of the most wonderful fantasies ever written, this play is loved by children, and is often the first play by Shakespeare they read. It is a play that should be seen. A magical film was made seventy years ago of this play, starring Mickey Rooney and James Cagney. Yes, Jimmy Cagney, playing a comic role—and he's *good*. The language is like jewels. This is from Act II, "I know a bank whereon the wild thyme blows, / Where oxlips and the nodding violet grows / Quite over-canopied with luscious woodbine / With sweet musk-roses, and with eglantine." Also from Act II, "I'll put a girdle round about the earth / in forty minutes." Some of the most memorable lines are the funniest, and that's partly due to Bottom who is turned into an ass. "Bless the, Bottom! Bless thee! Thou art translated," his companion says. And Puck, looking on, says, "Lord, what fools these mortals be!" And, finally, in Act V, "The lunatic, the lover, and the poet, / Are of imagination all compact."

Dramatis Personae:

Theseus, Duke of Athens
Egeus, father of Hermia
Lysander, in love with Hermia
Demetrius, in love with Hermia
Philosrate, Master of the Revels
Quince, a carpenter
Snug, a joiner
Bottom, a weaver
Flute, a bellows-mender

Snout, a tinker
Starveling, a tailor
Hippolyta, Queen of the Amazons;
    betrothed of Theseus
Hermia, in love with Lysander
Helena, in love with Demetrius
Oberon, King of Fairies
Titania, Queen of Fairies
Puck, or Robin Goodfellow

Peaseblossom, a fairy
Cobway, a fairy
Moth, a fairy
Mustardseed, a fairy

Other Fairies, attendants to Oberon
    and Titania
Attendants to Theseus and
    Hippolyta

ROMEO AND JULIET (1595)

This is the play of the "star-cross'd lovers." It has haunted readers
and viewers, and still does. Directors have progressively cast
younger leads to represent the actual ages of the pair. Because of
their strong love, this really does feel like a tragedy. *West Side
Story* was written after this play. There are some lovely words
here, and not just, "O Romeo, Romeo! Wherefore art thou
Romeo?" As usual, Shakespeare leaves us with some memorable
epigrams, such as, "He jests at scars, that never felt a wound."
And this is followed immediately in Act II by, "But, soft! What
light through yonder window breaks?" Also, probably the most
famous of all leavings, "Good night, good night! Parting is such
sweet sorrow." From Act III, "A plague o' both your houses!"
Parts of this story are mirrored to great and touching effect in the
movie, *Shakespeare in Love*.

Dramatis Personae:

Escalus, Prince of Verona
Paris, kinsman to Escalus
Montague
Capulet
Uncle to Capulet
Romeo, son of Montague
Mercutio, friend of Romeo
Benvolio, friend of Romeo
Tybalt, nephew of Lady Capulet
Friar Laurence
Friar John
Balthasar, servant to Romeo
Sampson, servant to Capulet
Gregory, servant to Capulet

Peter, servant to Juliet's nurse
Abram, servant to Montague
Lady Montague
Lady Capulet
Juliet, daughter of Capulet
Nurse to Juliet
An Apothecary
Three Musicians
An Officer
Pages to Paris and Officer
Citizens of Verona, Kinsfolk of
    both houses, Masquers
Guards, Watchmen, and Attendants
Chorus

RICHARD II (1595)

There is much rhyming in this play, more than is usual in Shakespeare's dramas. There is also much complaining by the king. This play has the well-known self-pitying lines, "For God's sake, let us sit upon the ground / And tell sad stories of the death of kings." But it also has what has become a verbal national anthem for England, the words spoken by John of Gaunt in Act II that begin, "This royal throne of kings, this sceptred isle, / This earth of majesty . . ." and contains the lines, "This blessed plot, this earth, this realm, this England."

Dramatis Personae:

King Richard the Second	Lord Ross
John of Gaunt	Lord Willoughby
Edmund of Langley, Duke of York	Lord Fitzwater
Henry Bolingbroke, Duke of Hereford; later Henry IV	Bishop of Carlisle
	Abbot of Westminster
Duke of Aumerle	Lord Marshal
Thomas Mowbray, Duke of Norfolk	Sir Stephen Scoop
	Sir Pierce of Exton
Duke of Surrey	Welsh Captain
Earl of Salisbury	Queen to King Richard
Lord Berkeley	Duchess of Gloucester
Bushy	Duchess of York
Bagot	Lady attending the Queen Lords,
Green	Heralds, Officers, Soldiers
Earl of Northumberland	Gardeners, Keepers, Messengers
Henry Percy, called Hotspur	Groom and other Attendants

KING JOHN (1596)

Here, one's destiny seems not to be under one's control. In this, the play is akin to Greek drama. Act III provided the words for a classic movie title, "Bell, book, and candle shall not drive me back, / When gold and silver becks me to come on." Some say the following lines from Act III are about Shakespeare's son, Hamnet, who had died a year or so earlier, "Grief fills the room up of my absent child, / Lies in his bed, walks up and down with me, / Puts on his pretty looks, repeats his words, / Remembers me of all his gracious parts." Also from Act III, "Life is as tedious as a twice-told tale."

Dramatis Personae:

Prince Henry, son to the king	Lewis, the Dauphin
Arthur, Duke of Britain; nephew to the king	Lymoges, Duke of Austria
	Cardinal Pandulph, Papal legate
Earl of Pembroke	Melun, a French lord
Earl of Essex	Chatillon, ambassador of France
Earl of Salisbury	Queen Elinor, mother of King John
The Lord Bigot	Constance, mother to Arthur
Hubert de Burgh	Blanch of Spain, niece of King John
Robert Faulconbridge	Lady Falconbridge
Philip the Bastard, his half-brother	Lords, Ladies, Citizens of Angiers
James Gurney	Sheriff, Heralds, Officers, Soldiers
Peter of Pomfreet, a prophet	Messengers and other Attendants
Philip, King of France	

THE MERCHANT OF VENICE (1596–97)

Easily, Shakespeare's most controversial play, and only gets more so. What was, for many, the norm of the times—anti-Semitism—is clearly not today. Is Shakespeare sympathetic to Shylock, or not? This is an endlessly debatable question. In Act III, it seems he is, when he has Shylock say, "If you prick us, do we not bleed? If you tickle us, do we not laugh? If you poison us, do we not die?" Then Portia, in Act IV, admonishes Shylock with these famous words, "The quality of mercy is not strain'd, / It droppeth as the gentle rain from heaven / Upon the place beneath: it is twice bless'd; / It blesseth him that gives and him that takes." In Act I, Shylock defines his limits, "I will buy with you, sell with you, talk with you, walk with you, and so following; but I will not eat with you, drink with you, nor pray with you. What news on the Rialto?"

Dramatis Personae:

Duke of Venice	Antonio, the merchant of Venice
Prince of Morocco	Bassanio, his friend
Prince of Arragon	Gratiano

Solanio	Stephano, Portia's servant
Solerio	Portia, a wealthy heiress
Lorenzo, in love with Jessica	Nerissa, a waiting-maid
Shylock, a wealthy Jew	Jessica, daughter of Shylock
Tubal, a Jew, his friend	Magnificoes of Venice, Officers of
Launcelot Gobbo, a clown,	the Court of Justice
servant to Shylock	Jailer
Old Gobbo, father of Launcelot	Servants to Portia
Leonardo, Bassanio's servant	Attendants
Balthasar, Portia's servant	
to Shylock	

1 HENRY IV (1596–97)

One of Shakespeare's most memorable pairings—that of Prince Hal and Sir John Falstaff—makes its debut here. And in Falstaff, we find possibly Shakespeare's greatest comic creation. Huge in girth and in appetite, he lives for pleasure and flees any chance of pain. He was an extremely popular character in Shakespeare's time as well. In Act IV, he utters a famous diatribe on the useless-ness of honor, and you can find it set to music in Giuseppe Verdi's last opera, *Falstaff*. He follows this in Act V by summing up his philosophy. "The better part of valor is discretion."

Dramatis Personae:

King Henry the Fourth	Sir Richard Vernon
Henry, Prince of Wales, called	Sir John Falstaff
Prince Hal	Sir Michael
Prince John of Lancaster	Poins
Earl of Westmoreland	Gadshill
Sir Walter Blunt	Peto
Thomas Percy, Earl of Worcester	Bardolph
Henry Percy, Earl of Northumberland	Lady Percy, wife of Hotspur
Henry Percy, called Hotspur	Lady Mortimer
Edmund Mortimer	Mistress Quickly
Richard Scroop	Lords, Officers, Sheriff, Vintner
Archibald, Earl of Douglas	Chamberlain, Drawers, Carriers,
Owen Glendower	Travelers, and Attendants

THE MERRY WIVES OF WINDSOR (1597-8)

Back by popular demand—some say at Queen Elizabeth's special request—we have Sir John Falstaff. Arrigo Boito, Verdi's librettist, drew heavily on this play for Verdi's last opera, *Falstaff*. "Why, then the world's mine oyster," he says in Act II, "which I with sword will open."

Dramatis Personae:

Sir John Falstaff	Pistol, follower of Falstaff
Fenton, a gentleman	Nym, follower of Falstaff
Shallow, a country justice	Robin, page to Falstaff
Slender, cousin to Shallow	Simple, servant to Slender
Ford	Rugby, servant to Doctor Caius
Page	Mistress Ford
William Page, son of Page	Mistress Page
Sir Hugh Evans, a Welsh parson	Anne Page, her daughter
Doctor Caius, a French physician	Mistress Quickly, servant to
Host of the Garter Inn	Doctor Caius
Bardolph, follower of Falstaff	Servants to Page and Ford

2 HENRY IV (1597-8)

Although this play features, once more, Sir John Falstaff, it is, in the end a sad play. Falstaff is rejected by Prince Hal, who, with the death of his father, becomes king. He can no longer tolerate Falstaff's irresponsible ways, and so the friendship is over. Orson Wells took Falstaff's lines from Act III, "We have heard the chimes at midnight" for the title of his movie about the man. No actor was better suited to play Falstaff than Wells, and his film is wonderful. Also from Act III, "Uneasy lies the head that wears the crown."

Dramatis Personae:

Rumour, the presenter	Thomas of Clarence
King Henry the Fourth	Prince John of Lancaster
Henry, Prince of Wales; afterwards	Humphrey of Gloucester
King Henry the Fifth	Earl of Warwick

Earl of Westmoreland
Earl of Surrey
Gower
Harcourt
Blunt
Lord Chief Justice
A Servant to the Chief Justice
Earl of Northumberland
Scroop, Archbishop of York
Lord Mowbray
Lord Hastings
Lord Bardolph
Sir John Coleville
Travers and Morton
Falstaff, Bardolph, Pistol, and a Page

Poins and Peto
Shallow and Silence, country justices
Davy, Shallow's servant
Mouldy, Shadow, Wart, Feeble, and Bullcalf, recruits
Fang and Snare, sheriff's officers
Lady Northumberland
Lady Percy
Mistress Quickly
Doll Tearsheet
Lords and Attendants
Officers, Messengers, Soldiers
Porter, Drawer, Beadles, Grooms, etc.
A Dancer Speaker of the Epilogue

MUCH ADO ABOUT NOTHING (1598)

This play is the famous battle of wits between Benedick and Beatrice. Love has a troubled journey finding its way home in this play, and often cruelty is substituted for wit. Typical is this pronouncement from Act II, "Would it not grieve a man to be over-mastered with a piece of valiant dust? To make an account of her life to a clod of wayward marl?" Act II also has a sweet song, "Sigh no more, ladies, sigh no more. / Men were deceivers ever; / One foot in sea, and one on shore." Also from ACT II, "As merry as the day is long." And from Act V, "For there was never yet a philosopher / That could endure the toothache patiently."

Dramatis Personae:

Don Pedro, Prince of Arragon
Don John, his bastard brother
Claudio, young lord of Florence
Benedick, young lord of Padua
Leonato, Governor of Messina
Antonio, brother of Leonato
Balthasar, servant to Don Pedro

Borachio, follower of Don John
Conrade, follower of Don John
Dogberry, a constable
Verges, a headborough
Friar Francis
A Sexton
A Boy

Hero, daughter of Leonato

Beatrice, niece of Leonato

Margaret, gentlewoman to Hero

Ursula, gentlewoman to Hero

Messengers, Watch, and
  Attendants

HENRY V (1598-9)

Prince Hal has become Henry V, and he is an aggressive ruler who invades France—not his enemy—and wages war. Hundreds of his men die. The chorus in this play utters some great lines, including, "O! for a Muse of fire, that would ascend / The brightest heaven of invention." From Act III, "Once more unto the breach, dear friends, once more, / Or close up the walls with our English dead!" And from Act IV, "We few, we happy few, we band of brothers."

Dramatis Personae:

King Henry the Fifth

Humphrey of Gloucester

Duke of Bedford

Duke of Exeter

Duke of York

Earls of Salisbury, Westmoreland,
  and Warwick

Archbishop of Canterbury

Bishop of Ely

Earl of Cambridge

Lord Scroop

Sir Thomas Grey

Sir Thomas Erpingham, Gower,
  Fluellen, Macmorris, Jamy

Bates, Court, Williams

Pistol, Nym, Bardolph

Boy

A Herald

Charles the Sixth, King of France

Lewis, the Dauphin

Dukes of Burgundy, Orleans, and
  Bourbon

The Constable of France

Rambures and Grandpré

Montjoy

Governor of Harfleur

Ambassadors to England

Isabel, Queen of France

Katherine, daughter of Charles
  and Isabel

Alice

Hostess of the tavern, wife of Pistol

Lords, Ladies, Officers, Soldiers,
  Citizens

Chorus

JULIUS CAESAR (1599)

If only he had listened when the soothsayer said, "Beware the ides of March." Some readers may not know that Marlon Brando played Marc Antony in a 1953 film version of this play. It is worth seeing. Everyone is on edge in this play, waiting for something to happen, and so the reader or viewer is, too. Dreams play an important role, as well. This play is rife with well-known lines. It may be that envy and betrayal sparked Shakespeare to great heights. In Act I, Caesar says, "Let me have men about me that are fat; / Sleek-headed men and such as sleep o' nights. / Yond Cassius has a lean and hungry look." Brutus has just been told that "The fault…is not in our stars / But in ourselves." And then, in Act III, Caesar's dying words, "Et tu, Brute?" After Caesar's death, Anthony gives his funeral speech that begins, "Friends, Romans, countrymen, lend me your ears," that has been parodied a thousand times, and yet is a masterpiece of insinuation. In it, Anthony says, "This was the most unkindest cut of all." Also from Act III, "Cry 'Havoc,' and let slip the dogs of war."

Dramatis Personae:

Julius Caesar
Octavius Caesar, Triumvir
Mark Antony, Triumvir
M. Aemilius Lepidus, Triumvir
Cicero, a senator
Publius, a senator
Popilus Lena, a senator
Marcus Brutus, a conspirator
Cassius, a conspirator
Casca, a conspirator
Trebonius, a conspirator
Ligarius, a conspirator
Decius Brutus, a conspirator
Metellus Cimber, a conspirator
Cinna, a conspirator

Flavius and Marullus, tribunes
Artemedorius, a Sophist of Cnidos
A Soothsayer
Cinna, a Poet
Another Poet
Lucilius, Titinius, Messala, Young
    Cato, Volumnius
Varro, Clitius, Claudius, Strato,
    Lucius, Dardanius, servants
    to Brutus
Pindarus, servant to Cassius
Calphurnia, wife of Caesar
Portia, wife of Brutus
Senators, Citizens, Guards,
    Attendants

AS YOU LIKE IT (1599–1600)

Here we find the famous forest of Arden in which an exiled Duke and his men live. It is a play about loyalty, and about being alone, and, ultimately, about redemption. This play has the well-known (but perhaps often unidentifiable) lines that begin, "All the world's a stage, / And all the men and women merely players: / They have their exits and their entrances; / And one man in his time plays many parts." This is the so-called "seven ages of man" speech. The images are wonderful, including, "creeping like snail / Unwillingly to school," and "the lover / Sighing like furnace." The whole thing ends with the most brilliant description of senility, "second childishness, and mere oblivion, / Sans teeth, sans eyes, sans taste, sans everything."

Dramatis Personae:

Duke Senior	Touchstone, a clown
Frederick, his brother; a usurper	Sir Oliver Martext, a vicar
Amiens, lord attending Duke	Corin, a shepherd
Jaques, lord attending Duke	Silvius, a shepherd
Le Beau, a courtier	William, in love with Audrey
Charles, a wrestler	Rosalind, daughter of the Duke
Oliver, son of de Boys	Celia, daughter of Frederick
Jaques, son of de Boys	Phebe, a shepherdess
Orlando, son of de Boys	Audrey, a country wench
Adam, servant to Oliver	Person presenting Hymen
Dennis, servant to Oliver	Lords, Pages, Foresters, and Attendants

HAMLET (1600–1)

This is arguably Shakespeare's most famous play, and it has fascinated critics ever since it was written. Every major critic—and many poets and novelists—have felt compelled to write about it and to try to unravel the mysteries of Hamlet's character. Read T.S. Eliot on this play, for example. *Hamlet* has considerably more than its share of famous lines. Almost everyone knows—and has probably said—"To be, or not to be." (This entire soliloquy has become famous.) The list goes on and on, including "O, what a rogue and peasant slave am I," "O! that this too too solid flesh would melt," and Hamlet's engaging directions to the players that begins, "Speak the speech, I pray you, as I pronounce it to you, trippingly on the tongue." Let's not forget Polonius's lines from Act I, "Neither a borrower nor a lender be. . . .This above all: to thine own self be true." "Something is rotten in the state of Denmark" comes from Act I, as does, "There are more things in heaven and earth, Horatio, / Than are dreamt of in your philosophy." From Act II, "Though this be madness, yet there is method in't." Also from Act II, "What a piece of work is man! How noble in reason! How infinite in faculty!" Spoken by Hamlet, normally with a skull in his hand, "Alas, poor Yorick!" from Act V. And finally, from Act V, "Goodnight, sweet prince."

Dramatis Personae:

Claudius, King of Denmark
Hamlet, Prince of Denmark;
   nephew of Claudius
Fortinbras, Prince of Norway
Horatio, friend of Hamlet
Polonius, Lord Chamberlain
Laertes, his son
Voltemand, a courtier
Cornelius, a courtier
Rosencrantz, a courtier
Guildenstern, a courtier
Osric, a courtier
A Gentleman
A Priest
Marcellus, an officer

Bernardo, an officer
Francisco, a soldier
Reynaldo, servant to Polonius
A Captain
English Ambassadors
Players
Two Clowns, gravediggers
Gertrude, Queen of Denmark
   and mother of Hamlet
Ophelia, daughter of Polonius
Lords, Ladies, Officers, Soldiers,
   Sailors, Messengers, and
   Attendants
Ghost of Hamlet's father

TWELFTH NIGHT, OR WHAT YOU WILL (1601)

Here, as in *As You Like It*, a woman—Viola—disguises herself as a man. In Shakespeare's time, when no women were allowed on the stage, you would have had a man playing a woman playing a man. That would have been a complex acting job, one might think. One of the most delightful of all Shakespeare's plays, it begins most engagingly with the lines, "If music be the food of love, play on." It also has a lovely little song in Act V with the refrain, "With hey, ho, the wind and the rain."

Dramatis Personae:

Orsino, Duke of Illyria
Sebastian, brother of Viola
Antonio, a sea captain
Valentine
Curio
Sir Toby Belch, uncle of Olivia
Sir Andrew Aguecheek
Malvolio, steward to Olivia

Feste, a clown; Olivia's servant
Olivia, a rich countess
Viola, in love with the Duke
Maria, Olivia's maid
A Sea Captain
Lords, Priests, Sailors, Officers,
    Musicians, and Attendants

TROILUS AND CRESSIDA (1602)

This play is set against the backdrop of the Trojan War. Shakespeare was true to his source, at least with Achilles, who is here, as he is in *The Iliad,* a prima donna. The character Pandarus provided the source for our word, "pander." From Act III, "Time hath, my lord, a wallet at his back, / Wherein he puts alms for oblivion."

Dramatis Personae:

Priam, King of Troy
Hector, son of Priam
Troilus, son of Priam
Paris, son of Priam
Deiphobus, son of Priam
Helenus, son of Priam
Margarelon, bastard son of Priam
Aeneas, Trojan commander
Anternor, Trojan commander
Calchas, Trojan priest
Pandarus, uncle of Cressida
Agamemnon, Greek general
Menelaus, brother of Agamemnon
Achilles, Greek commander

Ajax, Greek commander
Ulysses, Greek commander
Nestor, Greek commander
Diomedes, Greek commander
Patroclus, Greek commander
Thersites
Alexander, servant to Cressida
Helen, wife of Menelaus
Andromache, wife of Hector
Cassandra, daughter of Priam
Cressida, daughter of Calchas
Servants to Troilus, Paris, and
    Diomedes
Trojan and Greek Soldiers

MEASURE FOR MEASURE (1603)

Disguise plays a major role in this play as it did in *Twelfth Night*, though here the results are darker. Shakespeare also uses what has come to be call the "bed trick," in which a woman switches places with another in the dark to fool the male. It occurs in *All's Well That Ends Well*, too. This passage from Act III, is worthy of Prospero: "Thou hast nor youth nor age; / But, as it were, an after-dinner's sleep, / Dreaming on both. . . ."

Dramatis Personae:

Vincentio, Duke of Vienna
Angelo, his deputy
Escalus, an ancient lord
Claudio, a young gentleman
Lucio, a fantastic
Two Gentlemen
Provost
Thomas, a friar
Peter, a friar
A Justice
Varrius
Elbow, a simple constable

Froth, a foolish gentleman
Pompey, servant to Mistress
   Overdone
Abhorson, an executioner
Barnadine, a dissolute prisoner
Isabella, sister of Claudio
Mariana, betrothed to Angelo
Juliet, beloved of Claudio
Francisca, a nun
Mistress Overdone, a bawd
Lords, Officers, Citizens, Boy,
   and Attendants

OTHELLO (1603-4)

An actor's dream, this is another of Shakespeare's plays Verdi made into an opera. It has probably his greatest villain, too, Iago. It is both frustrating and fascinating to watch Othello slowly lose his confidence in his wife's, Desdemona's, love. There are those lines about jealousy in Act III, "O! beware, my lord, of jealousy; / It is the green-ey'd monster which doth mock / The meat it feeds on." This is followed in the same act by Othello's speech that ends, "Othello's occupation gone!" which is thunderously effective.

Dramatis Personae:

Brabantio, a senator
Other Senators

Gratiano, brother of Brabantio
Lodovico, kinsman of Brabantio

Othello, a noble Moor
Cassio, Othello's lieutenant
Iago, Othello's ancient
Roderigo
Montano, governor of Cypress
Clown, Othello's servant
Desdemona, wife of Othello

Emilia, wife of Iago
Bianca, Cassio's mistress
A Sailor
Messengers, Herald, Officers,
  Gentlemen
Musicians and Attendants

ALL'S WELL THAT ENDS WELL (1604-5)

This play is somewhat cynical, especially about women. Helena, rejected by Bertram, sets out to sleep with him by pure trickery. In Act IV, we hear the wisdom, "The web of our life is of a mingled yarn, good and ill together."

Dramatis Personae:

King of France
Duke of Florence
Bertram, Count of Rossillion
Lafew, an old lord
Parolles, a follower of Bertram
Steward to the Countess of
  Rossillion
A Clown
A Page

Countess of Rossillion, mother
  of Bertram
Helena, a gentlewoman under
  protection of the Countess
A Widow of Florence
Diana, daughter of the widow
Violenta, friend of the widow
Mariana, friend of the widow
Lords, Officers, Soldiers

TIMON OF ATHENS (1605)

Timon, one of the most generous of men, lavishes gifts on his friends. When he runs out of money, however, and asks his friends to help, they are nowhere to be found. The play has several worthy proverbs, including, "Nothing emboldens sin so much as mercy."

Dramatis Personae:

Timon, a noble Athenian
Lucius, a flattering lord
Lucullus, a flattering lord
Sempronius, a flattering lord
Ventidius, a false friend of Timon

Alcibiades, an Athenian captain
Apemantus, a churlish philosopher
Flavius, steward to Timon
Flaminius, Timon's servant
Lucilius, Timon's servant

Servilius, Timon's servant
Caphis, Philotus, Titus, Lucius,
    and Hortensius, servants of
    Timon's creditors
Poet, Painter, Jeweler, Merchant
An Old Athenian
Servants to Varro and Isidore
Three Strangers

A Page
A Fool
Phrynia, mistress of Alcibiades
Timandra, mistress of Alcibiades
Lords, Senators, Officers, Soldiers,
    Thieves, and Attendants
Cupid and Masque Amazons

KING LEAR (1605-6)

This is the role actors savor at the end of their careers. It becomes
one huge howl, and there is a storm raging outside for most of the
play to mirror Lear's rage within. "Nothing will come of nothing,"
Lear says to his reluctant daughter, Cordelia. And nothing is what
he gets. He does not like that, and says so, "How sharper than a
serpent's tooth it is / To have a thankless child." Just as aptly, he
inquires of the Fool, "Dost thou call me fool, boy?" And the Fool
replies, "All thy other titles thou hast given away; that thou / wast
born with." In Act III, "Blow, winds, and crack your cheeks!
Rage! Blow!"

Dramatis Personae:

King Lear of Britain
King of France
Duke of Burgundy
Duke of Cornwall
Duke of Albany
Earl of Kent
Earl of Gloucester
Edgar, son of Gloucester
Edmund, bastard son of Gloucester
Curan, a courtier
Oswald, steward to Goneril
Goneril, daughter of Lear

Regan, daughter of Lear
Cordelia, daughter of Lear
Old Man, Gloucester's tenant
Doctor
Fool
An Officer
A Herald
A Gentleman
Servants to Cornwall
Knights, Officers, Soldiers
Messengers and Attendants

MACBETH (1606)

It is hard for us now to feel the added perfidy of Macbeth's murder of Duncan, his king. Macbeth killed him in his own castle, after having granted Duncan his hospitality. This made it, in the minds of Elizabethans, doubly heinous. This play may vie with *Richard III* for the most famous opening lines of a play. They are spoken by a witch: "When shall we three meet again? / In thunder, lightning, or in rain?" In Act I, "Yet do I fear thy nature; / Is too full o' the milk of human kindness." In Act IV, a witch says, "Double, double toil and trouble; / Fire burn and cauldron bubble." Many others aside from William Faulkner have been drawn to Macbeth's speech in Act V of this murderous play that includes the lines, "To-morrow, and to-morrow, and to-morrow, / Creeps in this petty pace from day to day" and concludes with, "it is a tale / Told by an idiot, full of sound and fury, / Signifying nothing." And then, of curse, there is Lady Macbeth uttering, "Out, damned spot, out, I say!"

Dramatis Personae:

Duncan, King of Scotland
Malcom, Duncan's son
Donalbain, Duncan's son
Macbeth, a general
Banquo, a general
Macduff, a noble
Lennox, a noble
Ross, a noble
Menteith, a noble
Angus, a noble
Caithness, a noble
Fleance, son of Banquo
Siward, Earl of Northumberland
Young Siward, his son
Seyton, officer to Macbeth

Lady Macbeth
Lady Macduff
Hecate and Three Witches
Boy, son to Macduff
English Doctor
Scottish Doctor
A Sergeant
A Porter
An Old Man
Gentlewoman to Lady Macbeth
Lords, Gentlemen
Officers, Soldiers, Messengers
    and Attendants
Murderers
Banquo's Ghost, Apparitions

ANTONY AND CLEOPATRA (1606)

It was something for a Roman soldier, not to mention a general, to give up his duty and honor for a woman. This makes Mark Antony's love for Cleopatra even more memorable. Cleopatra expresses *her* love in Act I, "O! My oblivion is a very Antony, / And I am all forgotten." She speaks of "My salad days, / When I was green in judgment." And her entrance is described in Act II: "The barge she sat in, like a burnish'd throne, / Burn'd on the water; the poop was beaten gold." Also from Act II, "Age cannot wither her, not custom stale / Her infinite variety." And Anthony's death cry from Act IV, "I am dying, Egypt, dying."

Dramatis Personae:

Mark Antony, Triumvir
Octavius Caesar, Triumvir
M. Aemilius Lepidus, Triumvir
Sextus Pompeius - Pompey
Enobarbus, friend of Antony
Ventidius, friend of Antony
Eros, friend of Antony
Scarus, friend of Antony
Dercetas, friend of Antony
Demetrius, friend of Antony
Philo, friend of Antony
Maecenas, friend of Caesar
Agrippa, friend of Caesar
Dolabella, friend of Caesar
Proculeius, friend of Caesar
Thyreus, friend of Caesar
Gallus, friend of Caesar
Menas, friend of Pompey

Menecrates, friend of Pompey
Varrius, friend of Pompey
Taurus, a lieutenant-general
Canidius, a lieutenant-general
Silius, an officer
Euphronius, an ambassador
Alexas, attendant to Cleopatra
Mardian, attendant to Cleopatra
Seleucus, attendant to Cleopatra
Diomedes, attendant to Cleopatra
A Soothsayer
A Clown
Cleopatra, Queen of Egypt
Octavia, Antony's wife; sister of Caesar
Charmian, attendant to Cleopatra
Iras, attendant to Cleopatra
Officers, Soldiers, Messengers,
   and Attendants

PERICLES (1607)

Because of its disjointed nature, some scholars feel Shakespeare might have had a collaborator on this play. This is not considered one of his finer plays. From Act I, "The sad companions dull-ey'd melancholy."

Dramatis Personae:

Antiochus, King of Antioch
Pericles, Prince of Tyre
Helicanus, a lord of Tyre
Escanes, a lord of Tyre
Simonides, King of Pentapolis
Cleon, Governor of Tarsus
Lysimachus, Governor of Mytilene
Cerimon, a lord of Ephesus
Thaliard, a lord of Antioch
Philemon, Cerimon's servant
Leonine, Dionyza's servant
A Pander
Boult, the Pander's servant

Marshal
Daughter of Antiochus
Dionyza, wife of Cleon
Thaisa, daughter of Simonides
Marina, daughter of Pericles
Lychorida, Marina's nurse
A Bawd
Lords, Ladies, Knights, and
    Gentlemen
Sailors, Pirates, Fishermen
Messengers
Diana
Gower, as Chorus

CORIOLANUS (1608)

Male actors like playing the role of Coriolanus, because he's larger than life and consumes the stage. From Act III, "What is the city but the people?"

Dramatis Personae:

Caius Marcius, afterward Caius
    Marcius Coriolanus
Titus Lartius
Cominius
Menenius Agrippa
Sicinius Velutus
Junius Brutus
Young Marcius
A Roman Herald
Tullius Aufidius
Lieutenant to Aufidius
Conspirators

A Citizen of Antium
Two Volscian Guards
Volumnia, mother of Coriolanus
Virgilia, wife of Coriolanus
Valeria, friend to Virgilia
Gentlewoman attendant to Virgilia
Senators, Patricians, Aediles,
    Lictors, Citizens
Soldiers, Messengers
Servants to Aufidias and other
    Attendants

THE WINTER'S TALE (1609)

Leontes, the King of Sicily, is rash and makes some Othello-like decisions, including imprisoning his wife. There she dies—or so he thinks. Leontes may be rash, but he's also lucky, because in the end he finds his wife alive, and their love as well. And here, perhaps the most famous stage direction in the English language, from Act III, "Exit, pursued by a bear."

Dramatis Personae:

Leontes, King of Sicilia
Mamilius, Prince of Sicilia
Camillo, a lord of Sicilia
Antigonus, a lord of Sicilia

Cleomenes, a lord of Sicilia
Dion, a lord of Sicilia
Polixenes, King of Bohemia
Florizel, Prince of Bohemia

Archidamus, a lord of Bohemia
An Old Shepherd; reputed father of Perdita
Clown, his son
Autolycus, a rogue
A Mariner
A Jailer
Hermione, Queen to Leontes
Perdita, daughter of Leontes and Hermione

Paulina, wife of Antigonus
Emilia, a lady to Hermione
Mopsa, a shepherdess
Dorcas, a shepherdess
Lords, Ladies, and Gentlemen
Officers and Servants
Shepherds and Shepherdesses
Guards
Time, as Chorus

CYMBELINE (1610)

Deception is a major element in this play. The plot is complex to follow, and yet Shakespeare somehow unravels everything at the end. You may not have known the origin for this movie title, "Hark! Hark! The lark at heaven's gate sings." From Act III, "I have not slept one wink."

Dramatis Personae:

Cymbeline, King of Britain
Cloten, son of the Queen

Two British Captains
Two Lords, two Gentlemen of

Posthumus Leonatus, husband of Imogen	Cymbeline's court
	Two Jailers
Belarius, banished lord; disguised as Morgan	Queen, wife of Cymbeline
	Imogen, daughter of Cymbeline by a former queen
Guiderius	
Arviragus	Helen, a lady attendant to Imogen
Philario	Lords, Ladies, Roman Senators, Tribunes
Iachimo	
Caius Lucius	A Soothsayer
Pisanio	A Dutch Gentleman and a Spanish Gentleman
Cornelius	
A French Gentleman, friend of Soldiers	Musicians, Officers, Captains,
Philario	Messengers and Attendants
A Roman Captain	Apparitions

THE TEMPEST (1611)

This gorgeous play is said to be Shakespeare's farewell to the theatre. It has resonated with a great many poets. W.H. Auden's *The Sea and the Mirror: A Commentary on Shakespeare's The Tempest*, a long poem, is a good example and well worth reading. Auden was drawn to the illusions we humans have about art. *The Tempest* has a suitable farewell speech for Shakespeare in Act IV when Prospero speaks the speech that begins, "Our revels are now ended. These our actors, / As I foretold you, were all spirits and / Are melted into air, into thin air." It ends with "We are such stuff / As dreams are made on, and our little life / Is rounded with a sleep." The play also has the famous song, "Full fathom five thy father lies; / Of his bones are coral made / Those are pearls that were his eyes." From Act V, "Where the bee sucks, there suck I; / In a cowslips bell I lie."

Dramatis Personae:

Alonso, King of Naples	Master of a ship
Sebastian, his brother	Boatswain
Prospero, the rightful Duke of Milan	Mariners

Antonio, his brother; the usurping
    Duke of Milan
Ferdinand, son of the King
Gonzalo, an old and honest councilor
Adrian, a lord
Francisco, a lord
Caliban, Prospero's slave
Trinculo, a jester
Stephano, a drunken butler

Miranda, Prospero's daughter
Ariel, an airy spirit
Iris, a spirit
Ceres, a spirit
Juno, a spirit
Nymphs
Reapers
Other Spirits; attendants to
    Prospero

HENRY VIII (1613)

The action of this place takes place very close upon Shakespeare's
actual life. Henry's daughter was Elizabeth, Shakespeare's queen.
Though the lines in this play aren't as famous as some others in
other plays, perhaps they should be. These, for instance, "An old
man, broken with the storms of state / Is come to lay his weary
bones among ye; / Give him a little earth for charity."

Dramatis Personae:

King Henry the Eighth
Cardinal Wolsey
Cardinal Campeius
Capucius
Cranmer
Duke of Norfolk
Duke of Suffolk
Duke of Buckingham
Earl of Surrey
Lord Chamberlain
Lord Chancellor
Gardiner
Bishop of Lincoln
Lord Abergavenny
Lord Sandys
Sir Henry Guilford
Sir Thomas Lovell
Sir Anthony Denny
Sir Nicholas Vaux

Griffith
Three Gentlemen
Garter King-at-Arms
Doctor Butts
Surveyor to the Duke of
    Buckingham
Brandon
Door-keeper of the Council-
    chamber
Porter and his man
Page to Gardiner
A Crier
Queen Katherine
Anne Bullen
An Old Lady
Patience
Lords and Ladies in the Dumbshows
Women attending the Queen
Scribes, Officers, Guards, other

Cromwell

Secretaries to Wolsey

Attendants

Spirits

THE TWO NOBLE KINSMEN

Critics are in accord that this play is collaboration, and most think the collaboration was with John Fletcher, of Beaumont and Fletcher fame.

Dramatis Personae:

Theseus, Duke of Athens

Palamon, nephew of the King of Thebes

Arcite, nephew of the King of Thebes

Pirithous, an Athenian general

Artesius, an Athenian captain

A Doctor

Brother of the jailer

Friends of the jailer

A Gentleman

Gerrold, a schoolmaster

Hippolyta, wife of Theseus

Emilia, her sister

Three Queens

Jailer's Daughter

Valerius, a noble of Thebes

Six Knights

A Herald

A Jailer

Wooer of the jailer's daughter

Emilia's Servant

Country Wenches and Women
   personating Hymen, Boy

A Laborer

Countrymen, Messengers

A Man personating Hymen, Boy

Executioners, Guards,
   Soldiers, Attendants

CHAPTER 11

A Timeline of Great Works of Literature in English

INTRODUCTION

If you're at all like me, you are surprised and delighted to know that Cervantes and Shakespeare died in the same year, 1616. And also a bit startled. That's because the sensibilities of the two authors seem so different. Cervantes wrote in a way considerably more modern than Shakespeare did. It arouses my curiosity that these two very different giants should have existed at precisely the same time.

Curiosity about these matters is one reason why this chapter may be useful for you as a writer. Another is, simply, that it's helpful to know what was going on in the world of English literature at a certain time.

Just from a sociological point of view, a timeline can bring illumination to your ongoing study and absorption of literature. In 1925, Scott Fitzgerald published *The Great Gatsby*, his sweet, melancholy poem to the illusions a man can create of his own life. Set on the verdant estate of the mythical Jay Gatsby, the book may be the most gorgeous American novel ever written. Just eight years later, Erskine Caldwell published *Tobacco Road*. Spare, harsh, brutally truthful, this is the story of a family enveloped—buried—by poverty in rural Georgia. In those eight years between these two books, this country went through a convulsive change and decline. Lest we think this was mere stage drama, we can look to these two books, written so close in time to each other, for proof that it was no illusion. A year after Caldwell's brilliant work, James M. Cain published *The Postman Always Rings Twice*. Set in California, it left no doubt to readers that the South had no stranglehold on hard times.

Comparing books in this way can help remind us why we write the books, stories and essays we do. This list goes to 1995. After that, we feel less secure about putting a book on the same list along with, say, *Jude the Obscure*.

Pre-10th century	*Beowulf*	
1387–1400	*The Canterbury Tales*	Geoffrey Chaucer
1470	*Le Morte Darthur*	Sir Thomas Malory
1577–80	*Arcadia*	Sir Philip Sydney
1590–1609	*The Faerie Queene*	Edmund Spenser
1598	*Hero and Leander*	Christopher Marlowe
1599	*Julius Caesar*	William Shakespeare
1600	*Hamlet*	William Shakespeare
1601	*Twelfth Night*	William Shakespeare
1605	*King Lear*	William Shakespeare
1606	*Volpone*	Ben Jonson
1611	*The Tempest*	William Shakespeare
1611–12	*Anniversaries*	John Donne
1621	*The Anatomy of Melancholy*	Robert Burton
1667	*Paradise Lost*	John Milton
1678	*The Pilgrim's Progress*	John Bunyan
1681	*Miscellaneous Poems*	Andrew Marvell
1682	*Mac Flecknoe*	John Dryden
1700	*The Way of the World*	William Congreve
1711	*An Essay on Criticism*	Alexander Pope
1719	*Robinson Crusoe*	Daniel Defoe
1726	*Gulliver's Travels*	Jonathan Swift
1749	*The History of Tom Jones, a Foundling*	Henry Fielding
1755	*Dictionary of the English Language*	Samuel Johnson
1759–67	*Tristram Shandy*	Laurence Sterne

1766	*The Vicar of Wakefield*	Oliver Goldsmith
1777	*The School for Scandal*	Richard Sheridan
1791	*The Life of Samuel Johnson*	James Boswell
1794	*Songs of Innocence and of Experience*	William Blake
1798	*Lyrical Ballads*	William Wordsworth
1812	*Childe Harold's Pilgrimage*	Lord Byron
1813	*Pride and Prejudice*	Jane Austen
1817	*Biographia Literaria*	Samuel Taylor Coleridge
	Rob Roy	Sir Walter Scott
1818	*Endymion*	John Keats
	Frankenstein	Mary Shelley
1819	*Prometheus Unbound*	Percy Bysshe Shelley
1819–20	*The Sketch Book*	Washington Irving
1820	*Poems Descriptive of Rural Life and Scenery*	John Clare
1826	*The Last of the Mohicans*	James Fenimore Cooper
1843	*Past and Present*	Thomas Carlyle
1845	*The Raven and Other Poems*	Edgar Allan Poe
	Narrative of the Life of Frederick Douglass: An American Slave, Written by Himself	Frederick Douglass
1847	*Jane Eyre*	Charlotte Brontë
	Wuthering Heights	Emily Brontë
1847–48	*Vanity Fair: A Novel without a Hero*	William Makepeace Thackeray
1849–50	*David Copperfield*	Charles Dickens
1850	*In Memoriam*	Alfred, Lord Tennyson
	The Scarlet Letter	Nathaniel Hawthorne
	Representative Men	Ralph Waldo Emerson
1851	*Moby-Dick; Or, The Whale*	Herman Melville
1852	*Uncle Tom's Cabin*	Harriet Beecher Stowe
1853	*Poems*	Matthew Arnold
1854	*Walden; Or, Life in the Woods*	Henry David Thoreau
1855	*Leaves of Grass*	Walt Whitman
1862	Emily Dickinson actively writing; only a few poems published in her lifetime	
1864	*Apologia Pro Vita Sua*	Cardinal John Henry Newman

1865	*Alice's Adventures in Wonderland*	Lewis Carroll
1868	*The Ring and the Book*	Robert Browning
1872	*Middlemarch*	George Eliot
1881	*The Portrait of a Lady*	Henry James
1885	*The Adventures of Huckleberry Finn*	Mark Twain
1895	*The Importance of Being Earnest*	Oscar Wilde
1896	*Jude the Obscure*	Thomas Hardy
	A Shropshire Lad	A. E. Housman
1898	*The War of the Worlds*	H. G. Wells
1900	*Lord Jim*	Joseph Conrad
	Sister Carrie	Theodore Dreiser
1901	*Kim*	Rudyard Kipling
1903	*The Way of All Flesh*	Samuel Butler
1907	*Major Barbara*	George Bernard Shaw
1913	*Sons and Lovers*	D. H. Lawrence
1914	*North of Boston*	Robert Frost
1915	*Of Human Bondage*	W. Somerset Maugham
1918	*My Ántonia*	Willa Cather
1919	*The Wild Swans at Coole*	William Butler Yeats
	Winesburg, Ohio	Sherwood Anderson
1920	*The Age of Innocence*	Edith Wharton
	Main Street	Sinclair Lewis
1922	*Ulysses*	James Joyce
	The Waste Land	T. S. Eliot
1924	*A Passage to India*	E. M. Forster
	Desire Under the Elms	Eugene O'Neill
1925	*Mrs. Dalloway*	Virginia Woolf
	The Great Gatsby	F. Scott Fitzgerald
	Manhattan Transfer	John Dos Passos
1926	*The Sun Also Rises*	Ernest Hemingway
1929	*The Sound and the Fury*	William Faulkner
	Good-Bye to All That	Robert Graves
1930	*Poems*	W. H. Auden
1932	*Brave New World*	Aldous Huxley
1933	*Tobacco Road*	Erskine Caldwell
1934	*Tropic of Cancer*	Henry Miller
	The Postman Always Rings Twice	James M. Cain
1937	*Their Eyes Were Watching God*	Zora Neale Hurston
1939	*The Grapes of Wrath*	John Steinbeck
1940	*The Big Sea*	Langston Hughes
1943	*The Fountainhead*	Ayn Rand

1945	*Black Boy (American Hunger)*	Richard Wright
	Brideshead Revisited	Evelyn Waugh
1947	*A Streetcar Named Desire*	Tennessee Williams
1948	*The Heart of the Matter*	Graham Greene
1949	*1984*	George Orwell
	Death of a Salesman	Arthur Miller
1951	*The Catcher in the Rye*	J. D. Salinger
1952	*Waiting for Godot*	Samuel Beckett
	Invisible Man	Ralph Ellison
1953	*Go Tell It on the Mountain*	James Baldwin
	The Adventures of Augie March	Saul Bellow
1954	*Lord of the Flies*	William Golding
	Lucky Jim	Kingsley Amis
1955	*The Bride of the Innisfallen, and Other Stories*	Eudora Welty
1956	*Howl*	Allan Ginsberg
1957	*On the Road*	Jack Kerouac
1958	*The Naked and the Dead*	Norman Mailer
	Lolita	Vladimir Nabokov
1959	*Slaughterhouse-Five*	Kurt Vonnegut
	Naked Lunch	William Burroughs
1960	*The Golden Notebook*	Doris Lessing
	To Kill a Mockingbird	Harper Lee
1961	*Catch-22*	Joseph Heller
	The Moviegoer	Walker Percy
	The Alexandria Quartet	Lawrence Durrell
1962	*A Clockwork Orange*	Anthony Burgess
	One Flew Over the Cuckoo's Nest	Ken Kesey
	Ship of Fools	Katherine Anne Porter
1966	*Wide Sargasso Sea*	Jean Rhys
1969	*Portnoy's Complaint*	Philip Roth
	Deliverance	James Dickey
1973	*Gravity's Rainbow*	Thomas Pynchon
1975	*Ragtime*	E. L. Doctorow
	Heat and Dust	Ruth Prawer Jhabvala
1976	*The Woman Warrior*	Maxine Hong Kingston
1978	*The World According to Garp*	John Irving
	The Stories of John Cheever	John Cheever
1979	*A Bend in the River*	V. S. Naipaul

	Sophie's Choice	William Styron
1981	*Midnight's Children*	Salman Rushdie
	Rabbit Is Rich	John Updike
1982	*The Color Purple*	Alice Walker
1985	*Lonesome Dove*	Larry McMurtry
1987	*Beloved*	Toni Morrison
1989	*The Mambo Kings Play Songs of Love*	Oscar Hijuelos
1991	*A Thousand Acres*	Jane Smiley
1992	*The English Patient*	Michael Ondaatje
1993	*Ironweed*	William Kennedy
1995	*Independence Day*	Richard Ford

CHAPTER 12

Biblical Quotes and Books of the Bible

INTRODUCTION

A decent working knowledge of the Bible will help you better appreciate Western literature. It's as simple as that. This is particularly true of the literature written prior to 1800. The more you know about it, the better. One extreme, for example, is *Paradise Lost*. Milton probably assumed his readers knew the Bible almost as well as he did—which was by heart. At the other end of the scale is, for example, *The Sun Also Rises*. The title of Hemingway's first novel is from Ecclesiastes, though little else is from the Bible. Still, the Bible is the Rosetta Stone for much of our canon. Steinbeck's *East of Eden* will have far less resonance for you if you are not familiar with the story of Cain and Abel.

The Bible can be especially present in certain so-called regional literature. In literature from the American South, for example, the language of the Bible is on the page, and spoken by the characters who inhabit it, often to a high degree. William Faulkner at times seemed to be writing with the same pen that translated the Bible for King James. He admitted it was one of his greatest influences, and you can see it plainly at the most basic level—in his titles: *Go Down, Moses* and *Absalom, Absalom!*

Knowledge of the Bible is also helpful if you are going to be a good international traveler in the world of literature. The Bible's influence crosses borders and time spans fluidly. The verse from the Gospel of St. John that Dostoyevsky quotes at the beginning of *The Brothers Karamazov* is not from the "Russian" Bible. It's from *the* Bible, the same Bible you can open at any time and peruse. There is a kind of brotherhood of readers and writers as a result. It is thought provoking to realize that Dante, Shakespeare, Goethe, and other luminaries read and pondered the same Bible you can read today. And were inspired by it.

If you're a little rusty when it comes to the stories of the Bible, that's all right. The following chapter might be called Bible Study 101.

Note: The quotations here are from the Authorized Version, 1611.

> In the beginning God created the heaven and the earth. And the earth was without form, and void; and darkness was upon the face of the deep. And the Spirit of God moved upon the face of the waters.
> And God said, Let there be light: and there was light.
>
> [Genesis ch. 1, v. 1]
>
> And the evening and the morning were the first day.
>
> [Genesis ch. 1, v. 5]
>
> And God saw that it was good.
>
> [Genesis ch. 1, v. 10]
>
> It is not good that the man should be alone; I will make him an help meet for him.
>
> [Genesis ch. 2, v. 18]
>
> Bone of my bones, and flesh of my flesh.
>
> [Genesis ch. 2, v. 23.]
>
> Therefore shall a man leave his father and his mother, and shall cleave unto his wife: and they shall be one flesh.
>
> [Genesis ch. 2, v. 24]
>
> Now the serpent was more subtil than any beast of the field.
>
> [Genesis ch. 3, v. 1]
>
> In sorrow thou shalt bring forth children.
>
> [Genesis ch. 3, v. 16]
>
> In the sweat of thy face shalt thou eat bread.
>
> [Genesis ch. 3, v. 19]

For dust thou art, and unto dust shalt thou return.

[Genesis ch. 3, v. 19.]

Am I my brother's keeper?

[Genesis ch. 4, v. 9]

There were giants in the earth in those days.

[Genesis ch. 6, v. 4]

His hand will be against every man, and every man's hand against him.

[Genesis ch. 16, v. 12]

Ye shall eat the fat of the land.

[Genesis ch. 45, v. 18]

I have been a stranger in a strange land.

[Exodus ch. 2, v. 22]

A land flowing with milk and honey.

[Exodus ch. 3, v. 8]

Let my people go.

[Exodus ch. 7, v. 16]

Life for life,
Eye for eye, tooth for tooth.

[Exodus ch. 21, v. 23]

Thou shalt love thy neighbour as thyself.

[Leviticus ch. 19, v. 18.]

I am going the way of all the earth.

[Joshua ch. 23, v. 14]

Out of the eater came forth meat, and out of the strong came forth sweetness.

[Judges ch. 14, v. 14]

He smote them hip and thigh.

[Judges ch. 15, v. 8]

With the jawbone of an ass . . . have I slain a thousand men.

[Judges ch. 15, v. 16]

Intreat me not to leave thee, or to return from following after thee: for whither thou goest, I will go; and where thou lodgest, I will lodge: thy people shall be my people, and thy God my God: Where thou diest, will I die, and there will I be buried: the Lord do so to me, and more also, if ought but death part thee and me.

[Ruth ch. 1, v. 16]

A man after his own heart.

[I Samuel ch. 13, v. 14]

The beauty of Israel is slain upon thy high places: how are the mighty fallen!

[II Samuel ch. 1, v. 19]

The poor man had nothing, save one little ewe lamb.

[II Samuel ch. 12, v. 3]

And the king was much moved, and went up to the chamber over the gate, and wept: and as he went, thus he said, O my son Absalom, my son, my son Absalom! would God I had died for thee, O Absalom, my son, my son!

[II Samuel ch. 18, v. 33]

Then will I cut off Israel out of the land which I have given them; and this house, which I have hallowed for my name, will I cast out of my sight; and Israel shall be a proverb and a byword among all people.

[I Kings ch. 9, v. 7]

Behold, the half was not told me.

[I Kings ch. 10, v. 7]

But the Lord was not in the wind: and after the wind an earthquake; but the Lord was not in the earthquake:

And after the earthquake a fire: but the Lord was not in the fire: and after the fire a still small voice.

[I Kings ch. 19, v. 11]

Is thy servant a dog, that he should do this great thing?

[II Kings ch. 8, v. 13]

And the Lord said unto Satan, Whence comest thou? Then Satan answered the Lord, and said, From going to and fro in the earth, and from walking up and down in it.

[Job ch. 1, v. 7]

The Lord gave, and the Lord hath taken away; blessed be the name of the Lord.

[Job ch. 1, v. 21]

All that a man hath will he give for his life.

[Job ch. 2, v. 4]

There the wicked cease from troubling, and there the weary be at rest.

[Job ch. 3, v. 17]

Man is born unto trouble, as the sparks fly upward.

[Job ch. 5, v. 7]

I am escaped with the skin of my teeth.

[Job ch. 19, v. 20]

I know that my redeemer liveth, and that he shall stand at the
latter day upon the earth:
And though after my skin worms destroy this body, yet in my
flesh shall I see God.

[Job ch. 19, v. 25]

The price of wisdom is above rubies.

[Job ch. 28, v. 18]

Her ways are ways of pleasantness, and all her paths are peace.

[Proverbs ch. 3, v. 17]

Go to the ant thou sluggard; consider her ways, and be wise.

[Proverbs ch. 6, v. 6]

A wise son maketh a glad father: but a foolish son is the heaviness of his mother.

[Proverbs ch. 10, v. 1]

A virtuous woman is a crown to her husband.

[Proverbs ch. 12, v. 4]

Hope deferred maketh the heart sick.

[Proverbs ch. 13, v. 12]

He that spareth his rod hateth his son.

[Proverbs ch. 13, v. 24]

A soft answer turneth away wrath.

[Proverbs ch. 15, v. 1]

A merry heart maketh a cheerful countenance.

[Proverbs ch. 15, v. 13]

Better is a dinner of herbs where love is, than a stalled ox and
hatred therewith.

[Proverbs ch. 15, v. 17]

A word spoken in due season, how good is it!

[Proverbs ch. 15, v. 23]

Pride goeth before destruction, and an haughty spirit before a
fall.

[Proverbs ch. 16, v. 18]

There is a friend that sticketh closer than a brother.

[Proverbs ch. 18, v. 24]

Wine is a mocker, strong drink is raging.

[Proverbs ch. 20, v. 1]

Train up a child in the way he should go: and when he is old, he
will not depart from it.

[Proverbs ch. 22, v. 6]

Look not thou upon the wine when it is red.

> [Proverbs ch. 23, v. 31]

If thine enemy be hungry, give him bread to eat; and if he be thirsty, give him water to drink.

For thou shalt heap coals of fire upon his head, and the Lord shall reward thee.

> [Proverbs ch. 25, v. 21]

As cold waters to a thirsty soul, so is good news from a far country.

> [Proverbs ch. 25, v. 25]

Answer not a fool according to his folly, lest thou also be like unto him.

Answer a fool according to his folly, lest he be wise in his own conceit.

> [Proverbs ch. 26, v. 4]

As a dog returneth to his vomit, so a fool returneth to his folly.

> [Proverbs ch. 26, v. 11]

The wicked flee when no man pursueth: but the righteous are bold as a lion.

> [Proverbs ch. 28, v. 1]

He that maketh haste to be rich shall not be innocent.

> [Proverbs ch. 28, v. 20]

Where there is no vision, the people perish.

> [Proverbs ch. 29, v. 18]

There be three things which are too wonderful for me, yea, four which I know not:

The way of an eagle in the air; the way of a serpent upon a rock; the way of a ship in the midst of the sea; and the way of a man with a maid.

> [Proverbs ch. 30, v. 18]

Who can find a virtuous woman? for her price is far above rubies.

> [Proverbs ch. 31, v. 10]

Vanity of vanities; all is vanity.

> [Ecclesiastes ch. 1, v. 2.]

All the rivers run into the sea; yet the sea is not full.

> [Ecclesiastes ch. 1, v. 7]

The thing that hath been, it is that which shall be; and that which is done is that which shall be done: and there is no new thing under the sun.

> [Ecclesiastes ch. 1, v. 9]

To every thing there is a season, and a time to every purpose under the heaven:
A time to be born, and a time to die; a time to plant, and a time to pluck up that which is planted.

[Ecclesiastes ch. 3, v. 1]

A time to weep, and a time to laugh; a time to mourn, and a time to dance.

[Ecclesiastes ch. 3, v. 1]

A time to love, and a time to hate; a time of war, and a time of peace.

[Ecclesiastes ch. 3, v. 1]

A living dog is better than a dead lion.

[Ecclesiastes ch. 9, v. 4]

The race is not to the swift, nor the battle to the strong.

[Ecclesiastes ch. 9, v. 11.]

Wine maketh merry: but money answereth all things.

[Ecclesiastes ch. 10, v. 19]

Cast thy bread upon the waters: for thou shalt find it after many days.

[Ecclesiastes ch. 11, v. 1]

Of making many books there is no end; and much study is a weariness of the flesh.

[Ecclesiastes ch. 12, v. 12]

I am black, but comely.

[Song of Solomon ch. 1, v. 5]

The time of the singing of birds is come, and the voice of the turtle is heard in our land.

[Song of Solomon ch. 2, v. 10]

My beloved is mine, and I am his: he feedeth among the lilies. Until the day break, and the shadows flee away.

[Song of Solomon ch. 2, v. 16]

Love is strong as death; jealousy is cruel as the grave.

[Song of Solomon ch. 8, v. 6]

Many waters cannot quench love, neither can the floods drown it.

[Song of Solomon ch. 8, v. 7]

Though your sins be as scarlet, they shall be as white as snow.

[Isaiah ch. 1, v. 18]

They shall beat their swords into plowshares, and their spears into pruninghooks: nation shall not lift up sword against nation, neither shall they learn war any more.

[Isaiah ch. 2, v. 4.]

Whom shall I send, and who will go for us? Then said I, Here am I; send me.

[Isaiah ch. 6, v. 8]

The wolf also shall dwell with the lamb, and the leopard shall lie down with the kid; and the calf and the young lion and the fatling together; and a little child shall lead them.

[Isaiah ch. 11, v. 6]

How art thou fallen from heaven, O Lucifer, son of the morning!

[Isaiah ch. 14, v. 12]

Let us eat and drink; for to morrow we shall die.

[Isaiah ch. 22, v. 13]

For precept must be upon precept, precept upon precept; line upon line, line upon line; here a little, and there a little.

[Isaiah ch. 28, v. 10]

Is there no balm in Gilead?

[Jeremiah ch. 8, v. 22]

Can the Ethiopian change his skin, or the leopard his spots?

[Jeremiah ch. 13, v. 23]

They have sown the wind, and they shall reap the whirlwind.

[Hosea ch. 8, v. 7]

I will restore to you the years that the locust hath eaten.

[Joel ch. 2, v. 25]

Ye were as a firebrand plucked out of the burning.

[Amos ch. 4, v. 11]

What doth the Lord require of thee, but to do justly, and to love mercy, and to walk humbly with thy God?

[Micah ch. 6, v. 8]

Judge none blessed before his death.

[Ecclesiasticus ch. 11, v. 28.]

He that toucheth pitch shall be defiled therewith.

[Ecclesiasticus ch. 13, v. 1]

Let us now praise famous men, and our fathers that begat us.

[Ecclesiasticus ch. 44, v. 1]

The voice of one crying in the wilderness, Prepare ye the way of the Lord, make his paths straight.

[St Matthew ch. 3, v. 3]

Blessed are the poor in spirit: for theirs is the kingdom of heaven.
Blessed are they that mourn: for they shall be comforted.
Blessed are the meek: for they shall inherit the earth.

Blessed are they which do hunger and thirst after righteousness: for they shall be filled.

Blessed are the merciful: for they shall obtain mercy.

Blessed are the pure in heart: for they shall see God.

Blessed are the peacemakers: for they shall be called the children of God.

[St Matthew ch. 5, v. 3]

Ye are the light of the world. A city that is set on an hill cannot be hid.

[St Matthew ch. 5, v. 14]

Let your light so shine before men, that they may see your good works.

[St Matthew ch. 5, v. 16]

Resist not evil: but whosoever shall smite thee on thy right cheek, turn to him the other also.

[St Matthew ch. 5, v. 39]

Whosoever shall compel thee to go a mile, go with him twain.

[St Matthew ch. 5, v. 41]

Lay not up for yourselves treasures upon earth, where moth and rust doth corrupt, and where thieves break through and steal:

But lay up for yourselves treasures in heaven.

[St Matthew ch. 6, v. 19]

Where your treasure is, there will your heart be also.

[St Matthew ch. 6, v. 21]

No man can serve two masters . . . Ye cannot serve God and mammon.

[St Matthew ch. 6, v. 24]

Consider the lilies of the field, how they grow; they toil not, neither do they spin:

And yet I say unto you, That even Solomon in all his glory was not arrayed like one of these.

[St Matthew ch. 6, v. 28]

Judge not, that ye be not judged.

[St Matthew ch. 7, v. 1]

Why beholdest thou the mote that is in thy brother's eye, but considerest not the beam that is in thine own eye?

[St Matthew ch. 7, v. 3]

Neither cast ye your pearls before swine.

[St Matthew ch. 7, v. 6]

Ask, and it shall be given you; seek, and ye shall find; knock, and it shall be opened unto you.

[St Matthew ch. 7, v. 7]

Or what man is there of you, whom if his son ask bread, will he give him a stone?

[St Matthew ch. 7, v. 9]

Wide is the gate, and broad is the way, that leadeth to destruction, and many there be that go in thereat.

[St Matthew ch. 7, v. 13]

Strait is the gate, and narrow is the way, which leadeth unto life, and few there be that find it.

[St Matthew ch. 7, v. 14]

Beware of false prophets, which come to you in sheep's clothing, but inwardly they are ravening wolves.

[St Matthew ch. 7, v. 15]

By their fruits ye shall know them.

[St Matthew ch. 7, v. 20]

But the children of the kingdom shall be cast out into outer darkness: there shall be weeping and gnashing of teeth.

[St Matthew ch. 8, v. 12]

The foxes have holes, and the birds of the air have nests; but the Son of man hath not where to lay his head.

[St Matthew ch. 8, v. 20]

Let the dead bury their dead.

[St Matthew ch. 8, v. 22]

Neither do men put new wine into old bottles.

[St Matthew ch. 9, v. 17]

I came not to send peace, but a sword.

[St Matthew ch. 10, v. 34]

He that is not with me is against me.

[St Matthew ch. 12, v. 30 and St Luke ch. 11, v. 23]

A prophet is not without honour, save in his own country, and in his own house.

[St Matthew ch. 13, v. 57]

O thou of little faith, wherefore didst thou doubt?

[St Matthew ch. 14, v. 31]

If the blind lead the blind, both shall fall into the ditch.

[St Matthew ch. 15, v. 14]

Get thee behind me, Satan.

[St Matthew ch. 16, v. 23]

If thine eye offend thee, pluck it out, and cast it from thee.
[St Matthew ch. 18, v. 9]
For where two or three are gathered together in my name, there am I in the midst of them.
[St Matthew ch. 18, v. 20]
What therefore God hath joined together, let not man put asunder.
[St Matthew ch. 19, v. 6]
If thou wilt be perfect, go and sell that thou hast, and give to the poor, and thou shalt have treasure in heaven.
[St Matthew ch. 19, v. 21]
It is easier for a camel to go through the eye of a needle, than for a rich man to enter into the kingdom of God.
[St Matthew ch. 19, v. 24. See also St Luke ch. 18, v. 24]
With God all things are possible.
[St Matthew ch. 19, v. 26]
But many that are first shall be last; and the last shall be first.
[St Matthew ch. 19, v. 30]
For many are called, but few are chosen.
[St Matthew ch. 22, v. 14]
Render therefore unto Caesar the things which are Caesar's; and unto God the things that are God's.
[St Matthew ch. 22, v. 21]
Thou shalt love the Lord thy God with all thy heart, and with all thy soul, and with all thy mind.
This is the first and great commandment.
And the second is like unto it, Thou shalt love thy neighbour as thyself.
[St Matthew ch. 22, v. 38]
Ye blind guides, which strain at a gnat, and swallow a camel.
[St Matthew ch. 23, v. 24]
Ye are like unto whited sepulchres.
[St Matthew ch. 23, v. 27]
Well done, thou good and faithful servant.
[St Matthew ch. 25, v. 21]
It had been good for that man if he had not been born.
[St Matthew ch. 26, v. 24]
If it be possible, let this cup pass from me.
[St Matthew ch. 26, v. 39]
What, could ye not watch with me one hour?
[St Matthew ch. 26, v. 40]

Watch and pray, that ye enter not into temptation: the spirit indeed is willing but the flesh is weak.

[St Matthew ch. 26, v. 41]

All they that take the sword shall perish with the sword.

[St Matthew ch. 26, v. 52]

If a house be divided against itself, that house cannot stand.

[St Mark ch. 3, v. 25.]

He that hath ears to hear, let him hear.

[St Mark ch. 4, v. 9]

My name is Legion: for we are many.

[St Mark ch. 5, v. 9]

For what shall it profit a man, if he shall gain the whole world, and lose his own soul?

[St Mark ch. 8, v. 36.]

Suffer the little children to come unto me, and forbid them not: for of such is the kingdom of God.

[St Mark ch. 10, v. 14]

Physician, heal thyself.

[St Luke ch. 4, v. 23]

Love your enemies, do good to them which hate you.

[St Luke ch. 6, v. 27]

For the labourer is worthy of his hire.

[St Luke ch. 10, v. 7]

No man, when he hath lighted a candle, putteth it in a secret place, neither under a bushel, but on a candlestick, that they which come in may see the light.

[St Luke ch. 11, v. 33]

Soul, thou hast much goods laid up for many years; take thine ease, eat, drink, and be merry.

[St Luke ch. 12, v. 19]

Father, forgive them: for they know not what they do.

[St Luke ch. 23, v. 34]

To day shalt thou be with me in paradise.

[St Luke ch. 23, v. 43]

In the beginning was the Word, and the Word was with God, and the Word was God.

[St John ch. 1, v. 1]

Can there any good thing come out of Nazareth?

[St John ch. 1, v. 46]

Behold an Israelite indeed, in whom is no guile!

[St John ch. 1, v. 47]

Rise, take up thy bed, and walk.

[St John ch. 5, v. 8]

He that is without sin among you, let him first cast a stone at her.

[St John ch. 8, v. 7]

And ye shall know the truth, and the truth shall make you free.

[St John ch. 8, v. 32]

The poor always ye have with you.

[St John ch. 12, v. 8]

In my Father's house are many mansions . . . I go to prepare a place for you.

[St John ch. 14, v. 2]

I am the way, the truth, and the life: no man cometh unto the Father, but by me.

[St John ch. 14, v. 6]

Greater love hath no man than this, that a man lay down his life for his friends.

[St John ch. 15, v. 13.]

It is hard for thee to kick against the pricks.

[Acts of the Apostles ch. 9, v. 5]

God is no respecter of persons.

[Acts of the Apostles ch. 10, v. 34]

It is more blessed to give than to receive.

[Acts of the Apostles ch. 20, v. 35]

Hast thou appealed unto Caesar? unto Caesar shalt thou go.

[Acts of the Apostles ch. 25, v. 12]

A law unto themselves.

[Romans ch. 2, v. 14]

Let us do evil, that good may come.

[Romans ch. 3, v. 8]

For where no law is, there is no transgression.

[Romans ch. 4, v. 15]

The wages of sin is death.

[Romans ch. 6, v. 23]

If God be for us, who can be against us?

[Romans ch. 8, v. 31]

Vengeance is mine; I will repay, saith the Lord.

[Romans ch. 12, v. 19]

It is better to marry than to burn.

[I Corinthians ch. 7, v. 9]

Though I speak with the tongues of men and of angels, and have not charity, I am become as sounding brass, or a tinkling cymbal.

And though I have the gift of prophecy, and understand all mysteries, and all knowledge; and though I have all faith; so that I could remove mountains; and have not charity, I am nothing.

[I Corinthians ch. 13, v. 1]

Charity suffereth long, and is kind; charity envieth not; charity vaunteth not itself, is not puffed up . . .

Beareth all things, believeth all things, hopeth all things, endureth all things.

Charity never faileth

[I Corinthians ch. 13, v. 4]

When I was a child, I spake as a child, I understood as a child, I thought as a child: but when I became a man, I put away childish things.

For now we see through a glass, darkly; but then face to face: now I know in part; but then shall I know even as also I am known.

And now abideth faith, hope, charity, these three; but the greatest of these is charity.

[I Corinthians ch. 13, v. 11]

O death, where is thy sting? O grave, where is thy victory?

[I Corinthians ch. 15, v. 55]

God loveth a cheerful giver.

[II Corinthians ch. 9, v. 7]

For ye suffer fools gladly, seeing ye yourselves are wise.

[II Corinthians ch. 11, v. 19]

Be not deceived; God is not mocked: for whatsoever a man soweth, that shall he also reap.

[Galatians ch. 6, v. 7]

Be ye angry and sin not: let not the sun go down upon your wrath.

[Ephesians ch. 4, v. 26]

For by him were all things created, that are in heaven, and that are in earth, visible and invisible, whether they be thrones, or dominions, or principalities, or powers.

[Colossians ch. 1, v. 16]

Husbands, love your wives, and be not bitter against them.

[Colossians ch. 3, v. 19]

Let your speech be alway with grace, seasoned with salt.

[Colossians ch. 4, v. 6]

If any would not work, neither should he eat.

[II Thessalonians ch. 3, v. 10]

Use a little wine for thy stomach's sake.

[I Timothy ch. 5, v. 23]

For we brought nothing into this world, and it is certain we can carry nothing out.

[I Timothy ch. 6, v. 7]

The love of money is the root of all evil.

[I Timothy ch. 6, v. 10]

I have fought a good fight, I have finished my course, I have kept the faith.

[II Timothy ch. 4, v. 7]

Be not forgetful to entertain strangers: for thereby some have entertained angels unawares.

[Hebrews ch. 13, v. 2]

Faith without works is dead.

[James ch. 2, v. 20]

Let your yea be yea; and your nay, nay.

[James ch. 5, v. 12]

All flesh is as grass, and all the glory of man as the flower of grass. The grass withereth, and the flower thereof falleth away.

[*I Peter ch. 1, v. 24*]

But ye are a chosen generation, a royal priesthood, an holy nation, a peculiar people.

[I Peter ch. 2, v. 9]

Charity shall cover the multitude of sins.

[I Peter ch. 4, v. 8]

There is no fear in love; but perfect love casteth out fear.

[I John ch. 4, v. 18]

I am Alpha and Omega, the beginning and the ending, saith the Lord.

[Revelation ch. 1, v. 8]

And I looked, and behold a pale horse: and his name that sat on him was Death.

[Revelation ch. 6, v. 8]

These are they which came out of great tribulation, and have washed their robes, and made them white in the blood of the Lamb.

> [Revelation ch. 7, v. 14.]

God shall wipe away all tears from their eyes.

> [Revelation ch. 7, v. 17]

And when he had opened the seventh seal, there was silence in heaven about the space of half an hour.

> [Revelation ch. 8, v. 1]

And there appeared a great wonder in heaven; a woman clothed with the sun, and the moon under her feet, and upon her head a crown of twelve stars.

> [Revelation ch. 12, v. 1]

And that no man might buy or sell, save he that had the mark, or the name of the beast, or the number of his name.

> [Revelation ch. 13, v. 17]

Let him that hath understanding count the number of the beast: for it is the number of a man; and his number is Six hundred threescore and six.

> [Revelation ch. 13, v. 18]

Babylon is fallen, is fallen, that great city.

> [Revelation ch. 14, v. 8]

And the sea gave up the dead which were in it.

> [Revelation ch. 20, v. 13]

And God shall wipe away all tears from their eyes; and there shall be no more death, neither sorrow, nor crying, neither shall there be any more pain: for the former things are passed away. And he that sat upon the throne said, Behold, I make all things new.

> [Revelation ch. 21, v. 4.]

BOOKS OF THE BIBLE

Hebrew Bible (Old Testament)

Genesis	Judges	1 Chronicles
Exodus	Ruth	2 Chronicles
Leviticus	1 Samuel	Ezra
Numbers	2 Samuel	Nehemiah
Deuteronomy	1 Kings	Esther
Joshua	2 Kings	Job

Psalms	Ezekiel	Nahum
Proverbs	Daniel	Habakkuk
Ecclesiastes	Hosea	Zephaniah
Song of Songs	Joel	Haggai
(Song of Solomon)	Amos	Zechariah
Isaiah	Obadiah	Malachi
Jeremiah	Jonah	
Lamentations	Micah	

New Testament

Matthew	Ephesians	Hebrews
Mark	Philippians	James
Luke	Colossians	1 Peter
John	1 Thessalonians	2 Peter
Acts	2 Thessalonians	1 John
Romans	1 Timothy	2 John
1 Corinthians	2 Timothy	3 John
2 Corinthians	Titus	Jude
Galatians	Philemon	Revelation

Other Books of The Bible
HEBREW BIBLE APOCRYPHA

Of the numerous apocryphal works associated with the Old Testament, the most familiar are those that comprise the body of books known (primarily by Protestants) as the Apocrypha ("Hidden Books"). Protestants have rejected the authority of these works since the Reformation of the 16th century, but often include them as a separate section of the Bible. Roman Catholics and Greek Orthodox Christians embrace the holiness of a number of these books (usually 12 to 16 of them), which, when so considered, are called the Deuterocanonical Books ("Second-Level Books"). In addition, there are the works known collectively as the Pseudepigrapha ("False Writings"). These books, although associated with the Hebrew Bible, are regarded as strictly noncanonical.

Note: Because there is no universal agreement on which books belong to the Apocrypha, which books are recognized as authoritative, or even by which titles the books properly go, any classification of the apocryphal works is subject to dispute.

THE APOCRYPHA (INCORPORATING THE DEUTEROCANONICAL BOOKS)

1 Esdras
2 Esdras
1 Maccabees
2 Maccabees
3 Maccabees
Tobit
Judith
Ecclesiasticus (Sirach)

Wisdom of Solomon
1 Baruch (with Epistle of Jeremiah)
Prayer of Manasseh
Additions to Book of Daniel
Song of the Three Holy Children

Prayer of Azariah
Susanna
Bel and the Dragon
Additions to Book of Esther
Psalm 151

THE PSEUDEPIGRAPHA (SELECTED WORKS)

Jubilees
Letter of Aristeas
Books of Adam and Eve
Martyrdom of Isaiah
1 Enoch

2 Enoch
Testament of the Twelve Patriarchs
Sybilline Oracles
Assumption of Moses
2 Baruch

3 Baruch
4 Esdras
Psalms of Solomon
4 Maccabees (Story of Ahiqar)

NEW TESTAMENT APOCRYPHA

The extracanonical Christian writings associated with the New Testament are typically classified in accordance with the four major genres of New Testament literature: gospels, acts, epistles (letters), and apocalypses. Lacking a widely accepted definitive list of contents, this body of works includes the following books:

Gospels
Protoevangelium of James
Infancy Gospel of Thomas
Gospel of Peter
Gospel of Nicodemus
Gospel of the Nazoreans

Gospel of the Ebionites
Gospel of the Hebrews
Gospel of the Egyptians
Gospel of Thomas
Gospel of Philip
Gospel of Mary

ACTS

Acts of John
Acts of Peter
Acts of Paul
Acts of Andrew
Acts of Thomas

Acts of Andrew and Matthias
Acts of Philip
Acts of Thaddaeus
Acts of Peter and Paul

Acts of Peter and Andrew
Martyrdom of Matthew
Slavonic Act of Peter
Acts of Peter and the Twelve Apostles

Epistles

3 Corinthians (Letter of Paul)
Epistle to the Laodiceans
Letters of Paul and Seneca
Didache (Teachings of the
    Twelve Apostles)
Letters of Jesus and Abgar
Epistle of Barnabas

Epistle to Diognetus
Letter of Lentulus
Letters of Ignatius
Letters of Clement to the
    Corinthians
Epistle of Titus

Apocalypses

Apocalypse of Peter
Coptic Apocalypse of Peter
Apocalypse of Paul
1 Apocalypse of James
2 Apocalypse of James
Apocryphon of John

Sophia of Jesus Christ
Letter of Peter to Philip
Apocalypse of Mary
Apocalypse of Bartholomew
Apocalypse of Thomas

(Books taken from the New Revised Standard Version Bible
with Apocrypha. New York: Oxford University Press, 1991.)

CHAPTER 13

Major Mythological Characters

INTRODUCTION

Even more than the Bible, Greek and Roman mythology has served as a basis for stories, novels, plays, poems, and for their characters, for almost as long as people have been writing. The list is endless and continues to grow. Mythology's influence goes far beyond literature, of course. Recently, I saw Homer Simpson as Ulysses and, of all people, Ned Flanders as Priam. The basic (and correct) assumption, is that even today, in our electronic age, most children know the story of the Trojan War. They know Greek mythology as well. What does Sylvester Stallone name one of his opponents in *Rocky*? Apollo. And speaking of that, where would NASA be without mythology? Not to mention our galaxy. Or Walt Disney. Then there's that big shoe company. Just think— how many seafood restaurants would be affected if the name "Neptune" disappeared? This search for mythology's influence in our contemporary life is now a standard exercise in our grade schools, simply because the references are so ready that even an eight-year-old can find them.

Because so much of our culture is somehow connected with mythology, it behooves us to know something about these characters: Zeus, Poseidon, Hermes, Bacchus, Hera, Aphrodite, and so on down the Olympic line. These gods are directly involved in the events of the *Iliad* and the *Odyssey*, as well as in Greek drama.

Think of *The Bacchae*, for one. They are vain, easily offended, and prone to revenge. You didn't want to get the gods angry, but too often those haughty ancient Greeks did, and they would inevitably pay the price.

The simple fact is that the stories are fascinating and highly entertaining. That's reason enough to reacquaint yourself with this celestial cast of characters.

DEITIES OF CLASSICAL MYTHOLOGY
Greek

NAME	REALM, POSITION, OR SYMBOLISM
Adonis	god of the cycle of vegetation; personification of beautiful youth
Aeolus	god of the winds
Amphitrite	goddess of the oceans
Aphrodite	goddess of love and beauty
Apollo	god of youth, music, poetry, archery, and prophecy
Ares	god of war
Artemis	goddess of the hunt and the moon
Asclepius	god of medicine and healing
Athena	goddess of wisdom
Carpo	goddess of summer fruit
Chaos	personification of confusion
Chloris	goddess of flowers
Cronus	ruler of the Titans, after deposing his father, Uranus
Demeter	goddess of grains and harvest
Dionysus	god of wine
Enyo	goddess of war
Eos	goddess of the dawn
Eris	goddess of discord
Eros	god of love
Fates (or Moirai)	3 goddesses of human destiny (Atropos, Clotho, Lachesis)
Graces (or Charities)	personification of charm, grace, and beauty; 3 daughters of Zeus (Aglaia, Euphrosyne, Thalia)
Hades (or Pluto)	god of the underworld
Hebe	cupbearer of the gods
Hecate	goddess of dark places

Helios	god of the sun
Hephaestus	god of fire and the forge
Hera	queen of the goddesses; wife and sister of Zeus
Heracles	superhuman hero; performed 12 labors to win immortality
Hermaphroditus	a male-female deity, having been joined as one with the nymph Salmacis
Hermes	messenger of the gods
Hestia	goddess of the hearth
Hygeia	goddess of health
Hymen	god of marriage
Hypnos	god of sleep
Irene (or Eirene)	goddess of peace
Iris	goddess of the rainbow
Masyas	satyr flayed to death after losing flute-playing contest to Apollo
Metis	personification of prudence; first wife of Zeus
Morpheus	god of dreams
Muses	9 sisters; goddesses of arts/sciences:
Calliope	chief of the Muses
Clio	muse of history
Erato	muse of erotic poetry
Euterpe	muse of lyric poetry
Melpomene	muse of tragedy
Polyhymnia	muse of sacred poetry
Terpsichore	muse of dance
Thalia	muse of comedy
Urania	muse of astronomy
Nemesis	goddess of vengeance
Nereids	sea nymphs
Nereus	old sea god; father of the Nereids
Nike	goddess of victory
Nymphs	female spirits of nature
Nyx	goddess of night
Pan	god of shepherds, flocks, forests, and pastures
Persephone	queen of the underworld; goddess of spring
Pleiades	seven daughters of Atlas; changed into a cluster of stars by Zeus
Plutus	god of wealth
Poseidon	god of the oceans
Priapus	god of fertility

Psyche	female personification of Rhea, wife of Cronus; mother of Zeus
Satyrs	gods of the woodlands
Selene	goddess of the moon
Sirens	sea nymphs and enchantresses
Thanatos	god of death
Themis	personification of order and justice; daughter of Uranus and Gaia
Titans	children of Uranus, who helped, and then defeated, Cronus
Triton	trumpeter of the sea; son of Poseidon
Tyche	goddess of fortune
Uranus	god of heaven; father of the Titans
Zeus	chief god of Olympus

Roman

NAME	REALM, POSITION, OR SYMBOLISM
Aesculapius	god of medicine and healing
Apollo	god of youth, music, poetry, archery, and prophecy
Aurora	goddess of the dawn
Bacchus (or Liber)	god of wine
Bellona	goddess of war
Ceres	goddess of grains and harvest
Coelus	god of heaven
Cupid (or Amor)	god of love
Diana	goddess of the hunt and the moon
Discordia	goddess of discord
Fauna	goddess of the fields
Faunus	(or Inuus) god of shepherds and flocks
Flora	goddess of flowers
Fortuna	goddess of fortune
Graces (or Gratiae)	personification of charm, grace, and beauty; 3 daughters of Jupiter (Aglaia, Euphrosyne, Thalia)
Hercules	superhuman hero; performed 12 labors to win immortality
Janus	god of beginnings, especially of the year and the seasons
Juno	queen of the goddesses; wife of Jupiter
Jupiter (or Jove)	chief of all gods
Juturna	goddess of springs of water

Juventas	goddess of youth
Juventus	god of youth
Lares and Penates	household gods who watch over homes and cities
Lemures	spirits of the dead
Libitina	goddess of the underworld
Lucina	goddess of childbirth
Luna	goddess of the moon
Mars	god of war
Mercury	messenger of the gods
Minerva	goddess of wisdom
Mors	god of death
Neptune	god of the oceans
Nox	goddess of night
Orcus (or Pluto)	god of the underworld
Picus	god who could predict the future
Pomona	goddess of fruit trees and their fruit
Proserpina (Persipina)	queen of the underworld; goddess of spring
Psyche	female personification of the soul
Salacia	goddess of the oceans
Saturn	god of agriculture (equivalent of Greek Cronus)
Sol	god of the sun
Somnus	god of sleep
Silvanus (Sylvanus)	god of forests and uncultivated land
Tartarus	primeval god of the underworld
Terminus	guardian of boundaries
Trivia	goddess of dark places
Venus	goddess of love and beauty
Vesta	goddess of the hearth
Victoria	goddess of victory
Voluptas	goddess of pleasure
Vulcan	god of fire and the forge

Norse, Scandinavian, and Germanic Deities

NAME	REALM, POSITION, OR SYMBOLISM
Aegir	god of the sea and seashore
Aesir	principal race of Norse/Scandinavian gods (including Odin, Balder, and Thor)
Alfheim	elves of light

Arnamentia	goddess of springs
Asynjur	goddesses of the Aesir
Balder	god of the summer sun
Beiwe	goddess who heralded spring
Bertha	goddess of spinning
Bestla	mother of Odin
Bil	goddess of weaving
Bor	father of Odin
Bragi	god of poetry and music; chief poet of Odin
Brono	god of daylight
Buri	the first god, emerged from a cow-licked block of primeval ice
Dag	goddess of the day
Delling	god of the dawn
Donar	Germanic name for Thor
Eir	goddess of healing
Elle (or Elli)	personification of old age
Erda	goddess of the earth
Forseti	god of justice
Frey	god of fertility and weather; ruler of the Alfheim
Freyja (or Freya)	goddess of love, marriage, fertility, prosperity, magic, peace, and war
Frigg (or Frigga)	goddess of marriage and weaver of the clouds; wife of Odin
Fulla (or Volla)	maid and messenger of Frigg; caretaker of Frigg's shoes
Gefjon	goddess of fertility and virgins
Gerd (or Gerda)	goddess of light; personification of beauty
Gna	wind goddess and handmaiden of Frigg
Gondul	a Valkyrie who retrieved the souls of mortal kings slain in battle
Heimdall	god of the dawn and light; the watchman at Bilfrost (the Rainbow Bridge)
Hel (or Hella)	goddess of death and the underworld
Hermod	messenger of the gods
Hlin	goddess of consolation and protection
Hnoss	goddess of infatuation
Hod	blind god of winter
Hoenir	god who bestowed sense upon humans
Holda	goddess of spinning and weaving; patron of deceased children and witches

Holer (or Holler)	god of death, destruction, disease, and disaster
Idun (or Ithun)	goddess of spring and youth; keeper of the golden apples of eternal youth
Jabme-akka	goddess of the dead
Jord (or Fjorgyn)	goddess of the earth
Kajsa	goddess of the wind
Kvasir	god of wisdom; killed by dwarfs, who turn his blood into the mead of poetry
Laga	goddess of wells and springs
Lodur (or Ve)	god who bestowed appearance and speech upon humans
Lofn (or Lufn)	goddess of passion and forbidden love
Loki	god of mischief, trickery, chaos, and fire
Magni	god of strength
Mimir	god of wisdom and knowledge
Modi	god of courage
Nanna	goddess of the moon
Nat (or Nott)	goddess of the night
Nertheus	Germanic name for Njord
Njord (or Niord)	god of the wind, the sea, and navigation
Norns	3 virgin goddesses of destiny
Urd	goddess of the past
Verdandi	goddess of the present
Skuld	goddess of the future
Odin	chief of all gods; god of creation, victory, and the dead; leader of the Aesir
Poshjo-akka	goddess of the hunt
Ran	goddess of the sea and storms
Saga	all-knowing goddess
Sif	goddess of fertility and crops
Sjofn (or Vjofn)	goddess of passion and marital accord
Snotra	goddess of virtue and mistress of knowledge
Storjunka	god of the herds
Sunna	goddess of the sun
Syn	goddess of denial; defender of the accused
Thor	god of thunder, weather, agriculture, and the home
Tyr	god of war and strife
Ull (or Uller)	god of archery, the hunt, and skiers
Vali	god of vengeance
Valkyries	Odin's 12 handmaidens

Vanir	race of Norse/Scandinavian gods (including Njord, Frey, and Freyja); enemies, and later allies, of the Aesir
Var	goddess of insight; punisher of unfaithful spouses
Vidar (or Vithar)	god of vengeance
Vili	god who bestowed thought and motion upon humans
Vor	goddess of contracts, especially marriage; punisher of those who break promises
Waldmichen	woodland spirit (a Germanic form of Freyja)
Wotan	Germanic name for Odin
Yabme-akka	goddess of death, depicted as an old woman
Zisa	goddess of the harvest

Further References

Cotterell, Arthur. *A Dictionary of World Mythology.* New York: Oxford University Press, 1990.

Encyclopedia Mythica. "Norse Mythology," http://www.pantheon.org/mythica/areas/norse

DEITIES OF OTHER ANCIENT CULTURES

AUSTRALIAN	(TRIBE, OR REGION, IN PARENTHESES)
Altjira	sky father; god of the Dreamtime (Aranda)
Bunbulama	goddesses of the rain; endlessly pregnant (northern Australia)
Bunjil	god of creation (Kulin and Wurunjerri)
Djanggwul	divine trinity; 2 sisters, 1 brother (northern Australia)
Eingana	goddess of creation; mother of birth and death
Karora	god of creation (Bandicoot)
Kunapipi	mother goddess (northern Australia)
Mokoi	evil spirit (Murngin)
Pundjel	creator of all things; god of ceremonies (southeastern Australia)
Walo	goddess of the sun (widespread)
Wawalag	2 sisters; goddesses of fertility (northern Australia)
Yhi	goddess of creation and light (Karraur)
Yurlungur	great father; chief god of fertility; rainbow serpent (Murngin)

AFRICAN	(TRIBE IN PARENTHESES)
Abassi	god of creation (Efik)
Aha Njoku	goddess of yams (Ibo)
Anansi	god of trickery; "the Spider" (Ashanti)
Bumba	god of creation (Boshongo)
Chiuta	god of creation and rain (Tumbuka)
Chuku	god of creation and rain (Ibo)
Deng	god of creation, the sky, and fertility (Dinka)
Eshu	god of life's crossroads (Yoruba)
Faro	god of sky and water (Bambara)
Gamab	god of fate (Haukoin)
Huve	supreme god (Bushmen)
Jok	god of creation and birth (Alur)
Kaang	god of creation (Bushmen)
Kalunga	god of creation and the sky (Lunda)
Khonvoum	god of creation and the hunt (Pygmies)
Mbomba	god of creation and master of life and death (Mongo)
Nyalitch	god of the sky and lord of all spirits (Dinka)
Obatala	god of the disabled (Yoruba)
Quamta	supreme god (Xhosa)
Tore	god of animals and the hunt (Pygmies)
Wele	god of creation (Kavirondo)
Yansan	god of the wind (Yoruba)
Yemaja	mother goddess; goddess of fertility and birth

CELTIC	(G = GAUL; I = IRELAND; W = WALES)
Abnoba	goddess of forests, rivers, and the hunt (G)
Agrona	goddess of slaughter and strife (W)
Aine	goddess of love and fertility (I)
Amaethon	god of agriculture (W)
Andraste	goddess of war and victory (G)
Angus Mac Óg	god of love, beauty, and youth (I)
Arawn	god of the underworld (W)
Arianrhod	goddess of the full moon and rebirth (W)
Artio	goddess of wildlife; depicted as a bear (I)
Balor	god of death and king of a race of giants (I)
Banba	earth goddess; symbolic of the spirit of Ireland
Bebhionn	goddess of healing; patron of pleasure (I)
Belenus (Bel)	god of light; guardian of sheep and cattle (G, I)

Belisama	goddess of fire, light, and the forge (G, I)
Blodeuwedd	goddess of flowers in bloom (W)
Boann	goddess of fertility and abundance (I)
Borvo	god of hot mineral springs and healing (G)
Bran	god of prophecy and the arts (W)
Branwen	goddess of love and beauty (W)
Bres	god of agriculture and fertility (I)
Brigid (Brigit)	goddess of fire, poetry, healing, fertility, the forge, and martial arts (I, W)
Carman	goddess of evil sorcery (I)
Ceridwen	goddess of poetry, nature, and astrology (W)
Cernunnos	god of fertility, animals, wealth, and the underworld (G, I, W)
Cliodhna	goddess of beauty (I)
Creiddylad	goddess of love and summer flowers (W)
Dagda	father god and ruler of earth, life, and death (I)
Damona	goddess of fertility and healing (G)
Danu	mother goddess of the earth (I)
Dewi	god depicted as a red serpent or dragon (emblem of Wales)
Dian Cecht	god of healing; a physician and magician (I)
Don	mother goddess/god of the underworld (I, W)
Dylan	god of the sea (W)
Epona	goddess of horses, asses, mules, and oxen (G)
Eriu (Eire)	personification of Ireland
Fand	queen of the fairies and goddess of the sea (I)
Fodla	goddess who named Ireland
Gofannon	god of fire, smiths, and metalworking (W)
Gwydion	god of war and magic (I, W)
Lir (Llyr)	god of the sea (I, W)
Lugh	god of the harvest and lord of all skills (I)
Morrigan	goddess of war and strife; sometimes 3-fold, made up of Badb, Macha, and Nemhain (I, W)
Nantosuelta	goddess of nature and water (G)
Nuada (Nudd)	god of rivers and the sea (I, W)
Ogmios (Ogma)	god of academia and eloquence (G, I)
Pwyll	god of the underworld and lord of southwest Wales
Rhiannon	goddess and queen of horses and birds (W)
Rosmerta	goddess of fertility, fire, and wealth (G)
Shannon	goddess of the River Shannon (I)
Sirona	goddess of astronomy and healing (G)

Smertios	god of war (G)
Sucellus	god of forests, agriculture, and fertility (G)
Taliesin	god of poetry, music, and magic (W)
Taranis	god of thunder and master of the sky (G)
Tethra	god of the sea and lord of the otherworld (I)
Teutrates	god of war, wealth, and fertility (G)

EGYPTIAN

Amun (Amon)	king of the gods; patron of the pharaohs
Amun-Re	the gods Amun and Re considered as one
Anubis (Anpu)	god and guardian of burial grounds
Anuket	goddess of the Nile; nourisher of the fields
Bastet (Bast)	goddess of pleasure; patron of cats
Geb (Seb)	god of the earth
Hathor	goddess of the sky and art; patron of women
Horus	god (or multiple gods) of creation
Isis	queen of the gods; goddess of the day, grain, and fertility
Neb-Ti	2 goddesses (Nekhbet and Uatchit) who symbolize the unification of Egypt
Nephthys	goddess of the night; patron of the deceased
Nut	goddess of, and personification of, the heavens
Osiris	king of the gods; god of the underworld, resurrection, and fertility
Ptah	god of the moon; patron of craftspersons
Re (Ra)	god of, and personification of, the sun
Renenutet	goddess of the harvest and good fortune
Satis (Sati)	goddess of archery; personification of the Nile's waterfalls
Seshat	goddess of mathematics, writing, and building
Seth (Set)	god of deserts, night, war, and chaos
Sobek (Sebek)	god of water; symbol of the pharaohs' power
Taweret	goddess of childbirth
Tefnut	goddess of the dawn; personification of moisture
Thoth (Toth)	god of writing, wisdom, and the moon

INDIAN (HINDU)

Agni	god of fire and the spark of all life
Anuradha	goddess of fortune
Bhaga	goddess of prosperity; patron of marriage
Brahma	the senior supreme god; creator of the universe

Devi	mother goddess; nurturer and protector
Durgha	malignant form of Devi; mother of death
Ganga	goddess of the River Ganges
Ganesha	god of wisdom, literature, and fire
Hiranyagarbha	god of creation, which spawned Brahma
Indra	god of warlike deeds and the weather
Indrani	goddess of wrath; personification of jealousy
Kali	goddess of death; destroyer of ignorance and patron of spiritual knowledge
Karttikeya	god of war and virility
Kubera	god of prosperity and abundance
Lakshmi	goddess of fortune, beauty, and sensuality
Matarisvan	messenger of the gods
Nirriti	goddess of evil; personification of destruction
Parvati	goddess of the mountains; consort of Shiva
Rudra	god of wind and storms; incarnation of Shiva
Saranyu	goddess of the dawn
Sarasvati	goddess of rivers; patron of academia, poetry, and music
Soma	god of poets and the moon; exists as a plant and the liquor it yields
Shiva	a supreme god; destroyer of the universe
Surya	god of the sun
Trimurti	3 supreme gods: Brahma, Shiva, and Vishnu
Varuna	god of truth and justice
Vayu	god of the wind
Vishnu	a supreme god; preserver of the universe
Yama	god of death

JAPANESE

Amaturasu	Shinto goddess of the sun and (with Takami-Musubi) ruler of heaven and earth
Binzuru Sonja	god of eyesight and the alleviation of pain
Dainichi	Buddhist personification of wisdom and purity
Ekibiogami	god of the plague and other epidemics
Izanagi	Shinto god of all things light and heavenly
Izanami	Shinto goddess of the underworld; personification of earth and darkness
Jizo	Buddhist protector of travelers, children, and pregnant women

Juichimen	Buddhist god of mercy
Kura-Okami	god of rain and snow
Okuni-Nushi	Shinto god of magic and the harvest
Raiden	god of thunder (*rai*) and lightning (*den*)
Sae-no-Kami	group of gods who guard the roadways
Shichi Fujukin	7 Shinto gods of prosperity and the kitchen:
Benzai-Ten	goddess of wisdom and virtue
Bishamon	god of war; protector of the righteous
Daikoko	patron of farmers
Ebisu	patron of fishermen and farmers
Fukurokuju	god of wisdom
Hotei	god of laughter and contentment
Jurojin	god of longevity
Susanowa	Shinto god of the sea, wind, and storms
Takami-Musubi	Shinto god of creation and divine love; husband of Amaturasu
Takemikadzuchi	god of thunderstorms
Tsuki-Yumi	Shinto god of the moon
Uga-no-Mitama	goddess of agriculture
Wakahiru-me	goddess of the rising sun
Wata-tsu-mi	god of the sea

Further References

Cotterell, Arthur. *A Dictionary of World Mythology*. New York: Oxford University Press, 1990.

Encyclopedia Mythica. "Mythology,"
http://www.pantheon.org/mythica/areas/

Sykes, Egerton. *Who's Who in Non-Classical Mythology*. New York: Oxford University Press, 1993.

CHAPTER 14

A List of Great Print Resources for Writers That Can Be Found in (Most) Every Library

INTRODUCTION

With the advent of the Internet, the library now may be one of the most underused of resources for a writer. A writer ignores the library at his or her own peril. Unless and until the Internet contains all printed matter in an easily searchable form, there is simply too much critical material of interest to writers inside the four walls of the library.

Besides, writers belong in libraries.

So many writers first realized they were writers inside their local libraries. Where else can a young person's mind be free to roam around the world and throughout history, real or imagined, and alight wherever he or she fancies—in the form of a book? Not in a bookstore. A bookstore requires cash. A library only requires that you are a citizen of words. And that you have a library card. No other card will be easier to obtain or provide as much consistent pleasure for you.

As for research, the facts are simple. Books, still, are the ultimate form in which writing is judged—whether it be scholarly or creative. And, of course, more books are in libraries than anywhere else. There is still an inherent fleeting quality to the Internet. We know that books—printed books—have lasted hundreds of years. We have no idea yet about the longevity of what appears on the Internet. There is one direct benefit the Web has brought to libraries, though—most library catalogues are now available online. However, while you can do your search from home, you still have to get up and go. Many books are categorized as "reference only," and they can only be consulted at the library itself.

The simple—and appealing—fact is that, if you can imagine a reference book about a particular subject, it most likely exists. That is true even more so today than it was, say, ten years ago. There has been an impressive increase in the number of reference books, many delightfully particular and specific. Ask your librarian. He or she will love telling you about them.

Here follows a list of books that you should find at your local library and that you probably will, at one time or another, find useful when you put pen to paper. This list is eclectic, as are the interests of writers. Basic dictionaries and encyclopedias are not listed; as you surely already know about them.

The World Almanac and Books of Facts. New York: World Almanac, yearly.
The place to look when you can't figure out where else to look for it.

The Cambridge Illustrated History of Religions. New York: Cambridge U. Press,
Everything you ever wanted to know about Sikhism to Bahai.

The HarperCollins Bible Dictionary. San Francisco: Harper-Collins, 1996.
Includes both Old and New Testaments plus relevant names and places.

Gale Encyclopedia of Multicultural America. Detroit: Gale Research, 2002.
Essays on about 150 culture groups, with bibliography, museums, and URLs.

Statistical Abstract of the United States. Washington, D.C.: U.S. Government Printing Office, yearly.
A collection of facts and figures in one volume.

J.K. Lasser's Your Income Tax. New York: Macmillan, yearly.
You need all the help you can get.

The Oxford Guide to United States Supreme Court Decisions. New York: Oxford U.Press, 1999.
More than 400 of the most important decisions from 1789 until now.

United States Government Manual. Washington, D.C.: Office of the Federal Register, yearly.
Tells you how this government is organized, from top to bottom.

Occupational Outlook Handbook. Washington, D.C.: U.S. Dept. Labor, biennial.
Information on employment trends and outlooks.

Guide to Reference Books. Chicago: American Library Association, 1996.
An enormous resource broken down by diverse subject matter.
You will find books you never dreamed existed. Great resource.

Find It Fast 5th Edition: How to Uncover Expert Information on Any Subject Online or in Print: New York, HarperResource, 2000.
Some items may be out of date, but it's still worth a look.

The Biographical Dictionary of Scientists. New York: Oxford U. Press, 2000.
More than 1,200 entries in two volumes for scientists living and dead.

Astronomy Encyclopedia. New York: Oxford U. Press, 2000.
All aspects of astronomy, including historical developments.

Walker's Mammals of the World. Baltimore: Johns Hopkins U. Press, 1999.
Everything you wanted to know about mammals, past and present, in two volumes.

Miller-Keane Encyclopedia & Dictionary of Medicine, Nursing & Allied Health. St. Louis: WB Saunders, 2002.
Makes it all understandable.

Stedman's Medical Dictionary. Baltimore: Williams & Wilkins, 2000.
The gold standard.

Consumer Drug Reference 2004. Mount Vernon, NY: Consumers Union, yearly.
In plain English, more than 11,000 brand name and generic drugs.

Gardner's Art Through the Ages. New York: Harcourt Brace, 1995.
One of the best, with excellent illustrations.

The Oxford Companion to Music. New York, Oxford U. Press, 2002.
More than 8,000 entries on all sorts of music and musicians and composers.

A Handbook to Literature. Upper Saddle River, NJ: Prentice Hall, 2002.
More than 2,000 terms and facts in literature, linguistics, rhetoric, criticism, printing, bookselling, and information technology.

Simon & Schuster Handbook for Writers. Upper Saddle River, NJ: Prentice Hall, 2002.
Guidance on punctuation, grammar, structure, and a lot more.

Timelines of World History. New York: DK Publishing, 2002.
Heavily illustrated, as so many of this publisher's books are, it starts from the beginning and marches on.

Merriam-Webster's Geographical Dictionary. Springfield, MA: G. & C. Merriam, 1997.
Includes alternate and former names of countries and places.

Atlas of World History. New York: Oxford U. Press, 1999.
From 5,000,000 years ago to 1999.

Current Biography. New York: Wilson, annual.
Bios and obits of famous people.

The Native North American Almanac. Detroit: Gale Research, 2001.
This is precisely the kind of book you would never own. (Cost: $125.) But a library would. It contains an enormous amount of information on all aspects of Native Americans and their history.

The Hispanic American Almanac. Detroit: Gale Research, 1996.
Gale does the same for Hispanics. Remember, these kinds of books
simply did not exist twenty years ago. Consider yourself lucky.

The Asian American Almanac. Detroit: Gale Research, 1996.
Again, from Gale Research.

The African American Almanac. Detroit: Gale Research, 2003.
The 9th edition. From civil rights to science to sports.

*The Self-Publishing Manual: How to Write, Print, and Sell Your
Own Book* by Dan Poynter. Santa Barbara, CA: Para Publishing,
2003.
The 14th edition of this popular how-to book.

*Writer's Guide to Book Editors, Publishers, and Literary Agents:
Who They Are! What They Want! And How to Win Them Over!* by
Jeff Herman. Prima Publishing: Roseville, CA, 2002.
Updated annually.

*Artists & Writers Colonies: Retreats, Residencies, and Respites for
the Creative Mind* by Robyn Middleton and others. Portland, OR:
Blue Heron, 2000.
More than 260 programs across America.

The New Grove Dictionary of Music and Musicians by Stanley
Sadie and many others. New York: Grove, 2000.
Twenty volumes, and truly an amazing resource. Music nuts will
inevitably find some important facts and figures missing or slight-
ed, but where else can you find this range of scholarship?

The Grove Dictionary of Art by Jane Turner and a host of others.
New York: Grove, 1996.
Thirty-four volumes for this one! Nearly 200 pounds of essays,
facts and biographies, well illustrated. The last word on art,
Western and Eastern. *Note: There are electronic versions of these
two Grove behemoths. Your library may have a subscription. It's
worth inquiring, because, for searching at least, the electronic version is often more practical.*

*Rules of the Game: The Complete Illustrated Encyclopedia of All the
Sports of the World.* New York, St. Martin's, 1995.
From greyhound racing to curling.

CHAPTER 15

A List of Writers' Advocacy Organizations

INTRODUCTION

Writers need advocates. Aside from your bartender and some friends, there are very few people who care or understand what it's like to pursue this career. If you don't work at a university or college—and there's a Catch-22: need a book to get a job—or some other job, then you have the problem of health care, among other matters. What to do?

Not too long ago, some writers felt they were being unfairly treated by the *New York Times*. The *Times*, they felt, required too many rights to be bequeathed to them upon their purchase of an article. An individual would have no chance against the newspaper giant. But an organization like the Author's Guild, with a staff of lawyers and the dues from its members, would, and did.

It costs money to join groups like the Author's Guild or the National Writer's Union, but they scale their dues according to your income. It's worth investigating joining one or both of them. There are other organizations that advocate for writers, some specifically directed toward the genre in which you work. They can also be of assistance if you want to register a domain name online and set up your own Web page.

All these groups have their limitations, though. The profession of writing will never have the clout of, say, ice hockey, and neither will its unions and organizations. But they try their best, and they're getting more savvy. Every once in a while they even rack up some impressive victories for their constituents. Anything that connects you with the rest of the world in your solitary pursuit has to be a good idea.

American Society of Journalists and Authors
1501 Broadway, Suite 302
New York, NY 10036
Voice: (212) 997-0947
Fax: (212) 768-7414
http://www.asja.org/index.php

The Authors Guild
31 East 28th Street, 10th floor
New York, NY 10016-7923
Phone: (212) 563-5904
Fax: (212) 564-5363
E-mail: staff@authorsguild.org
http://www.authorsguild.org

National Writers Union
113 University Place, 6th floor
New York, NY 10003
Phone: (212) 254-0279
Fax: (212) 254-0673
E-mail: nwu@nwu.org
http://www.nwu.org

PEN American Center
588 Broadway, Suite 303
New York, NY 10012
pen@pen.org
Phone: (212) 334-1660
Fax: (212) 334-2181
http://pen.org

The Association of Writers and Writing Programs
George Mason University
MS 1E3
Fairfax, VA 22030-4444
Phone: (703) 993-4301
E-mail: awp@awpwriter.org
http://www.awpwriter.org

Society of Children's Book Writers & Illustrators
8271 Beverly Boulevard
Los Angeles, CA 90048
Voice: (323) 782-1010
Fax: (323) 782-1892
General Questions: scbwi@scbwi.org
http://www.scbwi.org

Writers Guild of America (West)
7000 West 3rd Street
Los Angeles, CA 90048
Phone within southern California:
(323) 951-4000
Outside southern California:
(800) 548-4532
Fax: (323) 782-4800
http://www.wga.org

Writers Guild of America (East)
555 West 57th Street, Suite 1230
New York, NY 10019
Phone: (212) 767-7800
Fax: (212) 582-1909
http://www.wgaeast.org

National Association of Women Writers
P.O. Box 700696
San Antonio, TX 78270
Phone: (866) 821-5829
Fax: (866) 821-5829
http://www.naww.org

Science Fiction and Fantasy Writers of America, Inc.
P.O. Box 877
Chestertown, MD 21620
(No phone)
Janet Jewell, Executive Director
E-mail: execdir@sfwa.org
http://www.sfwa.org

The Academy of American Poets
588 Broadway, Suite 604
New York, NY 10012-3210
Phone: (212) 274-0343
Fax: (212) 274-9427
E-mail: academy@poets.org
http://www.poets.org

Editorial Freelancers Association
71 West 23rd Street, Suite 1910
New York, NY 10010-4181
Tel: (212) 929-5400 / Toll free: (866) 929-5400
Fax: (212) 929-5439 / Toll free: (866) 929-5439
E-mail: info@the-efa.org
http://www.the-efa.org/index.html

Mystery Writers of America
17 East 47th Street, 6th floor
New York, NY 10017
Phone: (212) 888-8171
Fax: (212 888-8107
E-mail: mwa@mysterywriters.org
http://www.mysterywriters.org/

Romance Writers of America
16000 Stuebner Airline Road, Suite 140
Spring, TX 77379
Phone: (832) 717-5200
Fax: (832) 717-5201
E-mail: info@rwanational.org
http://www.rwanational.org/

Garden Writers Association
10210 Leatherleaf Court
Manassas, VA 20111
Phone: (703) 257-1032
Fax: (703) 257-0213
E-mail: info@gardenwriters.org
http://www.gardenwriters.org/

Horror Writers Association
P.O. Box 50577
Palo Alto, CA 94303
(No phone)
E-mai: hwa@horror.org.
http://www.horror.org/

International Food Wine & Travel Writers Association
(IFW&TWA)
1142 South Diamond Bar Boulevard #177
Diamond Bar, CA 91765-2203
Phone: (877) 439-8929
E-mail: admin@ifwtwa.orgWeb
http://www.ifwtwa.org

Poetry Society of America
15 Gramercy Park
New York, NY 10003
(No phone or e-mail)
http://www.poetrysociety.org/

Sisters in Crime
Beth Wasson, Executive Secretary
P.O. Box 442124
Lawrence, KS 66044-8933
E-mail: sistersincrime@juno.com
http://www.sistersincrime.org

Western Writers of America
Secretary-Treasurer, James Crutchfield
1012 Fair Street
Franklin, TN 37064
(No phone)
E-mail: tncrutch@aol.com
http://www.westernwriters.org/

Asian American Journalists Association
1182 Market Street, Suite 320
San Francisco, CA 94102
Phone: (415) 346-2051
Fax: (415) 346-6343
E-mail: national@aaja.org
http://www.aaja.org/

Writers of Color and Culture
(No address or phone)
E-mail: word@writersofcolor.org
www.writersofcolor.org/

National Association of Black Journalists
University of Maryland
8701-A Adelphi Road
Adelphi, MD 20783-1716
Phone: (301) 445-7100
Fax: (301) 445-7101
E-mail: nabj@nabj.org
http://www.nabj.org/

The National Association of Hispanic Journalists
1000 National Press Building
529 14th Street, NW
Washington, DC 20045-2001
Phone: (202) 662.7145
Fax: (202) 662.7144
Toll free: (888) 346.NAHJ
E-mail: nahj@nahj.org
www.nahj.org/home/home.shtml

National Association of Science Writers, Inc.
P.O. Box 890
Hedgesville, WV 25427
Phone: (304) 754-5077
Fax: (304) 754-5076
Diane McGurgan, Executive Director
E-mail: diane@nasw.org
http://www.nasw.org/

National Lesbian & Gay Journalists Association
1420 K Street, NW
Suite 910
Washington, DC 20005
Phone: (202) 588.9888
Fax: (202) 588.1818
E-mail: info@nlgja.org
http://www.nlgja.org/

Society of American Travel Writers
1500 Sunday Drive, Suite 102
Raleigh, NC 27607
Phone: (919) 861-5586
Fax: (919) 787-4916
E-mail: satw@satw.org
www.satw.org/satw/index.asp

The Society of Environmental Journalists
P.O. Box 2492
Jenkintown, PA 19046
Phone: (215) 884-8174
Fax: (215) 884-8175
E-mail: sej@sej.org
http://www.sej.org/

The Asian American Writers' Workshop
16 West 32nd Street, Suite 10A
New York, NY 10001
Phone: (212) 494.0061
Fax: (212) 494.0062
E-mail: desk@aaww.org
http://www.aaww.org/

Teachers & Writers Collaborative
5 Union Square West
New York, NY 10003-3306
Phone: 212-691-6590
Toll free: (888) BOOKS-TW
Fax: (212) 675-0171
E-mail: info@twc.org
www.twc.org

CHAPTER 16

How to Copyright Your Work

INTRODUCTION

To copyright or not to copyright, that is the question.

The quick answer is: that depends. You may not be aware that your work is copyrighted as soon as you write it. This may seem hard to believe, as there is an entire government agency, The United States Copyright Office, devoted to copyrights. But, yes, you automatically retain a copyright on your work.

Unfortunately, this automatic copyright seems to be virtually useless. For example, if you want to file a lawsuit for copyright infringement, your work must be registered with the U.S. government. Does this mean you will need or want to copyright every short story or poem you write? Probably not.

As of this writing, it costs $30 a pop to copyright anything. As a working writer in the real world where electric bills have to be paid, you will find yourself thinking twice before dropping $30 on a formality. After all, how many times have you or your friends had to sue anyone for copyright infringement? So, what should you do, and when? This chapter will explain some of the elements that go into making the decision of whether or not to apply for an official U.S. copyright.

The very first thing you should do is visit the Web page of the United States Copyright Office, which is at http://www.copyright.gov. As mentioned in Chapter 18, these government Web pages are, ironically, a model of efficiency, clarity, and practicality. We should give credit here where credit is due. Other organizations? should take a leaf from their book of Web user-friendliness.

The first thing you should do after pulling up their Web page is go to the Frequently Asked Questions section, and click on "Copyright in General." It explains what, exactly, is copyright: "a form of protection grounded in the U.S. Constitution and granted by law for original works of authorship fixed in a tangible medium of expression." You will learn, perhaps to your surprise, that it covers both published and unpublished works: "Your work is under copyright protection the moment it is created and fixed in a tangible form that it is perceptible either directly or with the aid of a machine or device."

What about sending a copy of the work to myself? "The practice of sending a copy of your own work to yourself is sometimes called a 'poor man's copyright.' There is no provision in the copyright law regarding any such type of protection, and it is not a substitute for registration."

Are copyrights transferable? What, legally, is meant by "the author"? How long does copyright last? Will my work be protected overseas? Is material on the Internet covered?

This Web site will answer just about any basic question you might have about copyrighting your work. It concerns not only literary works, but visual and audio works as well. There is also a substantial section containing the actual U.S. copyright laws, legal language and all. You can download, either in PDF or text format, "Subject Matter and Scope of Copyright," the general overview of the U.S. Copyright Law from Title 17 of the United States Code, for example, which covers a lot of ground. Or you can access something as specific as, say, "Sound Recordings and Music Videos" from the code. Before the advent of the Internet, we had to go through the laborious process of mailing off a request and postage for said documents to Washington, if we even knew they existed—but not anymore.

You can also search this database by author, title, and other variables for information about copyrighted works.

The real good news here is that it's very easy to copyright a work.

Just take a look at the government's instructions:

"Put into one envelope or package: a completed application Form TX or Short Form TX (choose which form to use), a $30 payment to 'Register of Copyrights,' and nonreturnable copy(ies) of the material." The Short Form TX is, in fact, blessedly short, can be used for most purposes, and can be filled out by an eight year-old. Both forms can be downloaded from the site.

How long does it take to obtain your copyright, you ask? Four to five months.

The National Writers Union feels very strongly that you should copyright your work, and it would be to your advantage to read what they have to say about it. After all, they're on the front lines protecting their members' work. Go to their website, http://www.nwu.org, where you'll find a document, "Copyright: A Guide for Freelancers" (find it by going to the site map), that spells out their point of view in detail. Here is the beginning of that section:

"The National Writers Union strongly recommends you register your work with the U.S. Copyright Office. While your work—published or not—is technically copyrighted the moment you create and document it, registration allows you to take legal action if your work is used without permission. In addition, the 1976 U.S. Copyright Law gives you control over copying, reproduction, distribution, derivative use, and public display of your work.

"You should aim to register your work within three months of its publication or prior to any publication infringement so you will be eligible to receive full compensation and damages if legal action becomes necessary. Because there is a fee involved each time you register (currently $30), the NWU recommends you submit all your work in one registration at least once a year."

The NWU has their own set of FAQs, and obviously they are not disinterested. Their interests are yours. They also provide links to other websites relating to copyright.

After studying both sites, you should be well versed in copyright strategy.

CHAPTER 17

A Common-Sense Guide to Manuscript Formats

INTRODUCTION

Despite the increased use of e-mail and attachments to both query editors and send them manuscripts, certain formal procedures need remain intact. You will encounter publishers and editors, notably those at university presses and journals, who are sticklers, for example, about the format in which a manuscript must be presented. In other instances, editors have a preference for a certain type of text format (rich text versus Word, for example), and this may have to do with the type of computers the organization uses. The instructions manuscript submission can read like a college admission application form. Editors have their reasons, and it's wise to remember that colleges and universities are as bureaucratic as any hefty corporation. Procedure must be followed.

The point is this: It's hard enough to get published these days. It's hard enough simply to get noticed. You don't want to blow your chances simply because you sent the manuscript out with the wrong margins. (Yes, some places are very exact about that.) If that happens, there should be no railing in the bar to anyone who will listen about the injustices of editors. All you had to do was to read this chapter.

I

Common sense is key. The first place that this most reliable of traits should lead you is to this rule: **Always include a cover letter.** When you meet someone new, you introduce yourself. This is polite as well as practical. A cover letter serves the same purposes, and then some. It gives you a chance to introduce yourself and to make a quick impression. If your letter is succinct and clear—I wholeheartedly emphasize *succinct*—then you've already got the editor on your side. An editor's most valuable commodity is time, and he or she will not waste it reading a rambling cover letter. Not including a cover letter is simply insulting, as well as suicidal.

II

Go to the organization's website. This can be a tad tricky, but anyone who has experience maneuvering through sites will be able to find their way. For example, let's look at Northwestern University Press, http://nupress.northwestern.edu. But we see no submission guidelines. We *do* see "Contact Us," however. And lo and behold, after clicking on that, we find "Manuscript Submissions"http://nupress.northwestern.edu/contact_sub.cfm#ms). Scroll down to "General Guidelines." Remember what we said in the introduction about publishers being particular? The second requirement on the list reads: "Use a clip or rubber band to hold your cover letter, manuscript, and biographical information together." Now, if you send them the next *Moby-Dick,* are they going to reject your manuscript because you didn't use a clip or rubber band? We both know you're not going to be sending them the next *Moby-Dick.* But we also know you don't want to irritate an editor who, on this given day, may just decide to throw your manuscript aside for the time being—the one that used a staple to keep everything together—and pick up one that's presented according to guidelines.

III

Kill a lot of birds with one stone. **Check the Web for a site devoted to submission guidelines** of many magazines or presses. Here's one from a website called Freelance Writing: http://www.freelance

writing.com/guidelines/pages. This links you to a page of categories, from "Boating" to "Workforce." These, in turn, link you to the actual guidelines of various publications. The only caveat here: Make sure the guidelines you read and act upon come straight from the publication or house itself, and that they are not interpretations made by a third-party website.

IV

When in doubt, query. If you have a question about what some of the requirements actually mean, don't hesitate to ask. Call or e-mail with your concerns. In this case, you have every right to inquire directly. It only shows that you want to get it all right.

V

Believe what they tell you. If the submission guidelines tell you something, then listen. Don't try to bend the rules. Here's an excerpt from the submission guidelines for *French Review,* the official journal of the American Association of Teachers of French:

"All articles are to be submitted to the Editor in Chief. The normal maximum for articles, *including endnotes,* is 5,000 words; the minimum, 2,500 words. The limit for submissions to 'In Your Corner: Focus on the Classroom' is 2,500 words. For 'Professional Issues' it is also 2,500 words. AATF membership is a prerequisite for the submission of articles. All articles must be accompanied by an Abstract of 100 words, maximum, in the same language as the manuscript's. Book review maximum: 650 words."

Notice that they have even put a visual emphasis on the phrase "including endnotes." You would think, then, that any writer submitting a manuscript to *French Review* would heed that warning. But I will bet you my last croissant that the editors could regale us with tales of submissions of manuscripts of 5,000 words, *excluding* footnotes. The writer simply didn't think they *meant* it.

Or a manuscript for "Professional Issues" that was 3,000 words, because, the writer supposed, the essay was *so* brilliant the *Review* would have to make an exception.

Oh?

This will get you a one-way trip to the "No" pile.

VI

Make sure you've got the right publication for what you've writ-ten. This may sound obvious, but why, then, do magazines and journals caution potential submitters to "please read us before you send anything"? Because, I'm sure, they get lots of manuscripts that are obviously unsuitable for their publication, remarkably so in some cases. Writers can be just plain lazy. They simply don't want to take the time to go to the library or to a bookstore to read the publication they intend to send their work to. That can be costly and a waste of time for all involved. There is a niche for what you've written, but it's important to give yourself the best possible chance for acceptance by eliminating publishers with no audience for your work. How else would you   know that unless you checked out the publisher?

VII

Always include a self-addressed stamped envelope. Or SASE, as it's called in the trade. And equally as important, make sure you include the correct return postage. Not including a SASE is the height of arrogance. Or the height of something undesirable. Its lack will immediately put editors in a foul mood. Which is not the state of mind you want them to be in when they begin reading your work.

VIII

If you are submitting a book proposal, be especially careful and thorough. Book proposals have become exceedingly wide-ranging documents. Because publishing has become so stringently profit-driven, editors want to be very confident that any book they accept for publication has a good chance of selling. It's essential that they are able to convey this to the people who control the money spent on their books. Thus, a book proposal has become more than just a simple, well-written explanation of what the book will be about. It's become a marketing tool. It must answer quite a few basic questions, such as: What is the competition here?, and Why will this book find a healthy spot among them? And so on. A good book proposal takes weeks, even months, to write. (It took Laura Hillenbrand four months just to write the book proposal for *Seabiscuit*.) So you need to do your research here, and do it well. There are any number of books on how to write a good book proposal, and you should avail yourself of at least two. You should also accept that, from the start, writing one will be no simple matter. But if you do it right, you could have that grail every writer dreams of: a contract.

IX

Again, this is just common sense, but for God's sake, check your manuscript very carefully for errors. Think everything is taken care of with your spell-checker? Think again. If you accidentally type in "two" when you meant "too," the spell-checker will think that it's not an error, and won't alert you. The point: When you miss something like this, it's so transparent that you have not gone over the manuscript carefully. It's then clear to the editor that you've accepted the spell-checker as your deity. You also might make an egregious error. If you've ever taken *one last quick look* at a manuscript and found that you had Sumatra placed in Africa or whatever, you know that heart-thumping feeling of narrowly escaping humiliation. Read your work carefully before you send it out. Twice.

X

Give the editor a decent amount of time to respond. Unlike you, the editor is not standing by the mailbox at dawn waiting for a letter. Time is often a writer's worst enemy. And isolation. Two days to writers can seem like two weeks, because they often think night and day about the manuscripts they have submitted. Suddenly, it's "Why haven't they gotten back to me?" even before the week is over. The best remedy? Start another project. Give your mind something else to do. And get out of the house.

CHAPTER 18

Great Websites for Writers

INTRODUCTION

There's no denying that the Web has changed writing, and changed it forever. So much information is available on the Internet that the chief problem now is one of culling and determining what, among the thousands of sites, is worthy or just marginal. The Web is metamorphosing as we speak. Websites move with the frequency of nomads in the dry season. Websites also perish without warning. One day you might consult a favored site, and the next day "This page not accessible" pops up like a tombstone. We all understand this transitory situation, so lists such as this are always affixed with the "subject to change without notice" caveat. However, certain websites have a ring of permanence to them—as least as much as can be said in this medium. Take the Library of Congress site, for example: http://www.loc.gov. This is a treasure, and the very simplicity of the address gives the user a sense of security, much as "1600 Pennsylvania Avenue" does.

However, even for the transient Web, there's recourse. You can go to the Internet Archive: http://www.archive.org and search (on the "Wayback Machine") for disappeared websites, and http://www.furl.net allows you to save websites and access them from other computers. Pray they both stick around.

In fact—and I find this ironic and wonderful at once—many U.S. government sites are among the best on the Web. Agencies that have the reputation of being slothful, unmanageable behemoths in three-dimensional daily life have produced the most efficient, lean, and accessible websites around. However this happened, we writers are the lucky beneficiaries. Just examine, for example, the order and simplicity of the main page of the U.S. Department of Defense: http://www.defenselink.mil. Many official documents are also available online, which makes obtaining them a much easier process than dealing with people. Remember, too, that all the government material is copyright free, an example of your tax dollars at work.

This chapter includes a basic list of websites helpful to writers. Just remember, such a list is always contracting and expanding, like the tides.

http://www.aldaily.com
Arts & Letters Daily, the website of the Chronicle of Higher Education.

http://www.yourdictionary.com
Scores of dictionaries of all types.

http://www.pw.org
Poets & Writers

http://writing.shawguides.com
A Guide to Writers Conferences and Workshops. Searchable by genre, country, and month.

http://www.awpwriter.org
The Association of Writers and Writing Programs. They publish the much-consulted AWP *The Writer's Chronicle*.

http://www.clmp.org
Council of Literary Magazines and Presses

http://sunsite.berkeley.edu/Libweb
Libweb, Library Servers from around the world via the World Wide Web.

http://vlib.org
World Wide Web Virtual Library, covering a vast array of subjects.

http://www.verbatimmag.com
Verbatim, the Language Quarterly

http://www.si.edu
The Smithsonian Institution

http://vlmp.museophile.com
Virtual Library Museum Pages from around the world.

http://www.firstgov.gov
The U.S. government's Web page, with gates to all the others.

http://www.nea.gov
National Endowment for the Arts

http://www.poets.org
The Academy of American Poets

http://www.pen.org
PEN American Center

http://www.smallpress.org
The Small Press Center

http://www.perseus.tufts.edu
The Perseus Digital Library

http://www.mla.org
The Modern Language Association

http://aaupnet.org
The Association of American University Presses

http://www.naa.org
Newspaper Association of America

http://writing-program.uchicago.edu/resources/grammar.htm
Grammar resources on the Web compiled by the University of Chicago.

http://www.ala.org
American Library Association

http://www.crl.uchicago.edu
Center for Research Libraries

CHAPTER 19

Forms of Address for Letter Writing

INTRODUCTION

Writers will write to editors, possible patrons, and grant givers for as long as they are trying to make their living. The recipients of these letters have traditionally been appreciative, not to say influenced, by a certain sense of respect afforded to them. This is just human nature. One of the most basic ways in which one can express this regard is in the form of a well-written letter. E-mail has made us all buddies at the drop of a hat. We might address the President with a "Hi, George!!!" in an e-mail, but that simply would not work in a letter. There are accepted ways and means of writing a real letter on real paper, placing it into a real envelope, and gluing on it a real stamp. This chapter details them for you. After reading it, you should have a basic grasp of the right way to write your future patron, your future editor, or your future grant giver.

If you want a classic example of how this is done, simply read Samuel Johnson's letter to his so-called patron, Lord Chesterfield. This letter, written by Johnson after his immense dictionary was completed, simply, clearly, and brilliantly condemns Chesterfield for his lack of assistance in the times when Johnson was struggling mightily and needed it most. Yet it never strays from a dignified polish, and makes its point with a devastating series of smoothly written, perfectly pointed sentences. With any luck, you'll never need to write such a letter. Your letter will be written to thank the

Committee for its long-standing support, to say that, without its help, your book would never have seen the light of day and won the Nobel Prize. And could you please have some more money, sir or madam?

GENERALLY ACCEPTED FORMS OF ADDRESS AND SALUTATIONS

Mr. = Ms. (unless addressee is known to prefer Miss or Mrs.), or if Mr. precedes a title, the female equivalent is Madam (or if addressee is foreign, then Madame)

Ambassador (American)
The Honorable _____
American Ambassador
or, if in Canada or Latin America,
The Honorable _____
The Ambassador of the United States of America
Sir or Madam:
Dear Mr. or Madam Ambassador:

Ambassador (foreign)
His or Her Excellency _____
Ambassador of _____
Sir or Madame:
Excellency:
Dear Mr. or Madame Ambassador:

Archbishop
The Most Reverend Archbishop of _____
or
The Most Reverend _____
Archbishop of _____
The Most Reverend _____:
Your Excellency:
Dear Archbishop:

Associate Justice (Supreme Court)
Mr. Justice _____
The Supreme Court of the United States
The Honorable Justice _____
The Supreme Court

Sir or Madam:
Dear Sir or Madam:
Dear Justice _____:

Attorney General
The Honorable _____
Attorney General
Department of Justice
or
Attorney General _____
Department of Justice
Sir or Madam:
Dear Sir or Madam:
Dear Mr. or Madam Attorney General:

Bishop (Catholic)
The Most Reverend _____
Bishop of _____
Most Reverend Sir:
Your Excellency:
Dear Bishop _____:

Bishop (Episcopal)
The Right Reverend _____
Bishop of _____
Right Reverend Sir:
Dear Bishop _____:

Bishop (Protestant, excluding Episcopal)
The Reverend _____
or
Bishop _____
Reverend Sir:
Dear Bishop _____:

Cabinet Officer
The Secretary of _____
or
The Honorable _____
Secretary of _____
Sir or Madam:
Dear Mr. or Madam Secretary:
Dear Mr. or Ms. _____

Chief Justice (Supreme Court, Federal)
The Chief Justice
The Supreme Court
or
The Chief Justice of the United States
The Supreme Court of the United States
or
The Honorable_____
Chief Justice of the United States
The Supreme Court
Sir or Madam:
Dear Sir or Madam:
Dear Mr. or Madam Chief Justice:

Clergy (Protestant)
The Reverend _____
or, with a doctorate,
The Reverend Dr. _____
or The Reverend _____, D.D.
Dear Mr. or Ms. _____:
Dear Dr. _____:

Commissioner
The Honorable _____
Commissioner
Dear Mr. or Madam Commissioner:
Dear Mr. or Ms. _____:

Council Member
The Honorable _____
Councilman or Councilwoman
or
Councilman or Councilwoman _____
Dear Mr. or Ms. _____
Dear Councilman or Councilwoman _____:

Governor
The Honorable _____
Governor of _____
or
Governor _____

or in some states,
His or Her Excellency, the Governor of _____
Sir or Madam:
Dear Sir or Madam:
Dear Governor _____:

Judge
The Honorable _____
Judge of the United States District Court of the _____ District of
_____
or
The Honorable _____
Associate Judge
United States District Court
Sir or Madam:
Dear Judge _____:

King or Queen
His or Her Majesty
King or Queen of _____
Sir or Madam:
May it please Your Majesty:

Lawyer
Mr. _____
Attorney at Law
or
_____, Esq.
Dear Mr. _____:

Mayor
The Honorable _____
Mayor of _____
Sir or Madam:
Dear Mayor:

Military Personnel (all titles)
Full or abbreviated rank, full name, comma, abbreviation for
branch of
service
Dear Rank _____:

Pope
    His Holiness Pope _____
    or
    His Holiness the Pope
    Your Holiness:
    Most Holy Father:

Premier
    His or Her Excellency _____
    Premier of _____
    Excellency:
    Dear Mr. or Madame Premier:

President of the United States
    The President
    The White House
    or
    The President of the United States
    The White House
    Dear Sir or Madam:
    Mr. or Madam President:
    Dear Mr. or Madam President:

Priest
    The Reverend _____
    or
    The Reverend Father _____
    Reverend Father:
    Dear Father _____:
    Dear Father:

Prime Minister
    His or Her Excellency _____
    Prime Minister of _____
    Excellency:
    Dear Mr. or Madame Prime Minister:

Professor
    Professor _____
    Department of
    or
    Dr. _____
    Department of _____

or
_____, Ph.D.
Professor of _____
Dear Professor _____:
Dear Dr. _____:

Rabbi
Rabbi _____
or, with doctorate,
Rabbi _____, D.D.
Dear Rabbi _____:
Dear Dr. _____:

Representative (State)
The Honorable _____
House of Representatives
Sir or Madam:
Dear Mr. or Ms. _____:

Representative (U.S. Congress)
The Honorable _____
United States House of Representatives
or
Representative _____
United States House of Representatives
Sir or Madam:
Dear Mr. or Ms. _____:
Dear Representative:

Senator (state)
The Honorable _____
The Senate of _____
Sir or Madam:
Dear Senator _____:
Dear Mr. or Ms. _____:

Senator (U.S. Senate)
The Honorable _____
United States Senator
or
Senator _____
United States Senate
Sir or Madam:

Dear Mr. or Madam Senator:
Dear Senator _____:
Dear Mr. or Ms. _____:

Speaker (U.S. House of Representatives)

The Honorable Speaker of the House of Representatives
or
The Honorable _____
Speaker of the House of Representatives
Sir or Madam:
Dear Mr. or Madam Speaker:
Dear Mr. or Ms. _____:

Vice President of the United States

The Vice President of the United States
United States Senate
or
The Honorable _____
The Vice President of the United States
or
The Honorable _____
The Vice President
United States Senate
Sir or Madam:
Dear Sir or Madam:
Mr. or Madam Vice President:
Dear Mr. or Madam Vice President:

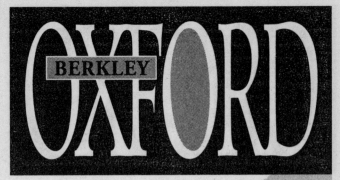

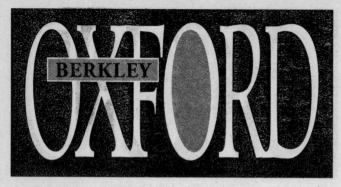

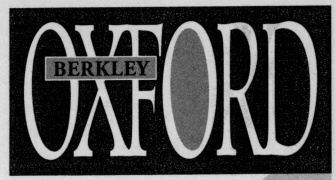

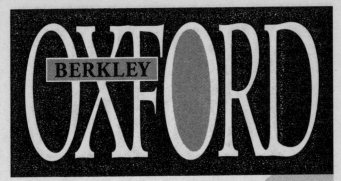

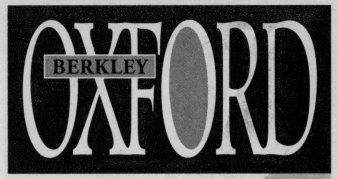

BERKLEY

OXFORD

THE WORLD TURNS TO OXFORD FOR ANSWERS.

THE OXFORD BUSINESS SPANISH DICTIONARY

0-425-19095-1

THE OXFORD ESSENTIAL DICTIONARY OF ABBREVIATIONS

0-425-19704-2

THE OXFORD ESSENTIAL DICTIONARY OF LEGAL WORDS

0-425-19706-9

THE OXFORD ESSENTIAL OFFICE HANDBOOK

0-425-19703-4

AVAILABLE WHEREVER BOOKS ARE SOLD OR AT
PENGUIN.COM

(B509)